Time Out

Cycle London

timeout.com

Rides by Patrick Field

Published by Time Out Guides Ltd, a wholly owned subsidiary of Time Out Group Ltd.
Time Out and the Time Out logo are trademarks of Time Out Group Ltd.

London 2012 emblems © The London Organising Committee of the Olympic Games and Paralympic Games Ltd (LOCOG) 2007. All rights reserved.

© Time Out Group Ltd 2011

10 9 8 7 6 5 4 3 2

This edition first published in Great Britain in 2011 by Ebury Publishing
A Random House Group Company
20 Vauxhall Bridge Road, London SW1V 2SA

Random House Australia Pty Ltd 20 Alfred Street, Milsons Point, Sydney, New South Wales 2061, Australia
Random House New Zealand Ltd 18 Poland Road, Glenfield, Auckland 10, New Zealand
Random House South Africa (Pty) Ltd Isle of Houghton, Corner Boundary Road & Carse O'Gowrie, Houghton 2198, South Africa

Random House UK Limited Reg. No. 954009

Distributed in USA by Publishers Group West
1700 Fourth Street, Berkeley, California 94710

For further distribution details, see www.timeout.com

ISBN: 978-1-84670-236-5

A CIP catalogue record for this book is available from the British Library

Printed and bound by Firmengruppe APPL, aprinta druck, Wemding, Germany

The Random House Group Limited supports The Forest Stewardship Council (FSC®), the leading international forest certification organisation. Our books carrying the FSC label are printed on FSC® certified paper. FSC is the only forest certification scheme endorsed by the leading environmental organisations, including Greenpeace. Our paper procurement policy can be found at www.randomhouse.co.uk/environment.

Time Out carbon-offsets all its flights with Trees for Cities (www.treesforcities.org).

The ultimate guide to London – **it's essential**

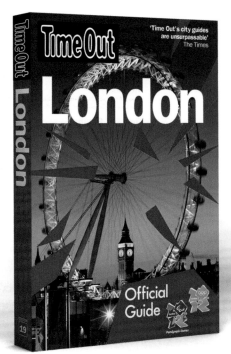

Time Out Guides Limited
Universal House
251 Tottenham Court Road
London W1T 7AB
Tel + 44 (0)20 7813 3000
Fax + 44 (0)20 7813 6001
Email guides@timeout.com
www.timeout.com

Editorial
Commissioning Editor Ruth Jarvis
Rides Author Patrick Field
Features Author Ellis Bacon
Deputy Editors Edoardo Albert, Cath Phillips
Listings Editors William Crow, Jamie Warburton
Proofreader Carol Baker

Managing Director Peter Fiennes
Editorial Director Ruth Jarvis
Business Manager Dan Allen
Editorial Manager Holly Pick
Management Accountants Margaret Wright, Clare Turner

Design
Art Director Scott Moore
Art Editor Pinelope Kourmouzoglou
Senior Designer Kei Ishimaru
Group Commercial Designer Jodi Sher

Picture Desk
Picture Editor Jael Marschner
Acting Deputy Picture Editor Liz Leahy
Picture Desk Assistant/Researcher Ben Rowe

Advertising
New Business & Commercial Director Mark Phillips
Account Manager Ben Holt

Marketing
Sales & Marketing Director, North America
& Latin America Lisa Levinson
Senior Publishing Brand Manager Luthfa Begum
Guides Marketing Manager Colette Whitehouse
Group Commercial Art Director Anthony Huggins

Production
Group Production Manager Brendan McKeown
Production Controller Katie Mulhern

Time Out Group
Director & Founder Tony Elliott
Chief Executive Officer David King
Chief Operating Officer Aksel Van der Wal
Group Financial Director Paul Rakkar
Group General Manager/Director Nichola Coulthard
Time Out Communications Ltd MD David Pepper
Time Out International Ltd MD Cathy Runciman
Time Out Magazine Ltd Publisher/MD Mark Elliott
Group Commercial Director Graeme Tottle
Group IT Director Simon Chappell
Group Marketing Director Andrew Booth

Contributors Sarah Cobbold, William Crow, Jamie Warburton.

Maps John Oakey. johnoakey1@gmail.com.

Cover photography by Jonathan Perugia; with thanks to the Towpath Café, Regent's Canal towpath, between Whitmore Bridge and Kingsland Road Bridge, N1 5SB; Cycle Surgery (www.cyclesurgery.com); and cyclists Simeon Greenway, William Crow, Sarah Cobbold.

Openers photography by Jonathan Perugia; and pages 240/241 Ben Rowe. Thanks to the cyclists: Barbarella Mendoza, Gabriel Cadogan, Ryan Cadogan (Short and Sweet); Ndaba Mazibuko, Lonnie Frisby, Jacob Goodman (At Your Leisure); Lowell Baricanosa, Vanessa Pfeiffer (Country Pleasures); London Baroudeurs Lowell, Stuart and Ben at Baroudeurs.cc (Allez, Allez!); Paul Rakkar (Central London Essentials).

Photography pages 3, 27 (top left), 58 (bottom right), 67 (bottom left), 68, 86, 96 (bottom) Jonathan Perugia; page 17 Abigail Lelliott; pages 18, 27 www.simonleigh.com; pages 19 (top), 38, 73 (bottom), 76 Scott Wishart; page 19 (bottom) Nigel Tradewell; pages 27 (top right), 33, 58 (left), 73 (top) Michelle Grant; pages 28, 67 (bottom right) Britta Jaschinski; page 37 Ed Marshall; page 43 (top) www.richardrowland.co.uk; page 43 (bottom right) Anthony Webb; pages 48, 50, 51, 85, 86 (top), 88, 106, 110, 117, 159, 160, 161, 165, 169, 177, 178, 179, 188, 189, 191, 198, 199, 207, 209 (bottom), 210, 238, 239 Ben Rowe; pages 49 (top), 58 (top right), 101 (top), 123 (right), 129 Nick Ballon; pages 57, 137 (left), 205 (left) Rob Greig; page 94 Jael Marschner; page 95 Belinda Lawley; page 98 Heloise Bergman; pages 101 (bottom), 134, 149 (bottom right) Ming Tang-Evans; page 104 Lee Valley Regional Park Authority; pages 111 (bottom), 225 ODA 2008; pages 120, 121 Elisabeth Blanchet; page 123 (left) Gary Jones; page 126 Laurence Davis; pages 135, 149 Charlie Pinder; page 137 (right) Tove K Breitstein; page 141 Alamy; page 150 Susie Rea; page 153 EMPICS Sport/PA Photos; page 162 (left) Oleg Skrinda/www.skindra.com; page 162 (right) Rod Currie; page 163 (left) RB Create; page 163 (right) www.georgeburgessphotography.com; pages 185, 186 (top), 187 (top) Julian Birch; page 196 RSPB- Images; page 201 John Dominick; page 205 (right) Danny Fitzpatrick/www.dfphotography.co.uk; page 217 Jake Davis; page 219 (left) www.gerardbrown.co.uk; page 219 (right) Slipstream Sports; page 222 Andrew Brackenbury; page 223 (top) Alastair Humphries; page 223 (bottom) www.edwalkerphotography.com; page 224 ODA.
The following images were provided by the featured establishments/cyclists: pages 49 (bottom), 87, 108, 109, 146, 209 (top), 214, 215, 220, 221, 281.

Introduction

Welcome to Cycle London. Who would have thought it? One of the world's least cycle-friendly cities has emerged over the last five years as one of its most biked-up. Whether through cost-saving, green intentions, fitness concerns or just a growing realisation that bikes are simply the best way to get from A to B in the city, the number of riders on the roads has shot up (by over 90% since 2000). You can see it on the streets: flotillas of cyclists on all types of bikes, in all types of clothing, with a bright and lively scene of rides, shops, cycle-crafts markets, cafés and cultural events developing in parallel. Interest can only grow with the staging of the London 2012 Olympic and Paralympic Games, at which Team GB's Cycling squad is expected to put in a headline-grabbing performance, and the legacy of the Olympic Park Velodrome.

We've designed this book to be useful for people at all points on the cycling spectrum, absolute beginners included. It's primarily a ride guide – that's what it's all about, after all. Experienced ride-maker Patrick Field has compiled 32 enjoyable routes in the capital and surrounding countryside that take you deep into London's inner life, show you the sights, drop you off at interesting stops and refuel you at some prime eating and drinking spots. But it also includes practical information on everything from the best locks to 'bike whisperers', along with insights into cycle culture.

The book is divided into sections to suit different types of cyclist, each containing appropriate rides, bike-buying advice and features. The first is Short and Sweet, in which all the routes are less than ten miles long and perfect for occasional riders, families with children and first-timers. But be warned: if this is your introduction to cycling, you may soon be accelerating your way through the sections, through longer urban rides to commuting and full days out in the country. You don't need to be terribly fit to get quite far on a bike, quite fast; and, once sampled, cycling in London becomes quickly addictive. The miles will fall pleasurably beneath your tyres, and you'll never see the city in the same way again.

Ruth Jarvis, Commissioning Editor

Meet the team

Patrick Field, Rides Author

Patrick Field is the originator of the landmark Dunwich Dynamo ride and has lived in, and ridden around, London since 1974. He authored the first modern guides to cycle-touring from London (*Breathing Spaces, Get Lost*) and runs the London School of Cycling.

Ellis Bacon, Features Author

Ellis Bacon has covered cycling in its many forms for almost a decade. He currently writes for *Cycling Weekly* and *Cycle Sport* magazines and is a former deputy editor of *Procycling*. In 2011 he covered his ninth Tour de France.

Contents

Short and Sweet   10

❶ Sailing through Southwark   12
Westminster Bridge to Tower Bridge. 2.9 miles
What Bike?   21
❷ Riding on Air   22
Hyde Park to Battersea Park. 5 miles
Kit Bag   31
❸ Towpaths & Toast   32
Soho to Stratford. 8 miles
Tips on Cycling in the Capital   41
❹ Dockland Diversions   42
Greenwich to Tower of London. 6 miles
Fixing a Puncture   50
❺ The City on Sunday   52
Monument to Old Spitalfields Market. 5 miles
Cycling in London: Love or Hate?   60
❻ Park & Ride   61
Kensington Gardens circular. 7.5 miles

At Your Leisure   70

❼ Meandering West   72
Kew Bridge to Hampton Court. 11 miles
What Bike?   80
❽ The Grand Junction   81
Paddington to Southall. 15 miles
Kit Bag   89
❾ Twin Peaks   90
Finsbury Park circular. 13 miles
At Your Service   99
❿ Time, Tide & Towpaths   100
Limehouse to Hertford. 28 miles
Pimp Your Ride   108
⓫ What Goes In Must Come Out   110
Stratford to Shooters Hill. 11 miles
Bike Polo   120
⓬ The World's Clock   122
Tower Bridge to Charlton House. 12 miles
Wandling Free   131
Wandsworth to Richmond Park. 13 miles

Country Pleasures 138

⑭ There... 140
  The Mall to Dorking. 43 miles
What Bike? 147
⑮ ...And Back Again 148
  Dorking to The Mall. 41.6 miles
Kit Bag 156
⑯ Far from the Madding Crowd 157
  Slough circular. 18.3 miles
The Cycling Calendar 162
⑰ King of the Hills 164
  High Wycombe to Berkhamsted. 38 miles
The Rapha Phenomenon 171
⑱ On the Straight and Narrow 172
  Stoke Newington to St Albans. 20 miles
Fit for Purpose 181
⑲ Riding to Roding 182
  Chingford circular. 29 miles
⑳ Eastward Hoo 190
  Gravesend to Rochester. 31 miles
Pack a Pocket or Two 198
㉑ Wheels over the Weald 200
  Purley to Brighton. 43 miles
㉒ Humbling the Hill 206
  Box Hill circular. 21 miles

Nuts and Bolts 240

Nuts & Bolts 242

Allez, Allez! 212

Road Racing 214
Mountain Biking 216
Tips from the Pros 218
Track Cycling 220
BMX 222
London 2012: Track & Road Racing 224

Central London Essentials 226

Central London Essentials 228
The Routes 229
Map: Central London Routes 230
Map: Central London Schematic 235
What Bike? 236
Kit Bag 237
The Word from the Streets 238

Map: Rides outside London 255
Map: Rides in London 256

Short and Sweet

For easy leisure cyclists of all ages

Saddle up for a rider's-eye view of central London, from its backstreets to its big attractions, on these short, easy routes. No fancy gear needed and no heavy traffic encountered. You don't even need to own a bike: several routes start and finish at cycle hire stations.

❶ 🚲 Sailing through Southwark

Using major roads you could cover this distance in ten minutes – but that would be to miss all the pleasures of this classic riverside route, which takes you past centuries of liquid and living history. Even if you're not inclined to take in a show at one of the many heavyweight arts venues along the way – the Royal Festival Hall, National Film Theatre, National Theatre, Tate Modern or Shakespeare's Globe – there's always that perpetually engaging spectacle, the theatre of the street. This stretch of riverbank is a magnet for human activity of every stripe.

In places the Thames Path is narrow and – when the sun shines – busy. So be prepared to avoid wandering pedestrians and to walk when necessary. Above all, don't hurry. This is a route to linger over. When the tide is out, there are even places where you can park, climb down to the river and stroll on the strand.

START Now, to begin. But wait. Before that initial push, take a look at the lion statue on Westminster Bridge, diagonally opposite the Houses of Parliament. It may look heroic, but it's a landmark with a bizarre pedigree. It was once painted bright red, being a commercial emblem that stood at the gate of the Red Lion Brewery on the site now occupied by the Festival Hall. It has been renamed the Southbank Lion in a snobbish attempt to obscure its low origins. Despite appearances, it's not chiselled from stone, or cast in metal. Rather it's a piece of Coade Stone, a proprietary ceramic material.

Cycling past the austere blocks of County Hall, formerly the seat of London's government and now, incongruously, host to the London Aquarium and a luxury hotel, among others, you'll quickly reach Jubilee Gardens, which is dominated by the Millennium Wheel – the ❶ London Eye – possibly the only turn-of-the-century 'M-word' attraction that has proved an unqualified success. Its scale and unmistakeable profile are a useful aid to orientation around Westminster, Whitehall and Waterloo. The riverside promenade here is popular with street performers of variable quality, but at least their proliferation adds value. For the passing cyclist, one low grade-act is a low-grade act, but half a dozen are a capering festivity.

As you ride over the well-worn flagstones with their regular little bumps and jolts, you'll soon pedal past the ❷ Royal Festival Hall, which faces the water

Start Westminster Bridge, SE1 7GP
Finish Tower Bridge, SE1 2UL
Time 1.5 hours minimum
Distance 2.9 miles
Connects with ❹ ❻ ⓬
Traffic & safety Mostly on paths shared with pedestrians – be ready to walk if it's crowded. Two short sections do not allow cycling. Two sections on busy roads
Terrain Flat
Transport *Start* Waterloo tube/rail. *End* London Bridge tube/rail
TFL bike-hire scheme *Start* Jubilee Gardens, South Bank. *End* Tooley Street, Bermondsey
Good for People who like stopping as much as riding

downstream of Hungerford foot and rail bridge. The Festival Hall was refurbished in 2007, improving the main auditorium's acoustics and establishing a new row of shops and restaurants at ground level. The success of this development led to speculation that the Hall's undercroft would also be tidied up and enclosed. The undercroft is a long-standing unofficial area for skateboarding, and a popular place to show off BMX freestyle riding. In response to the rumours, the skaters and bikers did some intensive lobbying and petitioning; the result was that the value of the informal usage was recognised and to some extent protected. Day or night you can while away a few minutes listening to the restful rumble of castors, waiting for somebody to fall and break something.

Under Waterloo Bridge (❶ 0.7 miles from the start) there's an open-air market selling books, prints and magazines. There are some stalls every day, but it's busiest at weekends. The stock ranges from charity-shop jumble via celebrity autobiographies to rare editions wrapped in cellophane. The British Film Institute – also snuggled under the bridge – has a bar and café with plenty of outdoor tables; a good early place to park the bike. Also look out for the statue of Laurence Olivier, a memorial to his role as founding director of the National Theatre in 1963.

The London edition of the worldwide, slow, noisy club-run Critical Mass leaves from under Waterloo Bridge on the last Friday of every month. The ride used to start at 6pm, but over the years this has drifted back and nowadays you can arrive at 7pm and not miss anything. The tree-lined Riverside Walk passes Gabriel's Wharf (❷ 0.9 miles) where timber huts house bars, cafés and quirky designer shops. The London Bicycle Tour Company persists here, even though its hire service has been undercut by Transport for London and its cycle-hire scheme.

Eat and ride

Depending on how you look at it, this ride has the advantage or disadvantage of providing so many eating options that you are at some risk of eating more calories during it than you burn off doing it. Gabriel's Wharf is home to ❸ Pieminister, which serves the old-time Londoners' delicacy of pie and mash. Beyond Gabriel's Wharf you can dismount and follow the waterfront on a narrow walkway past unusual design studios and shops. Alternatively, cross Bernie Spain Gardens and then ride the roads (and cobblestones) to rejoin the Thames by Tate Modern downstream of Blackfriars Bridge.

The riverside complex beyond the Gardens is topped by the Oxo Tower, whose distinctive illuminated windows were designed to get round a 20th-century prohibition on illuminated advertising. That they spelled out the name of a well-known convenience food was defended as pure coincidence. On the eighth floor of the Tower is an expensive restaurant and brasserie where – you may be sure – they make their own stock; it also has an alfresco terrace and wonderful views. Note that cycling is banned adjacent to the Oxo Tower.

❹ Tate Modern, formerly Bankside Power Station, reopened as the home of lots of important 20th-century art in 2000. Entry to the café and main collection is free. The Millennium Footbridge (❺ 1.75 miles) was another successful millennium project, although, after a wild opening weekend when the novelty of a new crossing drew crowds and queues, it was closed for an extended period while the engineers worked out how to damp the wobble that unforeseen impromptu synchronised walking produced. The bridge links Bankside to St Paul's Cathedral, whose dome nestles nervously among the skyscrapers of the City of London.

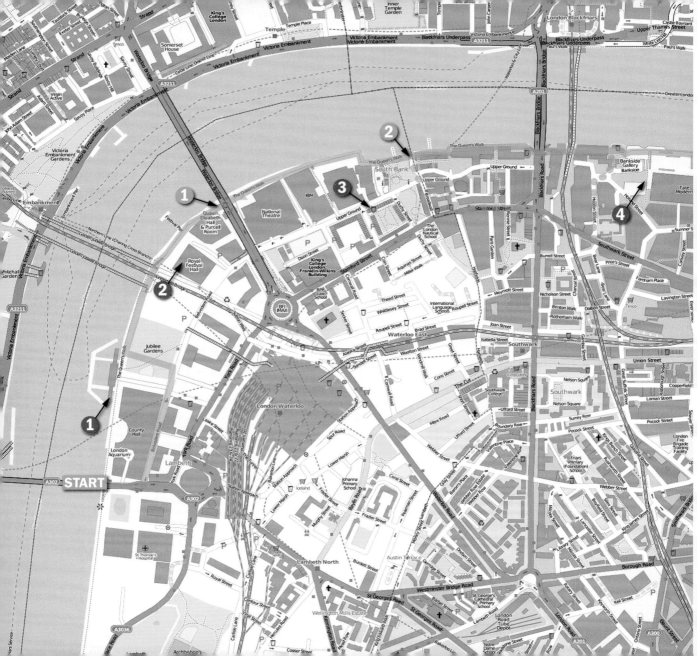

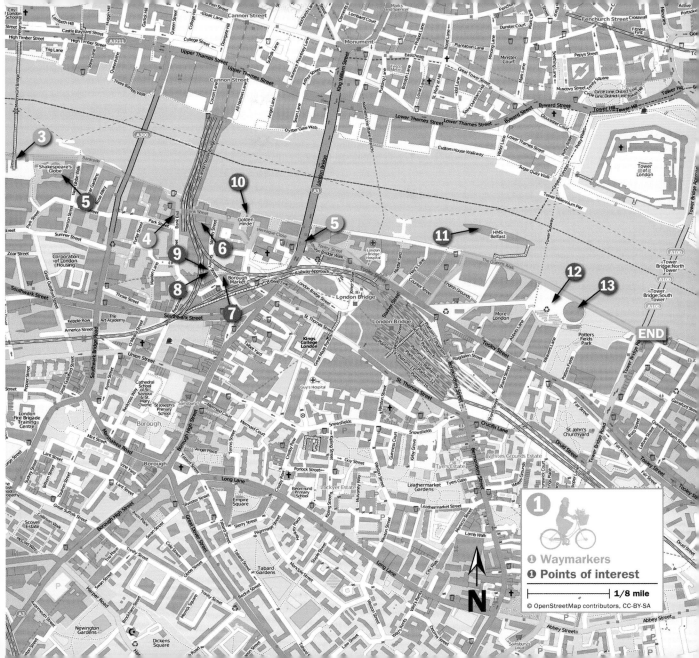

Route Directions

START at the south-east corner of Westminster Bridge, by the Lion statue

Straight on Westminster Bridge Road, away from the river

Traffic lights: left past the barrier into Belvedere Road (nervous riders can walk their bikes to here and start after the barrier)

Left just beyond exit barrier towards London Eye, into Jubilee Gardens

Right by London Eye (walking may be necessary) on to Thames Path

❶ **0.7 miles Pass** under Waterloo Bridge (by British Film Institute)

❷ **0.9 miles Pass** Gabriel's Wharf, dismount at Oxo Tower then continue on Thames Path if you don't mind walking narrow sections. (This route involves a well-signposted diversion with steps until building work on the new South Bank station is completed in late 2011)

> **Alternative route, instead of Thames Path:**
> *Right through Bernie Spain Gardens*
> *Left into Upper Ground*
> *Right into Hatfields*
> *Left into Stamford Street*
> *Traffic lights: straight into Southwark Street, crossing Blackfriars Road*

First left into Hopton Street, go round right-hand bend

T-junction: left into Hopton Street (on cobbles)

Up ramp on right to Tate Modern

Left towards river

Right to rejoin Thames Path

Under Blackfriars Bridge to Millennium Bridge (next to Tate Modern)

❸ **1.75 miles** Millennium Bridge (next to Tate Modern)

Right-hand bend, pass Anchor Pub

❹ **2 miles Left** into Clink Street – Pickfords Wharf

Right by *Golden Hinde* (walking may be necessary)

Left into Cathedral Street, round right-hand bend

Sharp left into Montague Close (keep the Cathedral on your right, unless you want to visit Borough Market, which you will find further down Cathedral Street)

❺ **2.3 miles Under** London Bridge, into Tooley Street

T-junction: left continuing on Tooley Street

Left into Battlebridge Lane, past Hays Galleria and barrier

Right into Thames Path and dismount – riding banned around City Hall

END 2.9 miles at Tower Bridge

The law stops south of the river

For most of London's history, entertainments within the City were strictly limited. Despite the wealth and dubious morals of its inhabitants, or perhaps because of them, no theatres or bawdy houses were permitted in the City, just churches and markets. The South Bank, however, lay beyond the walls and, even more viscerally, across the water; the City's ancient privileges and mores did not hold here. So when a young gallant's thoughts turned to pleasures and diversions, he'd hail a boatman and cross the river. One such boatman, Edward Sells, lived at the narrow, red-doored house named Cardinal's Wharf in the mid-18th century. The house was built around 1710, and a plaque proudly declares that Sir Christopher Wren lived here while he was building St Paul's. The timings suggest this is debatable, but nonetheless Cardinal's Wharf remains a pocket of 18th-century charm in the now fully redeveloped South Bank.

Rolling east there is ❺ Shakespeare's Globe, a Tudor wooden 'O' reconstructed close to its original site. In England – where old buildings are easy to find – reconstructions are generally considered cheap and nasty. It took an outsider to see past this prejudice: the Globe project was conceived and driven by Sam Wanamaker, an American film director and actor. You can watch Shakespeare's plays (modern material is also in the repertoire) at the Globe while being lightly drizzled on, but authenticity doesn't extend to bear–baiting spectaculars.

Continue down the river past the standard selection of restaurants. This newly developed section makes for a much smoother ride and lulls you into a false sense of security before you reach the cobblestones of old Southwark. Prepare for a bone-rattling ride past the Anchor Pub and down claustrophobic Clink Street (❹ 2 miles). As you jostle down the narrow streets, spare a thought for the thousands of prisoners that passed through Clink Prison between the 1144 and 1780. The ❻ Clink Prison Museum is located on the original site and explores what went on within the walls of the most notorious medieval prison.

Hearts of oak and steel

A right turn into Stoney Street takes you to ❼ Borough Market, a wholesale market where fine food is also sold retail from Thursday to Saturday. Stoney Street offers more food opportunities, including the ❽ Wright Brothers Oyster & Porter House, where you can take

London Eye.

South Bank, by the Royal Festival Hall.

an outdoor table on market days, and **➒** Feng Sushi for more exotic seafood. Back on Clink Street, which turns into Pickfords Wharf, there are more nautical echoes from the replica of Sir Francis Drake's **➓** *Golden Hinde*. This tiny sailing ship, squeezed into St Mary Overie Dock, prompts awe. They went around the world? In this? But even if, to modern eyes, it looks quaint, this vessel was the leading edge of technology in the 16th century, and its crew – out of contact for years – was more daring than any astronaut.

In mute commentary on where the values of the age lie, Southwark Cathedral is dwarfed by the Shard skyscraper shooting up behind it. Riding under London Bridge (**➎** 2.3 miles) on to Tooley Street takes you momentarily back to the busy world. A left turn into Battle Bridge Lane brings you back to the Thames. This section of the river, named the Pool of London, was once a bustling port (and portal for world domination when the cartographic pink of the British Empire covered a quarter of the globe), before shipping containers and coastal deep-water ports led to the collapse of commercial traffic in the Thames in the 1960s. Moored in the pool and open as a museum is **⓫** HMS *Belfast*, an 11,000-ton battlecruiser that was launched in 1939 – the year the British Empire reached its territorial peak. The Empire may have fallen, but its fall – the capital of centuries spent defeating Nazism – became it well.

Unfortunately, riding is banned on the section of the Thames Path around City Hall. Pass by the modern-day amphitheatre **⓬** the Scoop, where during the summer months you can enjoy free film screenings, theatre and other activities. Just beyond is **⓭** City Hall, the replacement – after an embarrassing interregnum when London had no elected regional government – for County Hall. The shape is to maximise the ratio of internal volume to surface area and thus conserve energy. It has a continuous spiral walkway running around the inside of the outer skin, so – in theory – you could ride a bike to the top. City Hall is small, in comparison to County Hall, but that doesn't mean that London is now run by fewer bureaucrats, just that they no longer all occupy the same complex.

The journey ends with the iconic view of Tower Bridge, and on the far bank, the Tower of London. If you want to get back to Westminster in a hurry, you can fly back via Southwark Street, Stamford Street and York Road, otherwise you can drift back the way you came. However slowly you got here you're sure to have missed something interesting on this endlessly fascinating window into London's past, present and future (**END** 2.9 miles).

❶ **Millennium Wheel – London Eye**
Riverside Building, next to County Hall, Westminster Bridge Road, SE1 7PB (0870 990 8883, www.londoneye.com). Open July, Aug, 10am-9.30pm daily. Sept-June 10am-8.30pm daily. Admission charge.
❷ **Royal Festival Hall**
Belvedere Road, SE1 8XX (0844 875 0073, http://ticketing.southbankcentre.co.uk/venues/ royal-festival-hall). Open 10am-11pm daily. Admission free. Shows charge.
❸ **Pieminister**
Gabriel's Wharf, 56 Upper Ground, SE1 9PP (7928 5755, www.pieminister.co.uk). Open 10am-5pm daily.
❹ **Tate Modern**
Millbank, SW1P 4RG (7887 8888, www.tate.org.uk). Open 10am-6pm daily; late opening 6-10pm first Fri of mth. Tours 11am, noon, 2pm, 3pm Mon-Fri; noon, 3pm Sat, Sun. Admission free.

❺ **Shakespeare's Globe**
21 New Globe Walk, SE1 9DT (7401 9919, 7902 1500 tours, www.shakespeares-globe.org). Tours Oct-Apr 10am-5pm daily. May-Sept 9am-12.30pm daily. Admission charge.
❻ **Clink Prison Museum**
1 Clink Street, SE1 9DG (7403 0900, www.clink.co. uk). Open June-Sept 10am-9pm daily. Oct-May 10am-6pm Mon-Fri; 10am-9pm Sat, Sun. Admission charge.
❼ **Borough Market**
Southwark Street, SE1 1TL (7407 1002, www.boroughmarket.org.uk). Open 11am-5pm Thur; noon-6pm Fri; 8am-5pm Sat.
❽ **Wright Brothers Oyster & Porter House**
11 Stoney Street, SE1 9AD (7403 9554, www.thewrightbrothers.co.uk). Open noon-11pm Mon-Fri; 11am-11pm Sat; noon-9pm Sun.
❾ **Feng Sushi**
13 Stoney Street, SE1 9AD (7407 8744, www.fengsushi.co.uk). Open 11.30am-10pm Mon, Sun; 11.30am-10.30pm Tue, Wed; 11.30am-11pm Thur-Sat.
❿ **Golden Hinde**
Pickfords Wharf, Clink Street, SE1 9DG (7403 0123, www.goldenhinde.com). Open daily; times vary. Admission charge.
⓫ **HMS Belfast**
Morgan's Lane, Tooley Street, SE1 2JH (7940 6300, www.iwm.org.uk). Open Mar-Oct 10am-6pm daily. Nov-Feb 10am-5pm daily. Admission charge.
⓬ **The Scoop**
The Queen's Walk, SE1 2AA (7403 4866, www.morelondon.com). Open 24hrs daily.
⓭ **City Hall**
Queen's Walk, SE1 2AA (7983 4000, www.london. gov.uk/city-hall/visitor-information). Open 8.30am-6pm Mon-Thur; 8.30am-5pm Fri. Admission free.

SHORT AND SWEET

What Bike?

Right. That's it. It's decided. It's time to dust down whatever you've got lurking at the back of the shed and get out on two wheels again. Chances are that all your old bike needs is its tyres pumped up and a drop of oil on the chain and you'll be ready to roll.

Of course, to enjoy Disney-esque, pedal-powered family outings, everyone will need a bike in good working order too, but as long as it's roadworthy, anything will do the trick: the old ten-speed, that retro ladies' bike, a BMX.

Expect to pay: nothing, if you're lucky – just the time it takes you to get it roadworthy, either by your own fair hand if you're feeling confident, or courtesy of your local bike shop for a small fee.

A new budget bike

If what you've already got just won't cut it, there are often some great deals to be had on cheap and cheerful bikes – more often than not mountain bikes – at larger local supermarkets. Look for familiar brand names, such as Shimano gears, but be aware that some of these cheaper bikes require assembly. There are plenty of specialist bike shops around London that will do this, provide you with advice and be happy to sell you a bike too.

Best brands: away from the supermarkets, stores such as Halfords and Decathlon offer decent, cheaper models, which will have had more knowledgeable hands construct them.

Those on a budget could do a lot worse than an Apollo Code men's hybrid bike from Halfords, with its racing bike-sized wheels and straight-handlebar comfort, along with those Shimano gears you're looking for. Or go for his 'n' hers Elswick bikes, which are even available from Asda.

Expect to pay: you're not going to get much change from £100 these days, but there are plenty of bikes that dip just below three figures, so shop around. You can often get last year's bikes at lower prices.

Family hangers-on

For smaller family members, trailers, child seats and even trailer bikes – 'half bikes', which attach to the back of a normal bike – will ensure that there's a way for them to come along for the ride too.

Best brands: for child seats, look for brands such as Hamax and WeeRide, while Halfords' own brand of bike trailers are worth a look, as is the Trail Gator – a 'tow bar' that attaches to the front of your little one's bike to create a rudimentary tandem.

Expect to pay: child seats are often the price of a cheap bike, but tend to last well, so can be used for younger siblings later. Trailers tend to be pricier still, so you'll be relieved when you're child is old enough to have their own bike – and a Trail Gator will help their confidence as they're starting out, well priced at around £50-£60. Again, shop around.

Bikes by the day

If all else fails, Londoners can always jump aboard a 'Boris bike'. Yes, the bikes are pretty unwieldy, but they're perfectly good for a family pootle.

Expect to pay: after an access fee, it will cost between nothing for half an hour to £50 for a maximum 24 hours' use. See www.tfl.gov.uk/cycling for further details.

Riding on Air

If you're coming back to biking after time on four wheels – or if you're just starting out – cycling in town can seem a pretty hairy proposition. This ride, with its mix of parks and residential streets, will increase your confidence and provide a thorough workout for those newly exercised bicycle muscles. The route links the spacious elegance of Hyde Park with the quirky variety of Battersea Park (if it had any more trees, it would be a wood not a park). And it can be extended at either end with scenic circuits away from motor traffic. Try it on a Sunday morning and wonder why you ever worried about riding in London.

Hyde Park is central London's biggest park. Its major features are two ornamental ponds – The Long Water and the Serpentine – which were landscaped in the 18th century by damming the Westbourne River. In summer, there's public swimming in the Serpentine, but those hardy souls who want to keep swimming all year round have to join the Serpentine Swimming Club. On summer evenings, well-organised, mass street-skates start from the park; on Fridays they depart from Hyde Park Corner, and on Wednesdays from Serpentine Road, which is also affectionately known as 'the Beach'.

START If you need to fuel up before kicking off, the ❶ Serpentine Bar & Kitchen serves seasonal food from an all-day menu. Even if you're not hungry, it's a convenient start point for the ride, standing at the east end of the lakes, where the north end of the dam meets Serpentine Road.

Note that Hyde Park has 'Boris bikes' for hire. Battersea Park lies outside the zone, but there's a hire station just north of the river on Flood Street.

The quickest way to the Albert Gate – where the Crystal Palace stood in 1851 – is to walk south, either along the top of the dam or through the secluded area beneath it known as the Dell. If you want to ride, set off west along Serpentine Road (in fact, a quiet boulevard) with the water on your left. When you join the road, use it to cross the bridge between the Serpentine and Long Water. Feel free to hop off your bike and take a photo: on a sunny day the pavements will be lined with others making the most of the scenic backdrop.

Opposite the Serpentine Gallery, turn east (❶ 0.8 miles) to cycle along the bike path beside the sandy, horse-exercising track known as Rotten Row – a rather

Start Hyde Park, W2 2UH
Finish Battersea Park, SW11 4NJ
Time 1 hour minimum
Distance 5 miles
Connects with ❻
Traffic & safety The park riding can be tricky when the parks are busy. The road riding is easy on Sunday mornings, but the roads are busy at other times
Terrain Flat
Transport *Start* Knightsbridge tube. *End* Battersea Park rail
TFL bike-hire scheme *Start* Albert Gate, Hyde Park. *End* Flood Street, Chelsea
Good for City riding virgins

delicious corruption of 'route du roi' or King's Road. If you just want to stay in the park, you can complete the fairly flat training circuit by continuing straight on, rejoining Serpentine Road just below the intimidating statue of *Achilles*, where a sharp left turn takes you back to the Beach and the Serpentine Kitchen. However, it's definitely not safe to go 'eyeballs-out' on this route. Expect unexpected random behaviour – be it from dogs, babies, drunks, in-line skaters or even other cyclists – but, at quiet times, riders who aren't super-fit can get a good workout. For longer, faster circuits, head up past *Achilles*, parallel to Park Lane, and join the last part of Ride ❻ near Speakers' Corner.

The open road

To continue this ride, keep going straight alongside Rotten Row past the east end of the Serpentine, with the wooded Dell area on your left. Turn right to roll a couple of smooth tracks across bumpy Rotten Row.

Exit the park through the Albert Gate (❷ 1.5 miles) in front of the French Embassy. Be careful here. The contra-flow bike lane in William Street puts you in 'the door zone'. Being hit when someone opens a car door is easily the most common accident for cyclists in London. At least here all the vehicles face towards you. If you hit a door opening towards you, it's more likely to slam shut than knock you down, but as soon as you get into Lowndes Square, check over your shoulder and take a safer, more prominent line clear of the doors' ambit.

If the mood strikes, you can do a spot of (window) shopping in the designer shops in Lowndes Square. Alternatively, you could take a small detour left down cobbled Motcomb Street to find art galleries and a selection of shops, cafés and pubs, including a gourmet delicatessen and specialist chocolate shop.

Consider the lives of the rich and famous as you ride along Cadogan Place: tennis courts on the right, palatial Victorian residences on the left... it feels a world away from central London. The Westbourne River, for most of its length, is one of London's lost waterways, its flow buried underground in pipes. The ride actually follows the river's course down to Sloane Square (❸ 2.3 miles), where the iron pipe that carries the river can be seen from the platform of Sloane Square tube station. The square itself isn't too much fun to ride around, so it's worth dismounting and taking a look to see what's playing at the ❷ Royal Court Theatre, next door to the tube station. The Royal Court can plausibly claim to be the most important English-language theatre in London.

En Route

The Princess Diana Memorial Fountain is laid on the slope between the bike track and the Serpentine. The Memorial is a pair of artificial streams, one placid and one turbulent, running in granite channels with a common start and a common finish, to form an oval. It opened in 2004, but modifications were needed to make it safer and to prevent flooding and erosion of the grass. At the time, the cost and delays – a consequence of building a dynamic feature that the public were encouraged to use – generated criticism. Some said it was an appropriate monument to Diana, being both 'dangerous and expensive', but it can now be considered a success. The cool sculptural quality makes an interesting contrast with the romantic faux-natural waterfall in the Dell at the other end of the Serpentine.

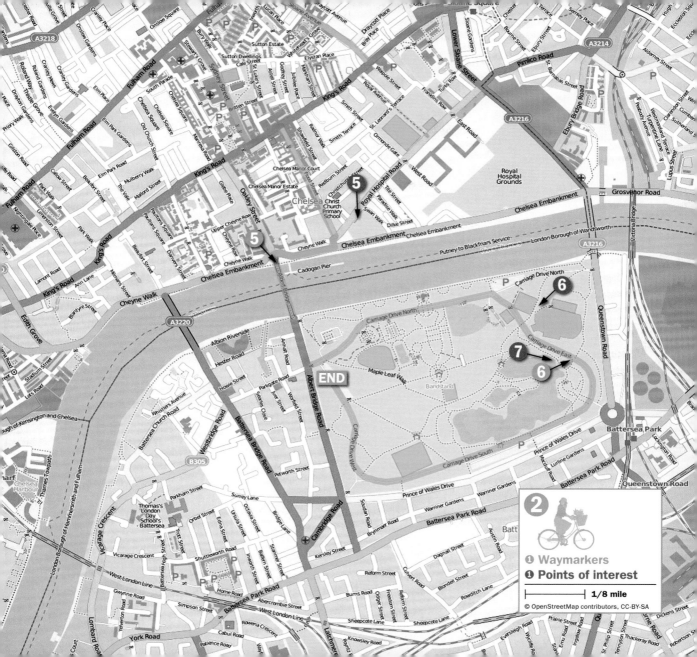

Route Directions

START at the Serpentine Bar & Kitchen at the eastern end of the Serpentine in Hyde Park
Ride west along Serpentine Road, 'the Beach', beside the north shore of the Serpentine
Pass barrier
Left physically straight on into the Ring
❶ 0.8 miles Left opposite Serpentine Gallery on to cycle track
Continue parallel to Rotten Row
Right just past the dam at the end of the Serpentine, to cross Rotten Row to Albert Gate

> **Alternative, direct route instead of cycling around the Serpentine:**
> *Walk south through the Dell beneath the dam at the end of the Lake to Rotten Row and continue to Albert Gate*

❷ 1.5 miles Traffic light: cross South Carriage Drive to Albert Gate
Traffic light: cross Knightsbridge into William Street – Lowndes Square – Lowndes Street
Right after the zebra crossing across Lowndes Street
Left into Cadogan Place
T-junction: right into Cadogan Place
❸ 2.3 miles T-junction: left into Sloane Street

Roundabout Sloane Square, fourth exit into King's Road
Right into Anderson Street – Sloane Avenue
❹ 3 miles T-junction: left by the Michelin Building into Fulham Road
Traffic light: left into Sydney Street
Traffic light, T-junction: left into King's Road
Right into Flood Street
T-junction: left into Royal Hospital Road
Right into Swan Walk (one-way street): dismount to walk down to Chelsea Physic Garden
T-junction: right into Chelsea Embankment; footway cycling is legal here
❺ 4.2 miles Traffic light: left on to Albert Bridge, cross the river
Left into Battersea Park through Albert Gate – Carriage Drive North
Mini roundabout by events area, second exit into Carriage Drive East. London Recumbents is on the left just after the Community Garden
❻ 5.2 miles La Gondola al Parco is on the right
Continue on Carriage Drive East – Carriage Drive South
END continue on Carriage Drive West to complete a training circuit

Ground-breaking plays such as *Look Back in Anger* and *The Rocky Horror Show* premiered here, and it continues to produce interesting new work. If you take a gamble on a new drama, the ticket will be cheaper and the performances fresher than at most West End theatres. Peter Jones, the department store opposite, was the first steel and glass building in Britain.

The King's Road, Chelsea's main radial route, was once a centre of London's bohemia. The Chelsea Arts Club Ball, latterly held at the Albert Hall, was suspended in 1959; it had become too riotous. The artistic tradition continues today, although in the more staid form of the ❸ Saatchi Gallery in the former Duke of York's Barracks, which is free to the public. It's on

Serpentine Gallery.

Serpentine Gallery

Serpentine Bar & Kitchen.

Princess Diana Memorial Fountain.

your left as you cycle past the designer and high street shops of the King's Road.

Cycling along Sloane Avenue you come to the ❹ Michelin Building at the junction with the Fulham Road (❹ 3 miles). The building's lurid colours may have faded since it was built in 1911, and some of the stained glass is missing, but the cartoon details remain. As you round the corner, you can appreciate it in its full glory, although you may need to cross the road to see the now-ubiquitous Michelin Man presiding over the grand entrance.

This is the modern world

In essence, the Michelin Building is a temple to modernism, and one of the key elements of an enjoyable bike ride, the pneumatic tyre. In the 19th century, a road was a bumpy stretch of stones, or mud or dust, and a tyre was an iron hoop encircling a wooden cartwheel. The idea of installing a bag of air around a wheel was ridiculous. People laughed. Street urchins threw stones and chanted 'bladder wheel'. But the first of the ceramic tiled panels on the Sloane Avenue wall shows the Michelin Company's first racing triumph, Charles Terront riding towards victory in the inaugural Paris-Brest-Paris race in 1891. In the panel, the roadside cross and the peasant woman's costume signify the wilds of Brittany that Terront was riding through. All over the industrial world, early-adopting riders were discovering that air tyres were faster and smoother and altogether more comfortable, but Terront's dominanting win in the Paris-Brest-Paris race was a key moment in changing public perception. In Paris they invented a ring-shaped pastry and called it the Paris-Brest. What's more, it really set the cash tills ringing for Michelin.

Nowadays, if you suggested a start-up company based on producing pneumatic tyres, publishing maps

and guidebooks, and inspecting restaurants, you'd be laughed out of your investment banker's expensively subsidised office. But back then, fired by the optimism that permeated the Edwardians, it seemed perfectly natural. After all, if you're touring on a bike, you need to know where to go (the Michelin Guides) and where to eat (the Michelin stars).

The Michelin Building celebrated its centenary in 2011. So it's taken a century to establish the limits of the cheap-energy economy. The motorised traveller can enjoy a five-star breakfast, and maybe manage a five-star lunch, but by dinner time the car driver is jaded. The cycle tourist is able to flit between walking in tight spaces, pootling along among strollers or acting as a vehicle on the road, freed from the drudgery of hiking or carrying bags, and all without sacrificing the pedestrian's ability to stop and savour any detail that catches the eye. What's more, all the exercise means you develop the appetite of a ditch digger and the figure of a dancer.

Modernism means constant change and the Michelin Building is no longer a garage or the offices of a tyre/publishing company. There's a bookshop that sells Michelin products and posters, a designer furnishing store, a florist, and a seafood stall, café, oyster bar and restaurant. Whether you go in to just enjoy the metal doors and ceramic mosaics, neck a coffee, buy a map or take on calories to get to Portsmouth, a whispered 'Vive Terront, vive Michelin, vive le Velo' is appropriate.

Turning left down Sydney Street, you'll find St Luke's Church with surrounding greens, a garden centre and Chelsea Town Hall at the bottom. In this central location, it almost feels like a village, albeit one with impeccably dressed inhabitants. A short run back up the King's Road ends with a right turn into Flood Street. The Arts and Craft building on this corner was once a gentleman's club. Until 2009, it housed Antiquarius, an indoor antiques market with 120 stalls. The closure of the market, which was replaced with a branch of fashion and furnishing chainstore Anthropologie, was mourned by many as the final step in the King's Road's mutation from louche hangout for artistic types to just another upscale, international shopping street.

A green and pleasant city

But if the King's Road is in danger of becoming Anyroad, the ❺ Chelsea Physic Garden at the foot of Flood Street (accessed via Swan Walk) serves to situate you in the unique currents of history and chance that make places what they are. The Chelsea Physic Garden was established by the Apothecaries Company in 1673 on grounds they had leased with the intention of building a boathouse for their ceremonial barge. The first heated greenhouse in England was erected here in 1681. Two years later, the first cedar of Lebanon trees in England were cultivated here, and, in the mid-18th century, cotton seeds from the garden established the crop in the new colony of North America. In 1848, tea plants from China were re-exported from the garden to India. If you're interested in horticulture or herbalism, you'll enjoy a visit. The café serves own-made cakes.

At the end of Swan Lane, you reach the Chelsea Embankment (which was designed by Joseph Bazalgette, the great Victorian civil engineer and the man who prevented London suffering another 'Great Stink', as a boulevard and intercept sewer), which opens up a panorama of the Thames and Battersea Park – our destination – on the South Bank. You can attempt a right-hand turn across the traffic, but it might be just as fast to turn left and cycle up to the nearby zebra crossing. You can then cycle either along the wide Chelsea Embankment or choose the slightly bumpier (but also quieter) cycle/pedestrian pavement.

Albert Bridge (❺ 4.2 miles) used to carry signs requesting bodies of marching men to break step to avoid shaking it down – Chelsea was once full of barracks and this is a route to Clapham Common, Aldershot and Portsmouth. An early Tom Stoppard play, *Albert's Bridge*, closes with this image, of too much order creating chaos, when an army of painters comes to restore the bridge with disastrous consequences. A sign on the Prince Albert pub, opposite the Prince Albert Gate to Battersea Park, alludes to the signs and the joke, requesting marching men to break step before entering the bar. The bridge – a curious three-span hybrid of suspension and cantilever systems – was fully overhauled and reconditioned in spring 2011 by a team whose actions were, presumably, carefully uncoordinated.

Battersea Park, which was reclaimed from marsh with spoil from the Royal Docks, is full of surprises. There's the Peace Pagoda, with its golden Buddha gazing serenely over the river (a gift to the people of London from the Nipponzan Myohoji Buddhist Order in 1985), the grand avenue of fountains, the massive odd rockery across the pond from ❻ La Gondola al Parco (❻ 5.2 miles), an unpretentious but very welcome Italian café-restaurant. The Carriage Drive perimeter makes for a lovely ride if you want to ride a training loop to the END. There's some interaction with parking motor traffic at the lap's south-eastern corner, but mostly it's broad, smooth and clear.

❼ London Recumbents offer non-standard bikes for hire from their shipping container base, so you can experiment with stretching the technological envelope in the manner of Charles Terront.

In historical terms, 120 years is a short time, little more than the blink of an eye. So you could say that the pneumatic tyre, with all its potential, really only hit the streets yesterday morning. The exciting implication of that is that the pioneer era is not yet over. We really do live in interesting times.

❶ Serpentine Bar & Kitchen
Serpentine Road, Hyde Park, W2 2UH (7706 8114, www.serpentinebarandkitchen.com). Open 8am-7pm Mon-Wed, Fri-Sun; 8am-8pm Thur.
❷ Royal Court Theatre
Sloane Square, SW1W 8AS (7565 5000, www.royalcourttheatre.com). Open 10am-8pm Mon-Sat.
❸ Saatchi Gallery
Duke of York's HQ, Duke of York Square, King's Road, SW3 4SQ (7811 3085, www.saatchi-gallery.co.uk). Open 10am-6pm daily. Admission free.
❹ Michelin Building
Bibendum, 81 Fulham Road, SW3 6RD (7581 5817 restaurant, 7589 1480 oyster bar, 7590 1189 café, www.bibendum.co.uk). Open Restaurant noon-2.30pm, 7-11pm Mon-Sat; 12.30-3pm, 7-10.30pm Sun. Oyster Bar noon-10.30pm daily. Café 8.30am-5pm Mon-Fri; 9am-noon Sat.
❺ Chelsea Physic Garden
66 Royal Hospital Road, entrance on Swan Walk, SW3 4HS (7352 5646, www.chelseaphysic garden.co.uk). Open Apr-Oct noon-5pm Wed-Fri; noon-6pm Sun, bank hol Mon. Admission charge.
❻ La Gondola al Parco
Battersea Park, SW11 4NJ (7978 1655, www.batterseapark.org). Open 8.30am-7pm daily.
❼ London Recumbents
Battersea Park, SW11 4NJ (7498 6543, www.londonrecumbents.co.uk). Open 10am-5pm Sat, Sun.

Kit Bag

Head protection

Helmets have come a long way since the Lycra-covered, polystyrene monstrosities of the 1980s and '90s. Today's helmets are bordering on cool – in both senses of the word – as well as being incredibly light. Although wearing a helmet is not compulsory, most cyclists in London do wear one.

Your local bike shop will be able to help with sizing and fitting. What you don't want to do is wear a helmet that is not properly adjusted and too loose (or too tight), or to wear it perched on the back of your head like an afterthought, as incorrect use is quite likely to do more harm than good.

Modern cycling helmets are shaped from polystyrene foam covered with a thin plastic shell. In an accident, they will either crack or break completely, but it is their function to do so: the foam is there to absorb the impact. It's important to replace your helmet if you crash as its effectiveness may have been impaired.

Helmet style

While today's helmets are designed to look stylish and discreet, urban hipsters will appreciate the throwback styling of the so-called 'p***-pot' style of helmet, which has made a triumphant return. Popular with skateboarders in the '70s, the style is now a fraction of the weight of its predecessor, while staying faithful to the original look.

Best brands: Giro and Bell are two of the best helmet brands, with years of experience behind them, and a huge range of lightweight, ventilated, good-looking models to choose from.

Expect to pay: prices vary, but all helmets on sale in the UK will have passed the EN 1078 standard – look for the label on the inside. The cost tends to tally with weight, ventilation and stylish good looks, but expect to pay anywhere from around £30 for the skater-inspired Bell Faction to a whopping £200 for top-end models such as the Giro Aeon.

Pack it in

As you're still a little way off from riding the Tour de France – at least for now – you'll probably not need a water bottle and holder (or bottle cage, to call it by its proper name) on your bike, but taking a bottle of something to drink in your rucksack may not be a bad idea. A rucksack is also a good place to keep your lock if you're planning on leaving your bike anywhere and, if you want to avoid having to walk, then you ought to have a puncture repair kit, a spare inner tube, tyre levers and a pump in there as well.

Less is more

That's just about all you need – nothing fancy. Comfy, grippy shoes will keep your feet happily on the pedals, and a bell is a courteous way of alerting pedestrians and slower-moving riders to your presence. The only other thing you'll need to remember is a bucketload of enthusiasm. If it's been a while since you last pushed on a pair of pedals, be prepared for your legs to cry out in pain a little at first – ditto your undercarriage, back, shoulders, neck, hands. But remember, the pain is only temporary; the smugness of having got out there and done it will last a lot longer.

Towpaths & Toast

This gentle ride along towpaths, parks and streets, through the dense texture of the inner city, provides opportunities to visit an unscientific sample of London's most innovative bike shops and to drop in on a random selection of coffee joints. In a fine example of the sort of joined-up thinking that bicycling engenders, there's even some overlap between the categories, allowing you to sip a cappuccino while discussing the merits of fixed-gear bikes. The route rounds off with the awe-inspiring spectacle of an overview of the site of the London 2012 Olympic and Paralympic Games.

START Before climbing on the saddle, get a quick caffeine zip with an espresso at ❶ Bar Italia – its 24-hour day means you can start the ride at any time, morning or night. The coffee bar opened in 1949 when espresso machines were an exotic rarity in the capital. The Italians who arrived in London from the Old Country and found cheap lodgings in Soho have now all moved to the suburbs – mostly tracking the Piccadilly Line north – but many still work in the area's bars and restaurants. If you can't get to Italy in May, this is the obvious place to watch the Giro d'Italia live on the big screen.

Saddled up and rolling, one of the most difficult tasks when cycling in Soho is keeping your attention on the road. The area is full of the self-conscious, and the self-consciously beautiful. Its cosmopolitan reputation dates, at least, from the arrival of the Huguenots (Protestant refugees) from France in the 17th century. Once London's primary red-light district – 164 establishments were listed in the area in 1981 – purges of corrupt policemen, stricter local licensing and a general relaxation of attitudes elsewhere have diluted Soho's concentration of strip joints and porn shops. The tradition persists in the area close to Piccadilly but in general Soho has now become a fashionable district of fancy offices, bars, restaurants and boutiques.

Sneaking through unpromising alleys takes you past ❷ St Giles in the Fields, built in 1733. This hidden Palladian church once dominated the area. It stands on the site of an isolated medieval leper hospital. Condemned prisoners being transported from London to their place of execution on the gallows at Tyburn (near present-day Marble Arch) were offered the 'Cup of Charity' as they passed

SHORT AND SWEET

Start Bar Italia, Frith Street, W1D 4RT
Finish Greenway, Stratford, E15 2PJ
Time 1.5 hours minimum
Distance 8 miles
Connects with ❾ ❿
Traffic & safety Mostly busy urban side streets, with some main roads. Park sections and paths shared with pedestrians
Terrain Flat with two short but steep hills
Transport *Start* Leicester Square tube/Charing Cross rail. *End* DLR (folding bikes only) Pudding Mill Lane
TFL bike-hire scheme Wardour Street, Soho
Good for Boulevardiers

Soho.

the hospital chapel. Rather appropriately, St Giles remains the patron saint of outcasts.

Crossing Charing Cross Road, a 19th-century improvement driven through unplanned slums, takes you out of Soho proper but Denmark Street, also known as 'Tin Pan Alley', is the centre for another local speciality, music. The Sex Pistols made their first demos while staying at 6 Denmark Street. The nine-year-old Mozart, giving Justin Bieber a run for his money on early world tours, gave afternoon recitals at 20 Frith Street while lodging there between 1764 and 1765. Music shops are still prominent in the area.

The redevelopment of St Giles Circus, sacrificed on the altar of traffic management in the 1960s, included the construction of Centrepoint, an early London skyscraper. The office block remained, notoriously, empty for ten years, while its owner waited for a single tenant to occupy all 34 floors. During the 1970s, this 'monument to capitalism's inefficiencies' was supposedly an important landmark for tour groups from Eastern Europe. The current building works are for the new Crossrail train link.

Oxford Street, on the line of a Roman road from Hampshire to Suffolk, is the A40, the road to Oxford, but it actually takes its name from Edward Harley, Earl of Oxford. New Oxford Street is another 19th-century

En Route

In an attic laboratory of the same building that houses Bar Italia, Scottish engineer John Logie Baird gave the first public demonstration of the transmission of moving images – the precursor of television – on 26 January 1926. A blue plaque high on the wall commemorates the event.

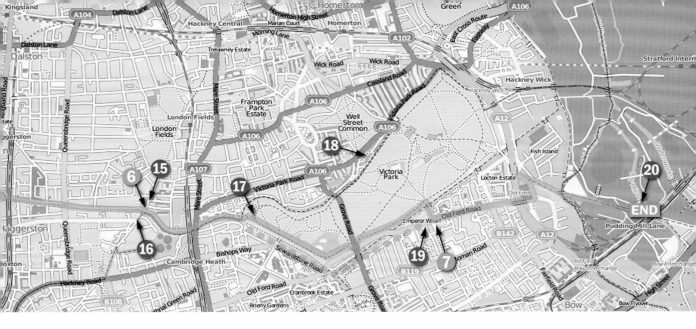

improvement, a bypass for St Giles High Street, and not a particularly pleasant road to cycle along. But the route soon turns into Bloomsbury, a district of elegant residential squares and terraces that has slowly been taken over by institutions.

The first of these was the ❸ British Museum (❶ 0.6 miles), which opened in 1759. A short detour up Lamb's Conduit Street takes you to ❹ Coram's Fields, a tranquil park that adults can visit only if accompanied by a child. The ❺ Foundling Museum behind the park is open to all, runs an eclectic programme of music and events, and tells the story of Thomas Coram's Foundling Hospital. To reach it, turn left into Guildford Street, right into Lansdowne Terrace and cut through the adults' section of Coram's Fields, where you pass the Brunswick Centre on your right. The concrete on this award-winning, modernist housing scheme, with shops and an

arthouse cinema, was hardly dry when it featured as an enigmatic location in Michelangelo Antonioni's 1975 film *The Passenger*.

Cycle shopping

Returning to Lamb's Conduit Street (❷ 1.1 miles), stop to enjoy the relaxed atmosphere engendered by this pleasing mix of pubs, cafés and independent shops. ❻ Bikefix, at no.48, specialises in stuff you can't find in bicycle chain stores: recumbents from the Netherlands and Germany, freight bikes from Norfolk and Amsterdam, trailers, tandems and upmarket folding bikes from all over. ❼ Condor Cycles in Gray's Inn Road is the southern European equivalent; its classic road bikes come with covetable Condor-branded rim tape.

❽ Danny's in Lamb's Conduit Street is good for healthy food and juice. Round the corner, at

Route Directions

START Bar Italia, 22 Frith Street, W1D 4RT
Left (south) on Frith Street
Left into Old Compton Street
Left into Charing Cross Road
Right into Phoenix Street
T-junction: left into Stacey Street
Right at the end of the road through barrier into Flitcroft Street
T-junction: right into Denmark Street
Walk across St Giles High Street
Right then left into Earnshaw Street
T-junction: right into New Oxford Street
Traffic lights: left into Museum Street
❶ 0.6 miles T-junction: right into Great Russell Street
T-junction: left into Southampton Row
Walk across Southampton Row at the traffic lights and continue into Cosmo Place.
Straight on across Queen Square into Great Ormond Street
❷ 1.1 miles Right into Lamb's Conduit Street (or left for Coram's Fields)
Traffic lights: left into Theobald's Road
Traffic lights: left into Gray's Inn Road
Traffic lights: right into Calthorpe Street (Coram's Fields detour rejoins here)
Traffic lights: left and immediate right into Lloyd Baker Street
❸ 2.1 miles Left into Amwell Street
  Detour to Bobbin Bicycles:
    Straight on River Street – Myddleton Square – Chadwell Street to join St John Street; Bobbin Bicyles is on the right, at no.397. Head left

along St John Street, left into Pentonville Road and right into Penton Street to rejoin the route

Traffic lights: straight on into Penton Street – Barnsbury Road
Right into Richmond Avenue
Immediate left into Thornhill Road
❹ 2.9 miles Right into Barnsbury Street
T-junction: left into Upper Street.
Immediate right into Richmond Grove
Straight on past barriers into Braes Street
T-junction: right into Canonbury Road – New North Road
  Detour to Mosquito Bikes:
    At Canonbury Road, turn right into Astey's Row to reach Essex Road; turn left for Mosquito Bikes at no.123. Continue on Essex Road, then turn right into New North Road to rejoin route
❺ 4 miles Left into Baring Street (or climb down steps to reach canal towpath)
Straight on into Curtiss Gardens – Canal Walk – continue to find ramp access to towpath
Follow Regent's Canal towpath, under Whitmore Road, Kingsland Road, Queensbridge Road
❻ 5.2 miles Pass Broadway Market Lock (Lock 7 is just over the bridge)
Left into Victoria Park, at Canal Gate
Right on to track to stay parallel to the canal. Keep to the right of the ornamental lake
  Alternative route when Victoria Park is closed:
    Stay on the towpath. Continue straight past the Old Ford Lock and take the steps just

before the first bridge to join Old Ford Road.
The routes rejoin at Old Ford Road at ❼

Exit the park by roundabout Old Ford Road/
Grove Road

Cross Grove Road on cycle track and re-enter park

Keep right to stay parallel to the edge of the park

Exit the park at Gunmaker's Lane through barrier
over the canal bridge. (You can avoid this tight gap
by following Old Ford Road at the last roundabout.
Bikeworks is in the industrial estate on the right)

❼ **6.7 miles T-junction: left** into Old Ford Road

Straight on over foot/cycle bridge over Crown
Close/A12

Roundabout: first exit Wick Lane

Right into Greenway

END 7.7 miles at View Tube and the
Container Café

19 Theobald's Road, is the more traditional delights
of, er, chip shop ❾ Fryer's Delight. Continuing on, turn
left into Amwell Street (❸ 2.1 miles) or follow River
Street and cross Myddleton Square to find ❿ Bobbin
Bicycles in St John Street. This new shop, with a
belle-époque aesthetic, stocks interesting products
for people who like to give their bikes names.

Bike shops haven't made big money since 1902.
Bikes are simple, last forever and the personal
element can be troublesome. After all, what do you
say to a customer who comes in to complain, 'This
bike you sold me last week is very slow going up
hills'? These are hard times for independent bike
shops squeezed by proliferating chain stores and
web-based mail-order houses. In Barnsbury (❹ 2.9
miles), ⓫ Micycle goes for the personal-consultancy
angle, offering coffee in its walled garden, courses
in riding and maintenance, and a membership
scheme that enables customers to wash and fettle
their bikes on the premises. Perhaps a business
model of the future?

In 1946, the southern section of the New River
was closed but its serpentine trail can be detected
across Islington as a string of open spaces or ponds.
Its course, which crosses Cannonbury Road at the
junction with Braes Street, is now a linear park and
playground. Follow the path – there are steps at
the end, so you'll have to dismount – for a short
cut to ⓬ Mosquito Bikes on Essex Road. Mosquito
grew from a workers co-operative in Dalston and
complements its handmade bikes with an expert
fitting service. As you wheel down from Islington
towards Hoxton and Shoreditch, the new apartment
block that you can see on the New North Road, where
it crosses the Regent's Canal (❺ 4 miles), stands
on the site of Gainsborough Pictures, where a young
Alfred Hitchcock began his directing career.

Regent's Canal towpath near Victoria Park.

Waterway

The Regent's Canal here has emerged from the Islington Tunnel and is dropping toward the River Thames at Limehouse. There's a tiny coffee bar, ⑬ Towpath Café, and adjacent compact bike workshop, ⑭ Route Canale Cycles, on the towpath just past the Whitmore Street Bridge. In general, the towpath is wide enough for you to pass pedestrians comfortably. It is popular with joggers, cyclists and pram-pushing parents, so watch out for oncoming traffic. The canal boats you see on the ride will all have engines. However, horses once towed the canal boats, walking along the towpath and dragging the boats behind them. As such, some of the paths underneath the bridges are very narrow, with low archways and often no chance to see anyone coming in the other direction until the last minute. Bells (or carefree whistles) are recommended.

At the next lock, the canal crosses a significant prehistoric trail, which connected the lowest safe crossing point on the Thames, in the area of London Bridge, with the equivalent on the River Lea, around the Lea Bridge Road. This corridor takes in the flower market of Columbia Road, Mare Street Narrow Way and Broadway Market, which leads to London Fields. On a Saturday, consider detouring to ⑮ Broadway Market (❻ 5.2 miles), where upmarket restaurants and specialist food stalls abut betting shops and convenience stores and sell gourmet produce. In the afternoon, it's packed with East London fashionistas. ⑯ Lock 7, a bike-shop/café that sells second-hand bikes, stands just over the bridge.

Cycling on, you'll soon come to ⑰ Victoria Park. This glorious example of, of course, Victorian landscaping is bisected by Grove Road. The western half of the park is more formal, the eastern big and open enough to offer a flat training circuit. ⑱ The Britannia pub has a garden for safe bike parking. Note that the exit gap through Gunmaker's Gate is too tight for tricycles. If your bike is wide and you can't or don't want to lift it over the 1.5-metre railing, use Old Ford Road.

⑲ Bikeworks (❼ 6.7 miles), housed in a couple of units on the newly built industrial estate on the right of Gunmaker's Lane, is a community organisation that fixes and rents bikes, runs training courses and provides guided bike tours around the perimeter of the Olympic Park. It is a rare reliable source of reconditioned cycles. Be careful when riding down Old Ford Road. It tapers to a steep foot-and-cycle bridge, defended by a barriered chicane, so – if you have a multi-speed bike – change down early to cross above the Blackwall Tunnel Approach Road. A few yards up another steep hill and you'll see six spear-shaped sculptures, marking the entrance to the Greenway. This walking and cycling route crosses the River Lea Navigation on a bridge guarded by a concrete pillbox from World War II, and passes the Olympic Stadium on an elevated embankment. A temporary building made from steel shipping containers houses the View

En Route

Lamb's Conduit Street is named for Thomas Lambe who, in 1557, financed the restoration of a local water supply system based on a dam in the River Fleet. In those days, water came from local wells, springs and streams or was delivered from the River Thames by carriers. Across the Fleet valley, Lloyd Baker Street climbs sharply by Mount Pleasant – it used to be a rubbish dump; the name is ironic – toward the terminus of the New River. Not a river, new in 1613, this 40-mile, man-made channel delivered sweet drinking water from Amwell in Hertfordshire to New River Head, a bluff that allowed water to be gravity-fed to the homes of paying customers. The New River was a speculative venture by rich entrepreneur and goldsmith Hugh Myddleton. When his funds were almost exhausted, King James I bought a share and became a sleeping partner in exchange for half the profits. The New River was a significant factor in London's rapid expansion north and west on to clay soil with few natural water sources.

Tube and, on the ground-floor, the ⑳ Container Café, which is a pleasant spot from which to survey the Olympic Park (**END** 7.7 miles).

❶ **Bar Italia**
22 Frith Street, W1D 4RF (7437 4520, www.baritaliasoho.co.uk). Open 24hrs daily.
❷ **St Giles in the Fields**
60 St Giles High Street, WC2H 8LG (7240 2532, www.stgilesonline.org). Open 9am-6pm daily. Admission free.

❸ British Museum
*Great Russell Street, WC1B 3DG (7323 8000,
7323 8299, www.britishmuseum.org). Open
Galleries 10am-5.30pm Mon-Thur, Sat, Sun; 10am-
8.30pm Fri. Great Court 9am-6pm Mon-Thur, Sun;
9am-11pm Fri, Sat. Admission free.*

❹ Coram's Fields
*93 Guilford Street, WC1N 1DN (7837 6138,
www.coramsfields.org). Open Summer 9am-7pm
daily. Winter 9am-dusk daily. Admission free.*

❺ Foundling Museum
*40 Brunswick Square, WC1N 1AZ (7841 3600,
www.foundlingmuseum.org.uk). Open 10am-5pm
Tue-Sat; 11am-5pm Sun. Admission charge.*

❻ Bikefix
*48 Lamb's Conduit Street, WC1N 3LJ (7405 1218,
www.bikefix.co.uk). Open 8.30am-7pm Mon-Fri;
10am-5pm Sat.*

❼ Condor Cycles
*49-53 Gray's Inn Road, WC1X 8PP (7269 6820,
www.condorcycles.com). Open 9am-6pm Mon, Tue,
Thur, Fri; 9am-7.30pm Wed; 10am-5pm Sat.*

❽ Danny's Gourmet Wraps
*31 Lamb's Conduit Street, WC1N 3NG (7404 5128,
www.dannysgourmetwraps.com). Open 7.30am-5pm
Mon-Thur; 7.30am-4pm Fri; 9.30am-4pm Sat.*

❾ Fryer's Delight
*19 Theobald's Road WC1X 8SL (7405 4114).
Open noon-11pm Mon-Sat.*

❿ Bobbins Bicycles
*397 St John Street, EC1V 4LD (7837 3370,
www.bobbinbicycles.co.uk). Open 11am-7pm
Tue-Fri; 11am-6pm Sat; noon-5pm Sun.*

⓫ Micycle
*47 Barnsbury Street, N1 1TP (7684 0671,
www.micycle.org.uk). Open 10am-5pm Tue-Sat;
noon-5pm Sun.*

⓬ Mosquito Bikes
*123 Essex Road, N1 2SN (7726 8765,
www.mosquito-bikes.co.uk). Open 9am-6pm
Mon-Wed, Fri; 9am-7pm Thur; 10am-6pm Sat.*

⓭ Towpath Café
*Regent's Canal towpath, between Whitmore
Bridge and Kingsland Road Bridge, N1 5SB
(no phone). Open 8am-dusk Tue-Fri; 9am-dusk Sat;
10am-dusk Sun.*

⓮ Route Canale Cycles
*Regent's Canal towpath, between Whitmore Bridge
and Kingsland Road Bridge, N1 5SB (no phone,
routecanalebicycles.wordpress.com). Open 9am-
6pm Tue-Fri; 10am-5pm Sat, Sun.*

⓯ Broadway Market
*Broadway Market, E8 4PH (www.broadway
market.co.uk). Open 8.30am-4.30pm Sat.*

⓰ Lock 7
*129 Pritchard's Road, E2 9AP (07515 360 721
mobile, www.lock-7.com). Open 8am-6pm Wed-Sat;
10am-6pm Sun.*

⓱ Victoria Park
*Old Ford Road, E3 5DS (8985 1957, www.tower
hamlets.gov.uk). Open 8am-dusk daily. Admission
free.*

⓲ Britannia
*360 Victoria Park Road, E9 7BT (8533 0040).
Open noon-11pm Mon-Thur; noon-midnight Fri;
11am-midnight Sat; noon-10.30pm Sun.*

⓳ Bikeworks
*Unit 8, Gun Wharf, 241 Old Ford Road, E3 5QB (8983
1221, www.bikeworks.org.uk). Open 8.30am-6.30pm
Mon-Thur; 8.30am-5.30pm Fri; 10am-5pm Sat.*

⓴ Container Café
*The Greenway, Marshgate Lane, E15 2PJ
(07834 275 687 mobile, www.theviewtube.co.uk).
Open 9am-5pm daily.*

Tips on Cycling in the Capital

If you're nervous about cycling in city traffic, then so much the better. It will keep you alert, and alert needs to become second nature when you're cycling in London. When it does – and it won't take long for this to happen – your riding skills will work unnoticed in the background and you'll have plenty of headspace left with which to relax and enjoy the journey. And hard though it might be to believe at first, it really can be fun.

● Be aware of other road- and pavement-users and anticipate their actions. The driver of a parked car may be about to open their door. The best policy is not to ride where a door can swing open unexpectedly and hit you. Where this is the only option, slow down. The headphone-wearing pedestrian, blithely oblivious to his or her surroundings, may be about to step into your path. Keep looking around for potential dangers, especially before manoeuvring.

● Don't assume that motorists – or cyclists – will signal their actions. But you always should, if there's other traffic around.

● Make sure other road users can see and hear you. Luminous kit is reassuring, but shouldn't be necessary if you have good lights. Get a bell and use it, but use your voice too, in a friendly way.

● A major danger, and the cause of most of the cycling fatalities in London, is when vehicles turn left across you. Never, ever go between a vehicle that has stopped at a junction and the curb. Long vehicles in particular have a blind spot and an unpredictable turning circle.

● Beware of heavy vehicles. Don't overtake one unless you're sure you can get past it. If a lorry is behind you, ride in the middle of the lane so the driver can't pass you without taking account of your presence.

● Use advanced stop lanes (the green boxes marked with a bike symbol out front at traffic lights). Move across the road, so that riders behind you also have access.

● Keep your brakes in good nick and remember they take longer to take effect in the wet. Look out for patches of oil/ice/wet leaves.

● Don't be shy about getting off and wheeling your bike along the pavement, if you feel that you might be in danger.

● Don't feel you have to ride so close to the edge of the road that you're in the gutter (and consequently have little room to manoeuvre around potholes and so on). You have a right to be on the road. Ride assertively. Make it easy for other people to see you by riding where they look.

● At all times, follow the rules of the road. At the very least, don't buzz pedestrians.

● Plan out unfamiliar routes in advance. Transport for London and the London Cycling Campaign provide a set of invaluable cycle-route maps that are available from bike shops, tube stations and www.lcc.org.uk.

● Consider taking some training on how to ride in London. Our rides author, Patrick Field, does double duty as the founder of the London School of Cycling (www.londonschoolofcycling.co.uk), whose courses are highly recommended.

SHORT AND SWEET

Dockland Diversions

The 'Isle' of Dogs is something of a misnomer. In fact, it is only isolated from the mainland by artificial channels; the peninsula hangs into the Thames like the tongue of a thirsty hound. This ride follows the artificial island's liquid border from Millwall to Canary Wharf, then heads west via Limehouse, Shadwell and Wapping to the Tower of London, bringing into focus the transformation of the city from a centre of physical trade to a financial hub. Half the riding is on wharves turned over to houses and restaurants, with occasional technical challenges from ramps and barriers; the rest is on ancient high streets with a few linking sections of new-town motor road or cycle path.

You can get to Greenwich by train from Charing Cross station or by boat with Thames Clippers – non-folding bikes carried at the captain's discretion – or ride down the Thames Path from Bermondsey. The red-brick domed building on the waterfront just west of the *Cutty Sark* is the entrance to the Greenwich foot tunnel. The recently refurbished tunnel is categorised as a public right of way, so it stays open all day, every day. By law, cyclists have to dismount and walk through it. The staffed lifts, which run from 10am to 5.30pm on Sundays and 7am to 7pm the rest of the week, are subject to occasional random breaks in service – so be prepared to carry your bike down and up each side's cast-iron spiral staircase. There are around 100 fairly wide, shallow steps, with eight landings along the way where you can catch your breath if need be.

   START The foot tunnel carries a good deal of chattering tourist traffic. Most, on leaving the tunnel, turn right into Island Gardens Park for its classic vista of Greenwich, but some will be visiting the tunnel itself; having featured in the photo booklet that accompanied the Who's album *Quadrophenia*, it's a pilgrimage site for mods. Others visit for the sheer novelty of walking 15 metres beneath the billions of litres of water that pass through the Thames on any given day. The short detour eastwards along the river wall into Island Gardens Park is rewarded with a view of the Old Royal Naval College framing Queen's House across the water. The ❶ Island Gardens Café serves own-made Caribbean food.

   Millwall Park, across the Isle of Dogs' perimeter road, was home to Millwall FC until 1910, when the club relocated to New Cross. A short steep climb made more

Start Greenwich foot tunnel, SE10 9HT
Finish Tower of London, EC3N 4AE
Time 2 hours minimum
Distance 6 miles
Connects with ❶ ❿ ⓬
Traffic & safety Half on wharves shared with pedestrians. Partly on old high streets and cycle tracks. A short section on new busy roads
Terrain Mostly flat with a few artificial ramps
Transport *Start* Greenwich rail. *End* London Bridge rail
TFL bike-hire scheme *Start* Wapping High Street, Wapping. *End* Tower Gardens, Tower Hill
Good for People who like architecture and cobblestoned streets

Greenwich Park and the Isle of Dogs.

Isle of Dogs.

Canary Wharf.

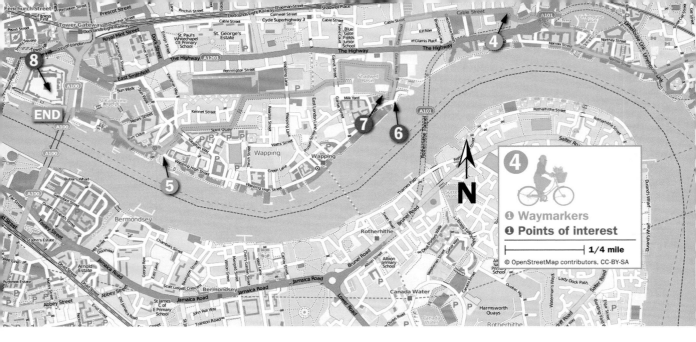

technical by two tight chicanes leads on to East Ferry Road. The low rise on the right is ❷ Mudchute Park & Farm, which can make a pleasant detour if you are cycling with children. The hill is made from mud dredged from the Millwall Docks. More man-made technical riding takes you down a ramp and under the DLR to climb and emerge on the rim of Millwall Outer Dock (❶ 1 mile).

Riding on the dock for the day

Docklands Watersports Centre directly opposite marks the site of the original main entrance to this dock complex. To your left, the arm under the arched wooden footbridge was a dry dock for repairing ships. Turn right to follow the edge of Millwall Outer Dock, which narrows as it approaches Glengall Bridge. North of the bridge is Millwall Inner Dock, although the

names no longer describe the two's relationship – access to the Outer is now available only through the Inner. However, since the fleets loaded with grain, timber and chemicals that used the docks in the past have been replaced with a few houseboats and a floating Chinese restaurant, it's not a big deal. Facing the water on your left as you continue around Millwall Inner Dock, ❸ Byblos Harbour is a friendly Lebanese café and grill.

After a second trip under the DLR, turn west on Marsh Wall by the clump of stainless steel and neon. Take note of the phone number on ❹ Lemongrass Kitchen across the road; in 1995, when the '01' London phone codes were divided into 0207 for inner London and 0208 for outer, west London's Shepherd's Bush was designated 0208, while this area of Tower Hamlets, which is actually further from

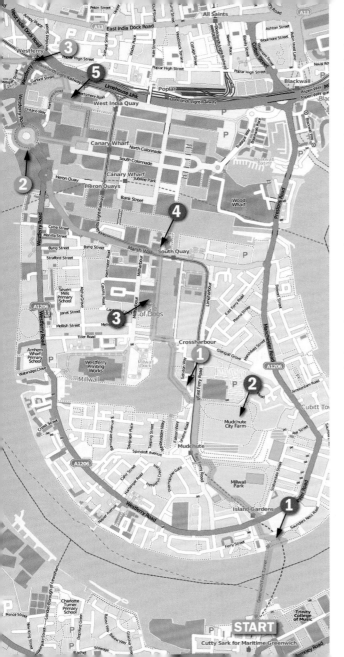

the centre of town, was designated 0207. This was widely interpreted as an attempt to boost the newly redeveloped Docklands. The original owners of Canary Wharf had gone bankrupt in 1992.

The French artist Pierre Vivant describes his zany *Traffic Light Tree*, installed at the junction of Marsh Wall and West Ferry Road (❷ 2 miles) in 1998, thus: 'The sculpture imitates the natural landscape of the adjacent London plane trees, while the changing pattern of the lights reveals and reflects the never-ending rhythm of the surrounding domestic, financial and commercial activities'. Thankfully, if rather surprisingly, this entertaining structure wasn't vetoed by a road-safety jobsworth.

The next roundabout is 'double-decked', with a car park below and roundabout above. Use extreme caution while on the roundabout as you'll need to stay in the right-hand lane to avoid the traffic, taking the first exit down to the car park. Turning right into Cabot Square takes you into Canary Wharf, where the fountains and public art are dwarfed by monolithic towers. The new land use often obscures what existed before, but the West India Docks – 'Import' dock to the north, 'Export' dock to the south – still exist, physically at least, and create a visual tension between the financial, administrative present and the heavy logistics of the past. The now-unused docks provide a moat that seems to emphasise the skyscrapers' isolation from 'real' life.

Turn left before 10 Cabot Square to walk down steps to the footbridge. (There's a lift, if required.) Behind on your right, 10 Cabot Square is clad with brick and stone providing a visual link between the masonry of the old docks and the glass and steel of the new financial district. Riding is prohibited on the footbridge, but that's not really a hardship as walking is recommended so that the surroundings can be

Route Directions

START at the south entrance to the Greenwich foot tunnel, which is situated just to the west of the *Cutty Sark*. Note that cycling is not allowed in the foot tunnel, so wheel your bicycle through it. Emerge from the foot tunnel and follow the river wall east into Island Gardens Park to view Greenwich

Exit Island Gardens Park, cross Saunders Ness Road through bollards into alley

Right into Manchester Road

Immediate left into Millwall Park beside Island Gardens DLR station

Follow the painted cycle track around the western (left) side of the park (beside the old railway viaduct)

Bear right then left to exit park up barriered ramp on Rope Walk

T-Junction: right into East Ferry Road (just past the lone brick chimney on the left)

❶ 1 mile Left down hairpin ramp under DLR

Up ramp to Millwall Outer Dock

Right along the dockside, following the cycle route

Left into Pepper Street, crossing over Glengall Bridge

Right to follow west side of Millwall Inner Dock. Take care by South Quay DLR station, walking may be necessary

Left into Marsh Wall

❷ 2 miles Roundabout: second exit into West Ferry Road

Up ramp to upper roundabout, keeping in the right-hand lane and using extreme caution when negotiating the roundabout

Alternative route, avoiding roundabout:
Dismount before you reach the roundabout, cross and walk around to the building on the right-hand side of the ramp, where there is a lift to the upper level. You can then continue straight on and turn right into West India Avenue

Second exit into West India Avenue

Left into Cabot Square

Left (just before 10 Cabot Square)

Walk down steps (lift available on left) and cross Import Dock on footbridge

Left into West India Quay

T-junction: right into Hertsmere Road

Left (just before CineWorld, signpost Poplar)

Under DLR

Immediate left (on footpath)

Left (back under DLR on blue cycle track) into Garford Street

Right on to blue cycle track that is running parallel to DLR

❸ 3 miles Cross West Ferry Road on light-controlled crossing into Salter Street,

Immediate left into Limehouse Causeway (signpost Tower Gateway)

Continue into Narrow Street on Cycle Super Highway 3

Right into contraflow lane on Horseferry Road (opposite the Narrow restaurant)

Right into cycle track (follow CS3 up over the bridge and through the park)

Cross Butchers Row at light-controlled crossing, right then

❹ 4 miles Immediate left into Cable Street
(on two-way cycle track)

At 'Give Way' sign on Hardinge Street

Left into Glamis Road

> **Diversion to see mural**
>
> *Continue on Cable Street to no.236, then retrace route and turn into Glamis Road*

Traffic lights: straight on across the Highway

Cross red bridge (Wapping Project on the right, Prospect of Whitby on the left)

Retrace to **re-cross** red bridge

Immediate left to follow edge of Shadwell Basin.

Follow the Basin the whole way around, then hairpin right down the ramp under the bridge

Bear slightly left diagonally through Wapping Woods on the red-brick path

Continue on the right of the canal (under the bridge)

Follow the channel until it ends in a flight of steps

Climb hairpins on the left

Continue on the left of the small basin

❺ 5 miles T-junction: right into Wapping High Street,

Immediate left into St Katharine's Way

Left (take care at 'No Entry' sign into two-way street passing in front of Devon House) – still St Katharine's Way

Cross drawbridge, with care

Continue through access tunnel

END 6 miles Left

Immediate right

Dismount and walk under Tower Bridge to Tower Wharf and the Tower of London

appreciated. Ahead are London's finest wharfside warehouses. These docks were constructed during the 19th-century downriver expansion. Their elegant detail – windows have clever metal grids to provide security without looking like a prison – date back to the Romantic period, when art and science were one subject. They now house popular watering holes for those who work long hours in the office towers behind you. The Marriott Hotel, to the right of the Georgian warehouses, bows gently like a pulling sail. The towers of Canada Square impress by scale alone.

Follow the quay past the **❺** Museum of London Docklands to exit past the floating church, wittily named St Peter's Barge.

Brick rather than glass

Picking up Cycle Super Highway 3 takes you along Limehouse Causeway (**❸** 3 miles) into Narrow Street. The expanse of blue paint signals that cycle traffic is expected and welcome – a good thing. The council estates of Shadwell come as a shock after miles of steel, glass and lovingly restored Georgian brick. Cable Street (**❹** 4 miles) is the site of a key event in British history. In 1936, the police were ordered to clear the street so that Oswald Mosley's British Union of Fascists, a dynamic organisation supported by many including the *Daily Mail*, the *Daily Mirror* and the motor-magnate Lord Nuffield, could march to Aldgate. This was a predominantly Jewish area and residents, workers and the wider East End population came together to resist the police assault; with human walls and barricades, they ensured that the Fascists did not pass. A big mural at no.236 commemorates the victory. You'll have to go further on along Cable Street to see it.

Glamis Road crosses a mighty drawbridge, and turns into fairly smooth cobblestones, passing the

Cable Street Mural.

❻ Prospect of Whitby, an atmospheric traditional pub serving beer and food. Opposite, behind the high brick wall, is ❼ the Wapping Project, a power station gallery free to the public. In its heyday, the power station generated pressurised water (rather than electricity, as one might presume), which was silently transported in cast-iron pipes to power cranes, lifts and theatre machinery as far away as Mayfair. Much of the plant is still in place in the hall that now houses a fancy restaurant. On a sunny weekend you can lock your bike to a rusting transformer in the yard and enjoy the spectacle of flocks of under-dressed trendies enjoying lunch sat amid the rusty relics of this strange technological cul-de-sac.

Retrace your tracks to cross the red steel bridge again, and turn left to follow the north wall of Shadwell Basin. On the right is St Paul's Church, once known as the Church of Sea Captains – there are more than 70 buried in the graveyard. As you leave the Basin, follow the course of an old canal through new housing, past the failed shopping mall of Tobacco Dock on your right, and eventually you will reach a flight of steps at the end of the canal. On the left, between the brick flower planters, runs Wapping's answer to L'Alpe-d'Huez – a rack of tight hairpins that can be negotiated with care on any solo bike.

The rattling cobbles of old Wapping High Street (❺ 5 miles) and St Katharine's Way lead to St Katharine Docks and a final technical challenge. The drawbridge across the dock's entrance has a steel grid and is signposted 'surface unsuitable for cycling'. Ride it – at your own risk – if you dare (narrow-wheeled road bikes in particular may struggle). Beyond, the service tunnel of the Tower Hotel is narrow and busy, but with care you can make it to a left-and-immediate-right-turn to dismount and walk under Tower Bridge to chill out on Tower Wharf between ❽ the Tower and the Pool of London (**END** 6 miles). If you are cycling back to London Bridge, you can turn right before Tower Bridge, go up the slip road and do a hairpin turn to cycle carefully across the bridge, taking in some of the best river views in London.

❶ Island Gardens Café
Island Gardens Park, Saunders Ness Road, E14 3EB (no phone). Open 10am-dusk (approx) Tue-Sun.
❷ Mudchute Park & Farm
Pier Street, E14 3HP (7515 5901, www.mudchute.org). Open 9am-5pm Tue-Sun.
❸ Byblos Harbour
The Waterfront, 41 Millharbour, E14 9NB (7538 4882, www.byblos-harbour.com). Open noon-11pm daily.
❹ Lemongrass Kitchen
185 Marsh Wall, E14 9SH (7537 9392). Open 11am-10pm Mon, Tue, Thur, Fri; 11am-5pm Wed; 6-10pm Sat, Sun.
❺ Museum of London Docklands
West India Quay, Hertsmere Road, E14 4AL (7001 9844, www.museumoflondon.org.uk/docklands). Open 10am-6pm daily. Admission free.
❻ Prospect of Whitby
57 Wapping Wall, E1W 3SH (7481 1095). Open noon-11pm Mon-Sat; noon-10.30pm Sun.
❼ Wapping Project
Wapping Hydraulic Power Station, Wapping Wall (7680 2080, http://thewappingproject.com). Open noon-midnight Mon-Sat; noon-6pm Sun. Admission free.
❽ Tower of London
Tower Hill, EC3N 4AB (0844 482 7777, www.hrp.org.uk). Open Mar-Oct 10am-5.30pm Mon, Sun; 9am-5.30pm Tue-Sat. Nov-Feb 10am-4.30pm Mon, Sun; 9am-4.30pm Tue-Sat. Admission charge.

Prospect of Whitby.

Wapping Project.

SHORT AND SWEET

Fixing a Puncture

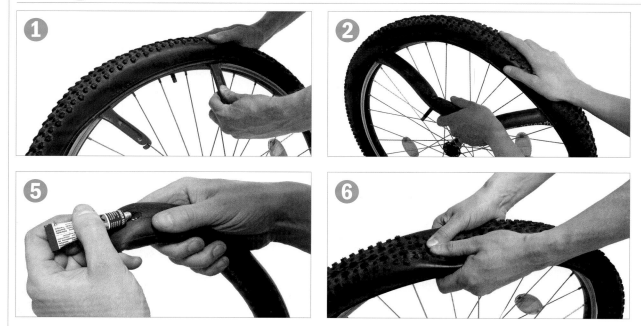

Apart from keeping your tyres sufficiently pumped up, repairing a puncture is the most likely bit of maintenance you're going to have to perform to keep your bike on the road. As with all other repairs, if you're unsure or uncomfortable about doing it yourself, then take your bike down to your friendly local bike shop.

❶ Having removed the wheel, insert the non-hooked end of your first tyre lever between the rim and the tyre bead, and push down with the palm of your hand so that you can hook the hooked end on to a spoke. Do the same with a second tyre lever a couple of inches further round the wheel, and then a third – at which point the second tyre lever will probably fall away on its own. Use the spare lever to run around the rest of the tyre.

❷ With one side of the tyre now fully unhooked from the rim, you will be able to remove the inner tube from the wheel, starting with the valve.

❸ Pump the tube up until you can locate the puncture. It may help to run the inflated tube close to your pursed lips. If you really still can't feel or hear anything, the ol' bucket of water trick will help.

❹ Use a biro to draw a ring around the hole, and then use the sandpaper that comes with your puncture repair kit to roughen the surface of the tube around the hole to help the puncture patch to stick. You may need to re-apply your biro mark after this, or just trust your eagle-eyed skill.

❺ Apply a thin layer of rubber solution at least an inch in diameter, with the hole at the centre.

❻ While the glue dries – give it at least a few minutes – try to identify the cause of the puncture. Check the outside of the tyre, then gently run your fingers around the inside, being particularly careful of any protruding glass, which is often the cause of punctures in urban areas.

❼ Remove the foil backing of your patch, and then press it down firmly over the hole. Next, pinch the patch until its plastic covering cracks, and then peel it away from the centre to the outside, leaving the patch in place.

❽ Pump a small amount of air into the tube, then replace it and the tyre, and pump the wheel back up to the recommended pressure (printed on the tyre sidewall), checking that the tyre is seated properly on the rim as you go.

❺ The City on Sunday

Sunday is a tale of two cities in London's historic heartland. In the financial district, an eerie calm descends. The throngs of workers are absent, the offices empty and the streets deserted: perfect for two-wheeled discovery of its monuments. But in the eastern fringes – once home to a Jewish population forbidden to touch money on a Saturday – traditional Sunday markets now encompass everything from household junk and stolen bikes to organic food and designer craftwork. Their colour and vitality provide a warm contrast to the desolate austerity of the capital's capital.

START What better place to begin a ride round the City than a monument to the event that devastated it. ❶ The Monument commemorates the Great Fire of London of 1666 and stands on Fish Street Hill, once a busy thoroughfare leading down to London Bridge. The 'Great' is important because in the narrow lanes and courts of the old wooden city, fires were not particularly rare, going back as far as AD 61 when the ancient British burned the Roman trading post. The City of London – the furthest point downstream on the Thames where land on both banks was dry enough for wharves, buildings and bridge footings – is the oldest part of the capital. A wooden bridge might have been here 1,900 years ago. In the Middle Ages, London Bridge was lined with houses, with a chapel in the centre important enough to have two priests and four clerks. The bridge had 19 arches and was destroyed by fire several times. Fire, redevelopment and – in the 20th century – enemy bombing, mean that little more than the names of streets and alleys remain from the old days.

Twin examples of the restless change that underlies the City's longevity are revealed as you ride west on Cannon Street. To the right, up New Change, is the ❷ One New Change shopping centre, Jean Nouvel's homage to the consumer gods of the 21st century. But resisting the blandishments of Mammon and some fine cafés – after all, you've only just started out on your ride – will reveal ❸ St Paul's Cathedral in all its grandeur. The cathedral is the fifth to be built on the site; the present building is actually smaller than its Norman predecessor, which gives you some idea of the extraordinary scale of Norman architecture. In 1663, Christopher Wren had been asked to survey the decaying old cathedral, which had been damaged by the Parliamentary army in the Civil War. He strongly

Start Monument, Monument Street, EC3R 8AH
Finish Old Spitalfields Market, E1 6AA
Time 1 hour minimum
Distance 5 miles
Connects with ❹
Traffic & safety Too busy during the week, but the streets are quiet on Saturdays and Sundays
Terrain Flat
Transport *Start* London Bridge rail, Cannon Street rail, Fenchurch Street rail, Liverpool Street rail. *End* Liverpool Street rail
TFL bike-hire scheme *Start* Lower Thames Street. *End* Norton Folgate, Liverpool Street
Good for Imaginative historians and street market hagglers

Route Directions

SHORT AND SWEET

START Straight (uphill) on Fish Street Hill
T-junction: left into Eastcheap
Traffic lights: straight on into Cannon Street
Pass St Paul's Cathedral
❶ **0.7 miles Right** into St Paul's Churchyard
Pass under Temple Bar into Paternoster Square
Cross Paternoster Square, exit to left of sundial
T-junction: right into Newgate Street – King Edward Street
Left into Little Britain
Straight on narrow cycle path/pedestrian walkway
T-junction: left into West Smithfield
T-junction: left into Giltspur Street to Golden Boy
Retrace to West Smithfield and continue, bearing left
❷ **1.3 miles T-junction: left** into Long Lane
Right into East Poultry Avenue
T-junction: right into Charterhouse Street – Charterhouse Square – Carthusian Street
T-junction: left into Aldersgate Street
Right into Fann Street
T-junction: left into Golden Lane
Immediate right into Fortune Street
Right into Whitecross Street
❸ **2.1 miles Straight on** from Whitecross Street into Silk Street, bearing left
T-junction: right into Moor Lane
T-junction: right into Fore Street
Bear left into Wood Street
T-junction: left into Gresham Street
Immediate right into Wood Street (walk one-way part)
T-junction: left into Cheapside
Immediate right into Bread Street
Left into Watling Street (walk if necessary)

Left into Queen Street
Straight on, crossing Cheapside, into King Street
Straight on into Guildhall Yard
❹ **3.2 miles T-junction: right** into Guildhall Buildings (take care, walk if necessary)
T-junction: right into Basinghall Street
T-junction: left into Gresham Street
Traffic lights: straight on into Lothbury
Right into Bartholomew Lane
T-junction: left into Threadneedle Street
T-junction: right into Bishopsgate
Traffic lights: left into Leadenhall Street
Right into Whittington Avenue
Left into Leadenhall Place
T-junction: left into Lime Street
Immediate right into Fenchurch Avenue
Right into Fen Court (take care, walk if necessary)
T-junction: left into Fenchurch Street
Left into Billiter Street
T-junction: right into Leadenhall Street
Left into Creechurch Lane
T-junction: left into Heneage Lane
❺ **4.1 miles T-junction: left** into Bevis Marks
Right into Goring Street
T-junction: right into Houndsditch
Left into St Botolph Street (Middlesex Street on left)
Left into Whitechapel High Street
Left into Osborn Street – Brick Lane (walk if crowded)
Left into Quaker Street
Left into Wheler Street
T-junction: left into Commercial Street
Right into Lamb Street – Spital Square
END 5.7 miles Bishopsgate

recommended demolition and rebuilding, but this was rejected. Wren drew up various renovation plans, one of which was accepted six days before the outbreak of the Great Fire. Following the fire, demolition was the only practical option available. The cathedral took 35 years to build.

The archway on St Paul's Churchyard (❶ 0.7 miles) was also designed by Wren. It once stood at Temple Bar, the western entry to the City where Fleet Street becomes the Strand. It was dismantled in 1878 – because of traffic congestion and the imminent construction of the Royal Courts of Justice – and then lay in a yard in Farringdon for ten years, before being erected as a gateway by the brewer Sir Henry Meux on his estate in Hertfordshire. Woods grew around it and by the 1990s it was hidden in a thicket like the lost remains of an ancient civilisation. The Meux family sold it to a trust for £1 and it was carefully reassembled in its current position in 2004.

Bombing it

Heading into King Edward Street, the ruins in the garden are further evidence of London's tumultuous past. Christ Church Greyfriars was destroyed in the Great Fire, rebuilt by Wren, only to be burned again during the wartime Blitz. A garden now fills the nave, but the tower and a wall remain.

The most notorious of all London prisons, Newgate, stood west of here until 1902, when it was replaced by the Central Criminal Court or 'Old Bailey'. Little Britain (where the Dukes of Brittany had a house) is a winding lane where booksellers once gathered. It leads into the pleasant labyrinth of lanes around St Bartholomew's Hospital, or 'Barts', the oldest in London. Wat Tyler, the leader of the Peasants' Revolt of 1381, was brought here after being stabbed by the Lord Mayor. The king's men

followed him in, dragged him out and beheaded him on the spot. So much for sanctuary.

Follow the hospital frontage around West Smithfield until you reach Giltspur Street. On the junction with Cock Lane, there is a small statue at first-floor level – the Golden Boy of Pye Corner – which marks the north-western limit of the Great Fire's range.

Returning to West Smithfield, you soon see the impressive edifice of Smithfield Market (❷ 1.3 miles). This is now the last of London's great 19th-century wholesale markets to remain operating on its original site. Refrigerated lorries unload meat here, and a slight scent of animal fat always hangs in the roadways. The Smithfield Nocturne (www.nocturneseries.com), a big Saturday night criterium bike race, is held here each summer, and the return coach service for the legendary Dunwich Dynamo night ride and beach party disgorges a few hundred, bleary-eyed zombies here on a Sunday afternoon each July. ❹ Smiths of Smithfield has a ground-floor café-bar serving hearty, no-fuss breakfasts and mugs of cappuccino.

Now rolling east, you'll come to the Barbican. This district was also completely flattened in the Blitz, then redeveloped in the 1960s and '70s with the ❺ Barbican Centre and accompanying housing. It's hard to believe now, but there was a time when architects seriously believed that reinforced concrete was a material of beauty. If you fancy seeing what's on, there's an entrance in Silk Street (❸ 2.1 miles) with plenty of cycle racks across the street.

Further evidence of the destructive power of German bombs is revealed by the tower of the church of St Alban, which is all that remains of the building. Next to it is Wood Street police station. The City of London, jealous of its historic and hard-won autonomy, retains its own police service separate from the Metropolitan

En Route

The Priory and Hospital of St Bartholomew were founded by Rahere – a jester to Henry I – who fell ill on a pilgrimage to Rome and vowed to lead a life of sober devotion in gratitude should he return home safely. Bartholomew Fair was originally a cloth market, held to earn money for the hospital, for three days from St Bartholomew's Eve, 23 August. Over the centuries, it developed into a general festival of entertainment. Ben Jonson's 1614 play of the same name gives a good idea of its atmosphere. The City of London ran a cattle market at the same time. The fair was suppressed in 1855 and replaced, in 1866, by Smithfield Market.

Police who operate in the rest of London. They wear distinctive helmets that supposedly channel those of Roman soldiers. Just before you turn left into Cheapside from Wood Street, look out for the small churchyard on your right. The church of St Peter West Cheap used to stand on the corner, but was destroyed in the Great Fire and never rebuilt. The plane tree in the courtyard is mentioned in Wordsworth's 'Reverie of Poor Susan'.

In the plain-speaking manner characteristic of the medievals, Wood Street sold wood, the parallel Milk Street sold milk, while across Cheapside – the old city's main market – is Bread Street. No prizes for guessing what was sold there. Watling Street is a narrow alley where you may have to get off your bike and walk. It's hard to believe that this is a fragment of what is, historically, the most important road in Britain, running from Dover to St Albans and out to the Welsh borders.

Jagging back north, you come to the medieval structure of the ❻ Guildhall (❹ 3.2 miles) – the City of London's 'town hall' – which survived severe damage in the Great Fire and the Blitz. As well as ceremonial and administrative functions, the building houses the Worshipful Company of Clockmakers' museum.

Although the Guildhall no longer wields its old power, we've all recently felt the repercussions of the decisions of the nearby, although not as old, Bank of England. 'The old lady of Threadneedle Street' was founded in 1694 to raise money for the Royal Navy. It now issues bank notes, holds gold reserves and tries to oversee and regulate financial dealings in the City.

In a generally flat route, the low hilltop at the crossroads of Bishopsgate and Cornhill, where you turn left into Leadenhall Street, stands out. This is the centre of the oldest part of the City and thus the oldest part of London. Food has been sold in Leadenhall Market since the 14th century. The current building dates from 1881.

It's worth dismounting to take a look at *The Gilt of Cain* – a piece of public art secluded in Fen Court – that is a rare acknowledgement of one of the roots of Great Britain's economic power; 17 granite sugar canes and a slave auctioneer's pulpit. The sculpture is located near St Mary Woolnoth Church, where the Reverend John Newton – author of the abolitionist hymn 'Amazing Grace' – delivered anti-slavery sermons. It's hard to believe now, but at the time the abolitionists were regarded as religious cranks by the sensible majority. The sculpture was unveiled in 2007 to mark the bicentenary of the abolition of the British transatlantic slave trade.

❼ Bevis Marks Synagogue (❺ 4.1 miles) was dedicated in 1701. It's the oldest synagogue in England still in use, and the only one in Europe that has had continuous services for more than 300 years.

St Paul's Cathedral.

It was originally built for the Sephardic community from Iberia, but it now claims flagship status for all Anglo-Jewry.

Real markets

If you're doing this ride on a Sunday or during the working week, you'll find Middlesex Street undergoing its weekly transformation into ❽ Petticoat Lane, the market's budget clothing and fabrics stalls sprawling into surrounding streets. You can enjoy a salt beef sandwich at ❾ Kossofs, the Jewish-owned café at no.91. After the isolation of the Sunday City, the commotion here reminds you what bustle Cheapside, Fish Street and Poultry – the souks of old London –

must once have held. You'll need to get off your bike here, and for stretches of the rest of the ride. ❿ The Tubby Isaacs jellied eel stall at the corner of Goulston Street and Whitechapel High Street offers another traditional refuelling opportunity.

For something more up to date, the ⓫ Whitechapel Gallery, just before you turn left off Whitechapel High Street, is a good port of call. Situated in an art nouveau building with a mosaic over the door, the gallery was established to bring good art to the East End. It also has a pleasant restaurant.

Nearing the end of the ride, refuelling becomes more urgent. Unfortunately, the curry houses of Brick Lane are generally disappointing, although many offer good

Brick Lane.

D & LEE TEXT

Petticoat Lane Market.

Old Spitalfields Market.

value for money. Try ⑫ Tayyabs in Fieldgate Street instead. But if Brick Lane's food isn't what it was, the walk – you'll almost certainly have to walk, since the street is perpetually crowded – will still bring the sounds and scents of the subcontinent flooding over you. As you pass the trendy Old Truman Brewery and near ⑬ Old Spitalfields Market, the vintage fashion, arts and crafts combine with Brick Lane to create a fashion-shoot-meets-Bangladeshi-bazaar vibe. The late 17th-century streets of Spitalfields – short for 'hospital fields' – were occupied first by Huguenot silk weavers. The occasional fading Germanic shop sign testifies to the Jews who moved through in the 19th and 20th centuries, to be overwritten by Bengali. Bishopsgate (**END** 5.7 miles), the City's eastern boundary, brings us back to another of the City's ancient roads: Ermine Street. Turn left for London Bridge and Kent or Surrey; turn right for Hackney, Hertford, York and Scotland.

❶ The Monument
Monument Street, EC3R 8AH (7626 2717, www.themonument.info). Open 9.30am-5pm daily. Admission charge.
❷ One New Change
1 New Change, EC4M 9AF (www.onenewchange. com). Opening times vary by store.
❸ St Paul's Cathedral
Ludgate Hill, EC4M 8AD (7236 4128, www.stpauls. co.uk). Open 8.30am-4pm Mon-Sat; for worship only Sun. Galleries, crypt & ambulatory 9.30am-4.15pm Mon-Sat. Closed for special services, sometimes at short notice. Admission charge.
❹ Smiths of Smithfield
67-77 Charterhouse Street, EC1M 6HJ (7251 7950, www.smithsofsmithfield.co.uk). Open 7am-11pm Mon-Fri; 10am-11.30pm Sat; 9.30am-10.30pm Sun.

❺ Barbican Centre
Silk Street, EC2Y 8DS (box office 7638 8891, cinema 7382 7000, www.barbican.org.uk). Open Box office 9am-9pm Mon-Sat; noon-9pm Sun. Admission Library free. Exhibitions, films, shows, workshops charge.
❻ The Guildhall
Corner of Gresham Street & Aldermanbury, EC2P 2UJ (7606 3030, www.corpoflondon.gov.uk). Open May-Sept 9.30am-5pm daily. Oct-Apr 9.30am-5pm Mon-Sat. Closes for functions; phone ahead to check. Admission free.
❼ Bevis Marks Synagogue
Bevis Marks, EC3A 5DQ (7627 1274, www.bevismarks.org.uk). Open 10.30am-2pm Mon, Wed, Thur; 10.30am-1pm Tue, Fri; 10.30am-12.30pm Sun. Admission charge.
❽ Petticoat Lane Market
Middlesex Street, E1 7EZ. Open 10am-4pm Mon-Fri; 9am-3pm Sun.
❾ Kossofs Bakery Café
91 Middlesex Street, E1 7DA (7247 7363). Open 7am-5pm Mon-Thur; 7am-3pm Fri; 7am-4pm Sun.
❿ Tubby Isaacs
Goulston Street & Whitechapel High Street (www.tubbyisaacs.co.uk). Open usually 10am-8pm Mon-Wed; 10am-10pm Thur-Sun.
⑪ Whitechapel Gallery
77-82 Whitechapel High Street, E1 7QX (7522 7888, www.whitechapelgallery.org). Open 11am-6pm Tue, Wed, Fri-Sun; 11am-9pm Thur.
⑫ Tayyabs
83 Fieldgate Street, E1 1JU (7247 9543, www.tayyabs.co.uk). Open noon-11.30pm daily.
⑬ Old Spitalfields Market
Commercial Street, E1 6AA (7247 8556, www.old spitalfieldsmarket.com). Open 9.30am-5pm Thur-Sun.

SHORT AND SWEET

Cycling in London: Love or Hate?

LOVE

1. Connecting the city
When you can see one neighbourhood change into another in a couple of streets, you start to connect the different parts of London into one thriving city.

2. Speed
Cycling is often faster than public transport.

3. Exercise
Why join a gym when you can get fit for free?

4. Cost
Once you've paid for your kit, cycling is free. No congestion charge, no road tax, no insurance…

5. Accessibility
On a bike you can reach all those secret gardens and historic alleyways off-limits to cars, without having to spend hours walking between them.

6. Camaraderie
There is often a mutual respect among cyclists – you feel like you're part of a secret club.

7. Fresh air
On more rural rides, take a deep breath of fresh air and feel the stressful, overcrowded London streets fade away.

8. Picnics
There is something quintessentially British about going for a bike ride with a basket full of bread, cheese, pork pies and ginger beer.

9. Spontaneity
Cycling makes the most of the journey rather than just the destination.

10. Emergency transport
Underground network shut down? Buses snarled up in Friday traffic? No problem.

HATE

1. Getting lost
London is a rabbit warren of one-way streets, dead-ends and confusingly named roads. A pocket *A-Z* (or smartphone) is essential to keep on route.

2. Hills
They're hard work, and rarely marked on maps.

3. Helmet hair
Enough said.

4. Cost
You may have a bike, but what about helmets, lycra, high-vis jackets, waterproofs, bike pumps…

5. Security
Stumbling across a hidden café is great, but if there's nothing to secure your bike to, you might as well just cycle on by.

6. Thieves
More than 400 bicycles are reported stolen in London every week. A good D-lock is vital.

7. Dirty air
The unique position cyclists hold on London roads, sandwiched between buses and black cabs, puts them in prime position to inhale traffic fumes.

8. Rain
This is perhaps the only time where you might look at those on a bus – warm and dry – with envy. The secret is to be prepared. Pack a poncho.

9. Cycling home again
The problem with being spontaneous is that you often end up having to cycle the whole way back.

10. Traffic
The safest thing is to assume that they really are all out to get you.

⑥ Park & Ride

London's best cycling role models used to be the aristocratic English women of SW1, SW7 and SW3. Wearing floral headscarves and quilted gilets, they rode through busy traffic, past pushy cab drivers and Belgravia white-van men, their effortless 'actually-I-do-own-the-road' nonchalance born from absolute certainty that their identity and status were assured. Perhaps they took their lead from the redoubtable Queen Victoria, during whose era the area acquired its current character, partly at the hands of her beloved husband, Albert. As well as showing you the monuments of her reign, this ride takes you past many of London's other major royal and political sights, and through the generous cycleways and stately landmarks of Kensington Gardens and Hyde Park.

When asked – on his death bed – if he desired a visit from Queen Victoria, Prime Minister and novelist Benjamin Disraeli is said to have replied: 'No, it is better not, she would only ask me to take a message to Albert.' Following the death of Albert, the Prince Consort, in 1861, aged 42, Victoria didn't appear in public for seven years and lived in black for another 40. The era's public preference for tight-laced sobriety came – in part – from the monarch's prolonged mourning for her German husband. Victoria's reign is the chain linking modernity with less familiar times. Victoria succeeded William IV, who served in the American War of Independence in silk stockings. She died in 1901, when bicycles with pneumatic tyres were unremarkable. Albert – Victoria's first cousin – was relatively progressive, being anti-slavery and in favour of universal education. He helped organise the Great Exhibition of 1851 whose profits were used to purchase the market gardens and nurseries south of Hyde Park on which 'Albertopolis', his planned cultural district, was built.

Gloucester Road, a continuation of **START** Palace Gate, marks the western limit of Albertopolis. This small strip of shops and cafés has everything from upmarket charity shops peddling designer cast-offs to independent pubs and cafés. Just off Gloucester Road is ❶ Launceston Place, the sort of restaurant to save for a treat after finishing your ride. The set lunch here is among London's best-value deals.

Behind the Albert Hall on Prince Consort Road, there's a statue of the man himself on a column listing his public works. Albertopolis – where personality cult

Start & finish Palace Gate, Kensington Gardens, W8 5NJ
Time 1.5 hours minimum
Distance 7.5 miles
Connects with ❷
Traffic & safety Busy city streets, backstreets and parks
Terrain Mostly flat, with some low hills
Transport High Street Kensington tube, Victoria tube/rail
TFL bike-hire scheme Palace Gate, Kensington Gardens
Good for History buffs and visitors to London

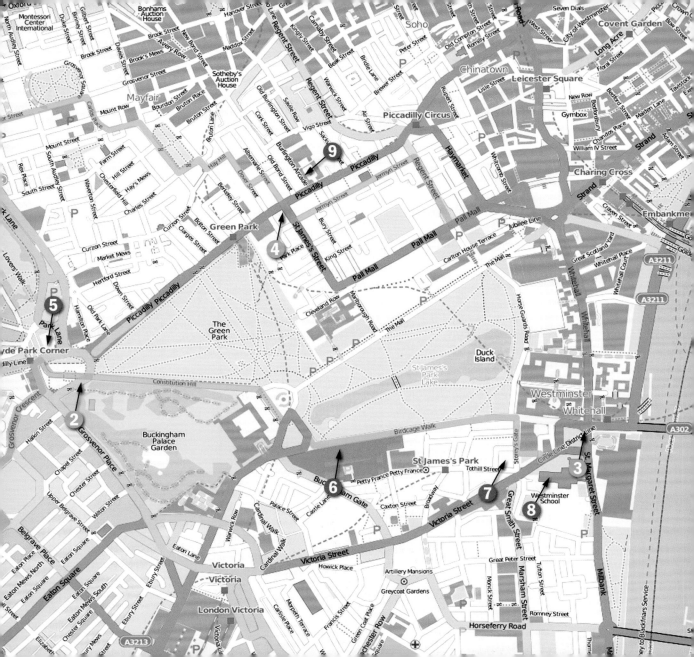

Route Directions

START Palace Gate – Gloucester Road
Left Elvaston Place
Left Queen's Gate
Right Prince Consort Road (use caution)
Right Exhibition Road
Immediate left Princes Gardens
Right on path in front of Imperial College Hall of Residence
T-junction: left on to path and through gap on right
Right into Ennismore Gardens Mews
Left into Ennismore Street – Rutland Gate Mews East
Right through gap and down three steps
Left into Rutland Street
T-junction: right into Montpelier Walk
T-junction: left into Cheval Place
T-junction: right into Montpelier Street
T-junction: left into Brompton Road
❶ **1.4 miles Right** into Hans Road
Hans Place roundabout 3rd exit still Hans Place
T-junction: left into Pont Street – Chesham Place
Belgrave Square roundabout 2nd exit into Grosvenor Crescent
Hyde Park Corner roundabout dismount, turn left to cross at pedestrian crossing to the central area
Pass under Wellington Arch using light controlled crossing
❷ **2.5 miles Straight** into Constitution Hill, flanked by four columns
Right into Buckingham Palace forecourt, continuing counter-clockwise around the fountain
Right into Spur Road (between two golden gates)
T-junction: left into Birdcage Walk
Right into Storey's Gate

Left in front of Queen Elizabeth Conference centre
T-junction: right into Little Sanctuary
Immediate left into Broad Sanctuary (Victoria Street)
❸ **3.7miles Parliament Square roundabout 2nd exit** into Parliament Street – Whitehall
Trafalgar Square 2nd exit into Cockspur Street – Pall Mall
Right into Waterloo Place – Regent Street
Left into Jermyn Street
T-junction: right into St James's Street – Albermarle Street
❹ **4.9 miles Straight** on across Piccadilly
Left into Stafford Street
T-junction: right into Dover Street
Left into Hay Hill
T-junction: right into Berkeley Street
Berkeley Square 3rd exit into Mount Street
Bear right on to Carlos Place
Grosvenor Square 2nd exit into Upper Grosvenor Street
❺ **5.8 miles T-junction: right** into Park Lane. Use cycle lane on the far pavement
Left into Hyde Park
T-junction: right on to bike path
Bear left past Speakers' Corner
Join The Ring road, parallel to Bayswater Road
Left on to the cycle track running parallel to the bridleway before reaching Victoria Gate
Cross bridge, continue to Alexandra Gate
Right on to cycle track in Kensington Gardens
❻ **7.4 miles Exit** the park at Queen's Gate
Right into Kensington Gore
END Left into Palace Gate – Gloucester Road

met the confidence of the high imperial age – was dedicated to the promotion of knowledge of science and arts; hence the Science, Natural History and Victoria & Albert Museums.

The quarter also includes the Royal College of Music and the Imperial College of Science, Technology & Medicine, whose extensive buildings dominate the area.

Glide down the hill in front of the Wilkinson Hall of Residence, Imperial College or cut through the small gardens in front. As you turn left into the seeming dead end, continue towards the distinctive railings and go down the ramp to your right. Follow it around the left-hand bend, and you'll come out at tranquil Ennismore Gardens Mews. These mews were backstreets that provided accommodation for horses, carriages, grooms and drivers. Horses probably coped with the cobbled streets better than modern-day bicycles.

Tea and sympathy

The big Italianate church further down Brompton Road on your right is known as the Brompton Oratory, although its correct title is the Church of the Immaculate Heart of Mary. It was consecrated in 1884 and was the centre of Roman Catholic activity in London until 1903, when Westminster Cathedral opened in Victoria. During the Cold War, KGB agents used it as a dead-letter box. Continue down the cobblestones right to the end of Rutland Gate Mews East, where the street becomes very narrow. On your right is a little archway with three steps leading down into Rutland Street. Follow the backstreets until you reach Brompton Road, where, unless you're feeling particularly brave, you can walk your bike across the pedestrian crossing and down the side of ❷ Harrods.

Harrods department store (❶ 1.4 miles) is illuminated spectacularly after dark, an unrepentant affront to artistic restraint and energy conservation. It grew rapidly from a village grocery store purchased by City tea merchant Henry Harrod in 1849 and was expanded to prominence by his son Charles. In 1894, it advertised itself with the bombastic slogan, 'Harrods serves the World'. The first escalator in London was installed inside in 1898. If you feel like you need a break, then ❸ Ladurée (on your left as you pass the back of Harrods) offers macaroons and delicate pots of tea in an opulent Parisian setting.

The Great Exhibition was a boon for all the shop-keepers of Knightsbridge, which was then merely a quiet hamlet on the Westbourne River. As you cycle across Sloane Street, look out for the ❹ Cadogan Hotel on your right.

'Forgive your enemies – nothing annoys them so much'

The hotel was newly built when Irish dramatist Oscar Wilde was arrested there. In 1895, John Douglas, 9th Marquess of Queensberry – a Scottish aristocrat also known for his endorsement of the code that regularised prize fighting – enraged by Wilde's association with his son Alfred, publically accused Wilde of being a homosexual, which was, at the time, a serious criminal offence. Wilde, whose comedy *The Importance of Being Earnest* was running to great critical acclaim, sued for criminal libel and Douglas was arrested. However, the private suit back-fired when the defence intimated that it had found evidence incriminating Wilde. Wilde dropped his case and the costs awarded to Douglas bankrupted the playwright. The police then arrested Wilde, he was prosecuted, found guilty and sentenced to two years in prison, where he wrote *De Profundis*. Wilde had been advised to flee the country, but was stricken with indecision. His arrest was commemorated by John Betjeman in 'The Arrest of Oscar Wilde at the Cadogan Hotel'.

Continue into Chesham Street until you reach Belgrave Square, at the heart of Belgravia. This exclusive district is named after Belgrave, a village – now a suburb of Leicester – where the Grosvenor family had an estate. The Grosvenors own this land, and more in Mayfair; they also owned and developed Pimlico, but that's no longer in the family. The current landlord is the 6th Duke of Westminster, who commissioned the statue of his ancestor, Robert, 1st Marquess of Westminster, that's on your left as you turn off from Belgrave Square. With him are two Talbot hunting dogs, which were immortalised forever when they were added to the Grosvenor coat of arms in the 17th century.

The triumphal Wellington Arch in Hyde Park Corner used to stand closer to ❺ Apsley House, the grand building next to the gates into Hyde Park. Apsley House – once known as 'Number One London', the first building east of a tollgate that stood here – was home to the Duke of Wellington who commanded the victorious forces at Waterloo. An oversized statue of the Duke once topped the arch, but that was removed to Aldershot in 1883 when the arch was rebuilt at the top of Constitution Hill. It was renamed Constitution Arch, but the name never stuck. Apsley House is open to the public as the Wellington Museum.

The New Zealand memorial – a cluster of cruciform bronze stakes in the far corner, pointing south – stands out as most original and least bellicose of Hyde Park Corner's monumental memorials. The normal request button on the pelican crossing (❷ 2.5 miles) into Constitution Hill is complemented by a higher one for horse riders. Class-conscious conspiracy theorists have suggested that the high button gives a quicker service. This is not true. As you roll down the hill, you will see Green Park on your left, Big Ben directly ahead and a high wall on your right – behind which are the 45 acres of Buckingham Palace Gardens. You can use the roadway of Constitution Hill or the parallel track in Green Park, depending on which is busiest.

Royal quarters

The frontage of Buckingham Palace – and the Victoria Monument complex of fountains and statures – dates from the building's last major makeover in 1913. The Mall, which runs away from the palace down to Admiralty Arch and Trafalgar Square, will host the start and finish of the London 2012 Olympic Cycling Road Race.

Birdcage Walk, named after the aviary that stood here during the reign of King James I, is anything but claustrophobic. Enjoy the expanse of the wide boulevard as you pass St James's Park on your left, the shadiest and most intimate of the Royal Parks, and the ❻ Guards' Museum on your right. As you turn right into Storey's Gate, you reach the cobblestones around the same time that you catch your first glimpse of Westminster Abbey. The grand ❼ Central Hall Westminster on your right, which under any other circumstances would be a major attraction in its own right, is the country's chief Methodist church and hosted the first assembly of the United Nations in 1948.

Parliament Square houses the Palace of Westminster, otherwise known as the Houses of Parliament. The world's first red/green traffic light regulated the exit from the Palace yard from 1868. A mounted statue of Oliver Cromwell – sword in one hand, Bible in the other – stands within the protection of Parliament's walls. Cromwell died of natural causes in 1658 and was buried in ❽ Westminster Abbey.

Buckingham Palace.

St James's Park.

Wellington Arch.

Albert Memorial.

Following the restoration of the monarchy, he was dug up and ceremonially beheaded on the 12th anniversary of the execution of Charles I. His severed head was displayed on a pole for 13 years. Statues standing free in the square include Winston Churchill and, the newest, Nelson Mandela.

Nearly 1,000 years ago, Edward the Confessor decided to relocate his palace from the City of London to Westminster. This had a profound influence on the development of London. The seat of political power was separated from the commercial centre; over the centuries, the countryside in between filled with law courts, markets, theatres, coffee houses, taverns, newspapers buildings and houses. 'Whitehall' (❸ 3.7miles) is not just a grand avenue; colloquially, it refers to the upper levels of the civil service, just as 'The City' refers to bankers, financiers and stockbrokers. If you see a crowd gathered in front of looming black security gates, slow down. Chances are you're in front of Downing Street, with the Prime Minister's residence at no.10. Directly opposite, you can see the London Eye, peeking out from behind the much older governmental buildings.

As you cycle (or maybe even walk – it can get very busy) around Trafalgar Square, you'll see Admiralty Arch on your left, with a distant vista of Buckingham Palace down the Mall.

Turning right into Waterloo Place, look out for the statues of Florence Nightingale, Sidney Herbert and the allegorical statue *Victory*. Up ahead are the flashing lights and images of the Trocadero, but turn left into Jermyn Street to enter the tranquil, exclusive streets of St James's. This district has a timeless air: gentleman's clubs on Pall Mall, shops along Jermyn Street selling bespoke shirts, panama hats and traditional male grooming products, although the area is not totally immune to demographic changes, to wit the Russian restaurant – complete with karaoke – at no.91 Jermyn Street. Piccadilly Arcade, a covered shopping walkway on the right, leads through to ❾ Burlington Arcade on the other side of Piccadilly (❹ 4.9 miles). Burlington Arcade dates from 1819, and could claim to be the oldest shopping mall in the world, although nothing so vulgar is likely.

On the west side of Berkeley Square are original buildings dating from the mid 18th century – nos.42-52, with modern interpolations at no.47 and no.48. No.44 was described by Nikolaus Pevsner, the doyen of architectural writers, as 'the finest terrace house of London'. Grosvenor Square is less atmospheric and is dominated by the modernist US Embassy, which stands in stark contrast to the grandiose buildings around it. The partial circuit of Hyde Park (❺ 5.8 miles) takes in Speakers' Corner – near Marble Arch – where a tradition of debate on politics and religion continues at the weekends. Regular orators bring their own soapboxes from which to address the sceptical, the bemused or the merely baffled passers-by.

Cross over the bridge between the Serpentine and the Long Water. As you glance left, you can see along the length of the Serpentine, with Big Ben and the Houses of Parliament in the distance. To your right is the Long Water, set in the grounds of Kensington Gardens. The ➓ Serpentine Gallery in Kensington Gardens is world-renowned for temporary exhibitions. Entrance to the gallery is free, and there are plenty of railings on which to secure your bike. It has just acquired another building, the Magazine, which – when it opens in 2012 – will double the available hanging space.

The ⓫ Albert Memorial – where else could a tour of Albertopolis end? – stands like a gaudy Gothic-revival space rocket opposite the Royal Albert Hall. The impromptu roller-hockey games on the roadway beneath it seem very sober in comparison. Finish the ride by either leaving the park at Queens' Gate (Ⓖ 7.4 miles) and cycling along busy Kensington Road, or strolling down to exit at Palace Gate **END**.

❶ **Launceston Place**
1A Launceston Place, W8 5RL (7937 6912, www.danddlondon.com). Open noon-2.30pm Tue-Sat, noon-3pm Sun; 6-10.30pm Mon-Sat, 6.30-9.30pm Sun.
❷ **Harrods**
87-135 Brompton Road, SW1X 7XL (7730 1234, www.harrods.com). Open 10am-8pm Mon-Sat; 11.30am-6pm Sun.
❸ **Ladurée**
87-135 Brompton Road, SW1X 7XL (3155 0111, www.harrods.com/visiting/restaurants/laduree). Open 9am-9pm Mon-Sat; 11.30am-6pm Sun.
❹ **Cadogan Hotel**
75 Sloane Street, SW1X 9SG (7235 7141, www.cadogan.com).

❺ **Apsley House Wellington Museum**
149 Piccadilly, W1J 7NT (7499 5676, www.english-heritage.org.uk). Open Apr-Oct 11am-5pm Wed-Sun & bank hols. Nov-Mar 11am-4pm Wed-Sun. Admission charge.
❻ **Guards Museum**
Birdcage Walk, SW1E 6HQ (7414 3271, www.theguardsmuseum.com). Open 10am-4pm daily. Admission charge.
❼ **Central Hall Westminster**
Storey's Gate, SW1H 9NH (7222 8010, www.c-h-w.com). Open 10am-4pm Mon-Sat; 1-4pm Sun. Admission free.
❽ **Westminster Abbey**
20 Dean's Yard, SW1P 3PA (7222 5152, 7654 4900 tours, www.westminster-abbey.org). Open Westminster Abbey June-Sept 9.30am-3.30pm Mon, Tue, Thur, Fri; 9.30am-6pm Wed; 9.30am-3.30pm Sat. Oct-May 9.30am-3.30pm Mon, Tue, Thur, Fri; 9.30am-6pm Wed; 9.30am-1.30pm Sat; worship only on Sun. Abbey Museum & Chapter House 10.30am-4pm daily. Cloisters 8am-6pm daily. College Garden Apr-Sept 10am-6pm Tue-Thur. Oct-Mar 10am-4pm Tue-Thur. Admission charge.
❾ **Burlington Arcade**
Burlington Arcade, W1J 0PZ (7630 1411, www.burlington-arcade.co.uk). Open 8am-6.30pm Mon-Wed, Fri; 8am-7pm Thur; 9am-5pm Sat; 11am-5pm Sun.
➓ **Serpentine Gallery**
Kensington Gardens (near Albert Memorial), W2 3XA (7402 6075, www.serpentinegallery.org). Open 10am-6pm daily. Admission free.
⓫ **Albert Memorial**
Hyde Park, Queen's Gate (7495 0916, www.royalparks.org.uk). Tours Mar-Dec 2pm, 3pm 1st Sun of mth. Admission Tours £6.

At Your Leisure

For Sunday riders

Follow Greater London's quiet roads and hidden routes – canal and river paths, disused railways and even a ferry – and discover its secret life, along with some of its loveliest monuments. Between 11 and 28 miles long, these rides are the perfect afternoon excursion.

❼ Meandering West

This spin to, and beyond, the limit of the tideway is flat. It hugs the River Thames as it loops around palaces and stately homes and spools through the sporting playgrounds of water-loving westerners. Some sections will be busy on fine summer weekends, but at other times it can be surprisingly quiet and bucolic. The riding surface varies from tarmac to soil to loose stones, but none of it is terrible. The bends of the river reveal new vistas turn by turn, and shelter you, intermittently at least, from any headwind. If you want to ride to the start from central London, the simplest route is via Hammersmith and Chiswick.

AT YOUR LEISURE

The strip of Brentford High Street running west from the north (Middlesex) side of **START** Kew Bridge, has the ❶ Kew Bridge Steam Museum and the ❷ Watermans arts centre – a theatre, cinema and gallery that, with an eye on many west Londoners' South Asian heritage, specialises in Asian arts; it also has a gallery dedicated to new media arts. The final link in this eclectic chain is the ❸ Musical Museum, a collection of automated musical instruments that includes a Wurlitzer cinema organ. If you want more evidence that the confluence of the Thames and the Brent is an important spot, consider the Brompton bicycle, manufactured nearby. The Brompton works is a real factory, with steel tubing going in one door and the famous folding bicycles popping out the other. Brentford is more interesting than some people think.

Kew Green, on the Surrey side of the bridge, is wonderfully scenic, and more so if there's a cricket match in play. Once you get on to the Thames Path you're soon shaking off buildings, with the Thames to your right and the ❹ Royal Botanic Gardens (Kew Gardens) on your left. Kew Gardens combines a scientific centre, an historic pleasure garden and generations of ground-breaking architecture. The gardens are worth a visit if you have the slightest interest in botany or horticulture, but overlooking their wonders from the riverbank is the next best thing.

Note that you are not legally permitted to ride along the section of the Thames Path between Kew and Richmond Bridges, even though lots of people do. The surface is good and pushing will not be a problem.

As you go along the river, you can see on the far bank the enormous brick chimney of the Kew Bridge Steam Museum, a 19th-century drinking-water pumping

Start Kew Bridge, Brentford, W4 3NG
Finish Hampton Court rail, KT8 9AE
Time 2 hours
Distance 11 miles
Connects with ⑭
Traffic & safety Mostly on cycle paths. Note that cycling is officially banned between Kew Bridge and Richmond Bridge. Minimal contact with motor traffic, apart from around Kingston town centre
Terrain Flat
Transport *Start* Kew Bridge rail. *End* Hampton Court rail
Good for Dreamers

Route Directions

START South from Kew Bridge along Kew Road
Right into Kew Green
Hairpin right before the Rose & Crown pub
back into Kew Green
Left into alley running along the wall of Kew Bridge
Left then
Immediate right
T-junction: left on to Thames Path. Note: cycling
is officially banned between here and Richmond
Continue on Thames Path
❶ **2.6 miles** Richmond Lock
Continue on Thames Path, taking care in Richmond
town centre
Keep to tarmac path through Buccleuch Gardens
Continue on London Thames Cycle Route to...
❷ **6 miles** Teddington Lock
Continue on Thames Path
Join Lower Ham Road
Continue on Thames Path to Kingston upon Thames
In Kingston upon Thames follow signs for
Thames Path
Left into Down Hall Road, dismounting if necessary
Right into Skerne Road going under railway bridge
Traffic lights: straight on into Wood Street
Bear left on to traffic-free section of Wood Street
T-junction: right into Clarence Street
Left in to Horse Fair
❸ **8 miles Cross** Kingston Bridge on cycle path
Left into Barge Walk
Continue on Barge Walk
END 11 miles T-junction: left on to Hampton
Court Bridge
Cross bridge to Hampton Court railway station

Royal Botanic Gardens (Kew).

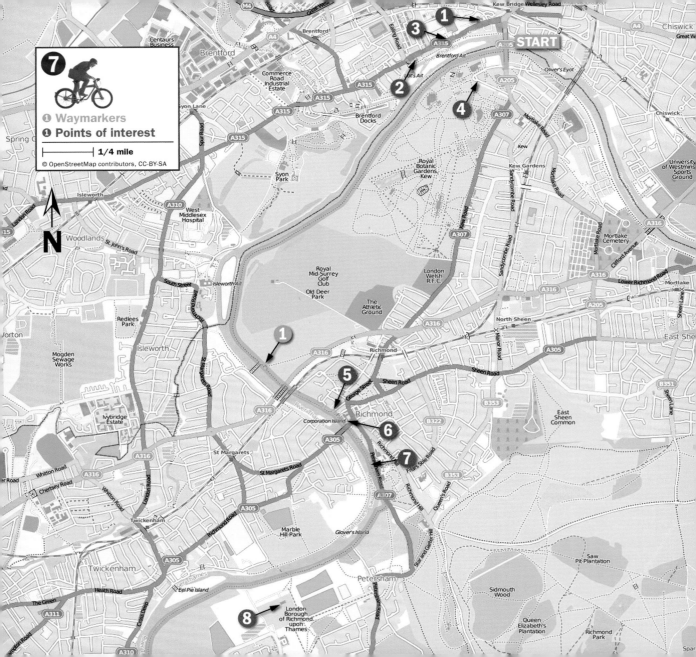

Richmond Lock.

station, and Thames Lock, where the Grand Union Canal meets the tideway. Further upstream, another lock marks the mouth of the River Brent, pouring down from Barnet. Kew Gardens was developed from the grounds of two royal palaces that were landscaped by Lancelot 'Capability' Brown, the doyen of the 'natural' style. Brown also worked on the privately owned Syon Park across the river, which has its own botanical gardens. The Thames' banks became popular as royal and aristocratic residences because travel by boat was safe, comfortable, private and reliable. Syon House provided interior locations for the film *Gosford Park*.

On the left is the Old Deer Park. A cleft stainless-steel monument marks the Royal Meridian, used to set the King's time before the standardisation of Greenwich Mean Time. The Old Deer Park is the home of the Exiles (London Welsh RFC). Heading west, leaving Chelsea, Fulham and Brentford behind, rugby replaces association football as the sport of choice.

Half full or half empty

Isleworth village on the outside of the bend is very pretty and around the corner is Richmond Lock (❶ 2.6 miles), a moveable barrage like a mini 1890s Thames Barrier, but here the function isn't to keep the water out, it's to hold it in; 19th-century improvements downstream meant that when the tide fell, water ebbed faster, leaving Richmond with only mud. The barrage is open for two hours either side of high tide, otherwise it's closed – which keeps the last four miles of the tidal Thames at least half full at all times. It also provides a footbridge, if you don't mind steps. A side lock allows boats to pass at any time.

Beyond Twickenham Bridge is Richmond, where the town spills down to the water. Bordered by parks and the river, Richmond has the feeling of a quintessential Surrey town. Richmond Bridge – the oldest surviving on the Thames – dates from 1774.

Richmond riverside has the ❺ White Cross, a Fuller's pub serving hearty food. If you want something more relaxing, ❻ Tide Tables, right under the bridge, offers parking and a terrace. ❼ Stein's, a Bavarian beer garden by the river, serves sausages. You can only order a beer if you also eat. Beyond Richmond, formal gardens give way to bumpy meadow, but you do pass the Stuart splendours

Hampton Court Palace.

of ❽ Ham House. The first hamlet on your left is Petersham, where George Vancouver is buried. Vancouver sailed to Hawaii with James Cook and later mapped the north-west coast of the Americas. Disputes with well-connected former shipmates forced him into early retirement here, deep in Surrey, where he could at least watch the tide rise and fall and dream of the Pacific. He died in 1798 aged 40. You can take a ferry over to Twickenham if you fancy a novelty. It costs £1, plus 50p for a bike.

Twickenham Ait lies against the far bank. 'Ait' (sometimes spelled 'aight' or 'eyot', but always pronounced 'eight') is an Old English word for a river island, most associated with the Thames. Twickenham Ait is better known by its latter-day name of Eel Pie Island. The island's hotel was once a famous music venue where the Rolling Stones and the Who played in the 1960s.

Around the bend is Teddington Lock (❷ 6 miles), a significant point of the river as the Port of London Authority's jurisdiction ends here. Behind is the tidal Thames, departure for pirates, explorers and empire builders; ahead is the upper Thames, home of straw boaters, punts and the wind in the willows. There's a place to hire tandems up ahead (❾ River Route Tandem Hire).

Kingston upon Thames is unpleasant for cyclists. The town's nucleus at the foot of Kingston Bridge is a brutal and anonymous underpass; cycle tracks take you around it but it's an ugly ride. If you insist on heading for this Surrey town on the River Hogsmill, push on to the central streets south of Kingston Bridge (❸ 8 miles) – otherwise roll over the bridge and continue upstream on the Middlesex bank.

The last leg is a loop around Bushey Park while Kingston becomes Surbiton across the water. The

building with the extravagant gold topping is St Raphael's Roman Catholic church. Lancelot Brown apparently never got this far, as Bushey Park still has strict Renaissance formality radiating from Sir Christopher Wren's ❿ Hampton Court Palace. In winter and spring, you can see the green globes of mistletoe infesting the park trees. The gilded gates designed to impress water-borne arrivals are behind an extra set of municipal railings, which rather defeats their function as gates and status symbols. The old red-brick Tudor palace around the back comes into view as you reach Hampton Court Bridge (END 11 miles). Head right if you want to visit the palace or the park; left for East Molesey and trains.

If you want a quick route home, ride past the palace and through the park to cut off the Kingston corner. There are hotels, bars and cafés on both sides of the river, so you can stroll around or sink a slow one while deciding where to cruise next. When one really should be in the office, a ride along the river to Thames resorts such as this (similarly Maidenhead, Windsor and Henley) to spend an afternoon by the water feels utterly splendid.

❶ Kew Bridge Steam Museum
Green Dragon Lane, Brentford, Middlesex TW8 0EN (8568 4757, www.kbsm.org). Open 11am-4pm Tue-Sun, bank hols. Admission charge.
❷ Watermans
40 High Street, Brentford, Middlesex TW8 0DS (8232 1019, box office 8232 1010, www.watermans.org.uk). Open noon-midnight Mon-Fri; 10am-midnight Sat, Sun.
❸ Musical Museum
399 High Street, Brentford, Middlesex TW8 0DU (8560 8108, www.musicalmuseum.co.uk). Open 11am-5.30pm Tue-Sun. Admission charge.

❹ Royal Botanic Gardens
Richmond, Surrey TW9 3AB (8332 5655, 8940 1171 information, www.kew.org). Open Apr-Aug 9.30am-6.30pm Mon-Fri; 9.30am-7.30pm Sat, Sun. Sept-Oct 9.30am-6pm daily. Early Feb-late Mar 9.30am-5.30pm daily. Late Oct-early Feb 9.30am-4.15pm daily. Admission charge.
❺ White Cross
Riverside, (Off Water Lane), Richmond, Surrey TW9 1TH (8940 6844, www.youngs.co.uk). Open noon-11pm Mon-Sat; 10am-10.30pm Sun.
❻ Tide Tables
2 The Archways, Riverside, Richmond, Surrey TW9 1TH (8948 8285, www.tidetablescafe.com). Open 9am-6pm daily.
❼ Stein's
55 Richmond Towpath, Richmond, Surrey TW10 6UX (8948 8189, www.stein-s.com). Open Summer noon-10pm Mon-Fri; 10am-10pm Sat, Sun. Winter noon-5pm Sat, Sun. Times vary depending on weather, call to check.
❽ Ham House
Ham Street, Ham, Surrey, TW10 7RS (8940 1950, www.nationaltrust.org.uk). Open House Apr-Oct noon-4pm Mon-Thur, Sat, Sun. Gardens Mid Feb-Oct 11am-5pm daily. Jan-early Feb, Nov-mid Dec 11am-4pm daily. Tours (pre-booking essential) phone for details. Admission charge.
❾ River Route Tandem Hire
YMCA Hawker Centre, Lower Ham Road, Kingston, Surrey KT2 5BH (8296 9747, www.tandemhire.com). Open 9am-9pm Mon-Fri; 9am-7.30pm Sat, Sun.
❿ Hampton Court Palace
East Molesey, Surrey KT8 9AU (0844 482 7777, www.hrp.org.uk). Open Palace Mar-Oct 10am-6pm daily. Nov-Feb 10am-4.30pm daily. Park dawn-dusk daily. Admission charge.

What Bike?

Having outgrown, outperformed or even simply outlasted your old bike, what should the newly enthusiastic leisure cyclist be looking for?

Best of both worlds

Those returning to cycling after a long lay-off are likely to be pleasantly surprised by the quality of today's bikes, with their powerful brakes and beautifully shifting gears. Long gone are the days of squeezing brakes frantically to produce a minimal decrease in speed. Nowhere is this better exemplified than in the hybrids. These combine the speed and efficiency of a drop-handlebar racing bike with the more upright position of a mountain bike, complete with a large range of gear ratios to make cycling uphill easier.

The flat handlebars of hybrid bikes house standard-looking brake levers together with more modern-looking twist-grip or trigger-style gear shifters, giving you the choice of anywhere between 18 and 24 gears. That sitting-up-straight position may not be as aerodynamic as the forward tuck of a racer, but the extra height it offers, enabling you to survey the traffic ahead much more clearly, inspires confidence.

Best brands: today's hybrid bikes – such as those from Trek and Specialized – are mainly made from aluminium. As a result, your machine is not going to rust away like bikes of old, but you'll still need to clean and oil the chain now and again.

Expect to pay: as with most things, you tend to get what you pay for, but spending at least a few hundred pounds should get you something decent.

Horses for courses? Nah...

Of course, the hybrid's parents – racing bikes and mountain bikes – also perform well on a daily basis. Some might find the more stretched-out position of a racer less comfortable, but there's no need to think that a racing bike is too delicate to get you quickly and efficiently about town.

Mountain bikes are more durable, but that equates to a slower, more sluggish ride. The heavily treaded tyres can always be swapped for a pair of slick ones if you plan to ride more on the road than off, while the flat handlebars and huge range of gears of an MTB make it a comfortable, everyday-style bike to suit everyone.

Let's go Dutch!

Increasingly popular are the sit-up-and-beg, or 'Dutch', bikes of the past. These heavy, robust bicycles have made a comeback, particularly in London, and it's not unusual to spot young women slowly pedalling through Islington with tiny dogs perched in their wicker baskets. They come in traditional men's and women's designs, the latter with a step-through frame to allow for long skirts. Racks and panniers adorn the already hefty machines, which were designed for shifting heavy loads around town long before the invention of the car, while a clunky traditional bell tops off the look.

Best brands: staunchly British company Pashley is a popular choice, but real-deal Dutch brands such as Gazelle deserve a look too.

Expect to pay: quite a lot. Around £500-£600 for a ladies' Pashley Princess.

⑧ 🚲 The Grand Junction

According to Jim Morrison, 'the west is the best'. He may have come to that conclusion more on the basis of rhyme than reason, but this ride allows you to see if it applies in a London context. What's more, the terrain is as level as you could possibly want. The Paddington arm of the Grand Junction Canal forms the basis for this ride. The straightforward navigation (keep the water beside you), pan-flat riding and the lack of motor traffic are all obvious attractions, but there's a more mysterious quality too. Moving from place to place on a corridor that has become largely irrelevant to modern land use means that you pop up in locations you weren't expecting. The mystery is enhanced because some of these places – Kensal Green Cemetery, the Ace Café, Southall High Road – have a slightly bizarre character all of their own.

START From the Great Western Railway terminus of Paddington it's a very short ride to the Paddington arm of the Grand Junction Canal – not so surprising when you think that both forms of engineering sought the same level ground to dig their ways. Access is through Sheldon Square, a new office complex with an elegant, but underused open-air auditorium and public art. If you're passing through on a weekday you can easily distinguish Sean Henry's enigmatic oil-painted bronze 'standing man' figures from the real-life office workers standing around in animated knots: the sculptures are the ones not smoking.

The lagoon a few yards north is where the Regent's Canal and Grand Junction Canal meet and is the reason this part of Maida Vale is known as Little Venice. Turning west, cycle traffic is prohibited for a short section of path that is parked up with houseboats; either walk or use parallel Delamere Terrace, then continue into Westbourne Green Open Space. The distinctive neo-Gothic brick church is St Mary Magdalene, designed by George Edmund Street (who was also responsible for the Royal Courts of Justice on the Strand).

The canal brushes the elevated Westway – a fragment of the unfinished Ringway scheme that aimed to put a motorway box around inner London. ❶ Great Western Studios, wedged between the canal and the motorway, is a purpose-built complex where the 'creative industries' host shows, talks, sales and other events open to the public. As the name might suggest, ❷ Meanwhile Gardens (❶ 1.7 miles) was

Start Paddington Railway Station, W2 1RH
Finish Brent Meadow, Southall, Middlesex, UB1 3ER
Time 2.5 hours
Distance 15 miles
Traffic & safety A few hundred metres on busy roads, then canal path until the last two miles on Uxbridge Road
Terrain Flat
Transport *Start* Paddington rail. *End* Hanwell rail
TFL bike-hire scheme North Wharf Road, Paddington
Good for Transcendentalists

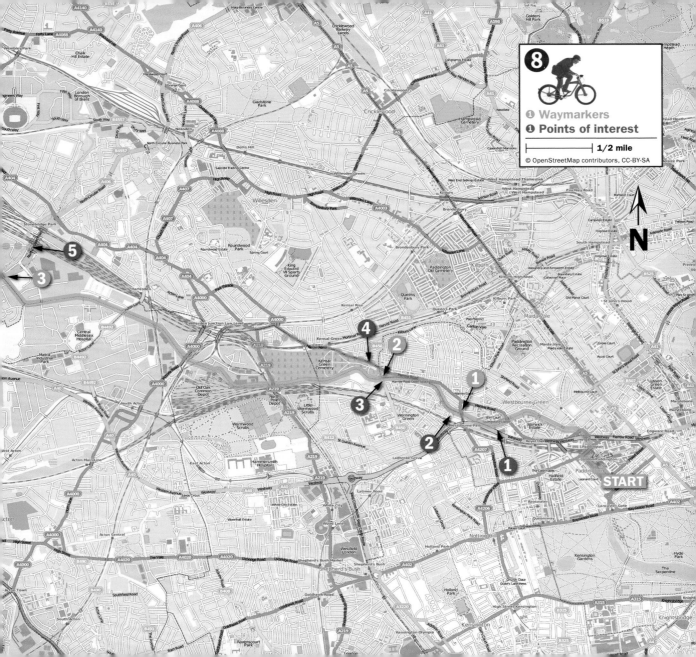

Route Directions

START Leave Paddington Station via eastern ramp
Right into Praed Street
Immediate right into Eastbourne Terrace
Traffic lights, T-junction: right into Bishop's Bridge Road
Left into Sheldon Square (past barrier)
Right (at the bottom of the ramp)
Immediate right
Left to reach canal path
T-junction: left on to towpath
Exit left at 'No Cycling' sign to continue on Delamere Terrace parallel to canal
Straight on where the road bends left, going into Westbourne Green Open Space on dual use path
Rejoin towpath to continue
❶ 1.7 miles Pass Meanwhile Gardens
Continue on towpath
❷ 2.4 miles Continue on tow path or
   To visit Kensal Green Cemetery
    Right on Ladbroke Grove (bridge 4)
    Traffic lights: left into Harrow Road
    (cemetery entrances are on the left)
    Left into Trenmar Gardens
    Right into Waldo Road
    Left into Scrubs Lane
    Rejoin towpath down steps on right
❸ 5.6 miles Continue on towpath to aqueduct over North Circular
   To visit Ace Café
    At next footbridge cross canal –
    Grand Union Walk (alley)
    T-junction: right into Mount Pleasant
    Immediate right into Beresford Avenue
    T-junction: right to Ace Café
    Retrace to footbridge to continue
❹ 9 miles Pass Black Horse Inn on left
Continue on towpath going under A40
Left up alley before bridge 20
❺ 12.6 miles T-junction: left on Uxbridge Road
Through Southall and under big steel railway bridge
END 14.6 miles Left into Brent Meadow before River Brent bridge

only ever intended to be a temporary community garden built on land awaiting development; that was in 1976 – it's now quite a mature project. Behind is Trellick Tower (finished in 1972), designed in the Brutalist style by Ernö Goldfinger. The steep bridge ramp just before Ladbroke Grove is for the entrance to Portobello Dock (❷ 2.4 miles) where the ❸ Dock Kitchen provides seasonal lunches seven days a week and themed dinner menus.

If you want to visit ❹ Kensal Green Cemetery, cross the canal on Ladbroke Grove to find the entrances on Harrow Road. If you return to the canal via Scrubs Lane, you'll have to use steps, but they do have a gutter running along the side to make it easier to wheel a bike up or down.

If you stay on the canal, you pass an out-of-town Sainsbury's with free mooring for canal-borne customers, then another steep, in this case redundant, bridge. It used to allow access to the now filled-in Gas Works Basin. The canal passes through Park Royal. Beyond the Grand Junction Arms pub standing on Acton Lane is a winding hole –

a place wide enough to spin a boat around. Cycling on, look to the right for the arch of Wembley Stadium as it appears through buildings. The section of a canal between locks is called a pound, and this one stretches for no less than 27 miles by worming across the landscape at a constant height. An aqueduct is required to take the canal over the valley of the River Brent, which also holds the North Circular Road (❸ 5.6 miles). For the span, the channel is divided in two, and the bridge is marked with the crown and three blades coat of arms of the now sadly defunct Middlesex County Council. Half hidden in brush on the north-west corner of bridge is a concrete (pillbox) fortification from World War II, marking the River Brent as a 'stop line' in counter-invasion plans.

Biker bikes

From the next exit over a footbridge, it's a short spin on back streets to the ❺ Ace Café on the North Circular Road. Housed in a modernist brick building, it serves all-day fried breakfast as well as the likes of grilled chicken breasts with broccoli. The staff dress uniformly in blue jeans and T-shirts, and the place is festooned with information about forthcoming events broadly themed around cars, motorcycles and rock 'n' roll. The Ace was once a notorious destination for motorcycle outlaws or 'ton-up boys'. It was a setting for the 1963 film *The Leather Boys*. The café closed in 1969, but on the 25th anniversary of its closure, 12,000 motorcycle riders held a reunion rally outside the building, which was by then operating as a tyre depot. The success of the reunion led to a full reopening in 1998. Today, it's a café, social centre, music venue and place of pilgrimage for 'rockers' of all ages, as well as a slightly odd 'living museum' of a much mythologised strand of 20th-century life. Staff are friendly and the parking is good.

Southall.

Kensal Green Cemetery.

Once across the North Circular, the terrain becomes greener thanks to gardens, golf courses and open spaces. The ❻ Black Horse (❹ 9 miles) at Greenford is the first pub you'll pass on the south side. Its garden, cradled in a left-hand bend, is another reason to consider a stop, and the fact that it marks the northern limit of the trip; from now on the line begins to turn south. Finding a mosque in London isn't hard, but the Mohammedi Park Mosque across the canal in Northolt is big by any standards. The weird grass-covered earthworks beside the A40 are Northala Fields; a park opened in 2007 that was constructed using rubble from the old Wembley Stadium.

The bridges are numbered but in an unusual manner. The plain numbers are bridges that were built with the canal around 1800, while those that have letters are later additions. The canal, which allowed traffic to move from London to the Midlands without the tortuous Thames trip to Oxford, was a great success. Don't go under bridge 20 (❺ 12.6 miles); it carries the Uxbridge Road which takes us through Southall.

Southall is a great destination, akin to south Asia, without the long-haul travel, in a red-brick suburban setting. If you want to eat, there's plenty of choice. On your right running into town is ❼ Mirch Masala, part of a small chain; it has parking outside. If you want takeaway and a picnic, try the tiny ❽ Shahi Nan Kabab on the left as you're leaving town. The best place for eating your takeaway is a little further on, under the giant steel railway bridge and down to the River Brent; on your left before the river bridge is ❾ Brent Meadow (END 14.6 miles), a waterside hay field dominated by Isambard Kingdom Brunel's Wharncliffe Viaduct, carrying trains into Paddington. It would be fair to say that IKB was a particular man; he gave clear instructions for the disposal of spoil around the viaduct, so that it would create a pleasing vista.

He didn't just want to make the Great Western Railway (also known as 'God's Wonderful Railway' or 'Brunel's billiard table'), he was creating a work of art. Munch your samosas and enjoy the view. If it's warm, you can paddle. For those sitting 65 feet above staring out of the window of a First Great Western train, Paddington is only minutes away. But if travel is a pleasure – and bicycles are proof that it is – why get the journey over so quickly?

❶ Great Western Studios

65 Alfred Road, W2 5EU (7221 0100, www.greatwesternstudios.com). Open 9am-6pm Mon-Fri. Admission free.

En Route

Park Royal's rather fanciful name comes from a short-lived attempt to establish a permanent showground for the Royal Agricultural Society. When this failed, the Park Royal was the site of munitions factories during the Great War and it remains an industrial zone. The green areas here are not cherished city parks or gardens, but odd bits of land too small, or the wrong shape, for another factory. There are, however, blackberries in the autumn.

Ace Café.

Wharncliffe Viaduct.

❷ Meanwhile Gardens
156-158 Kensal Road, W10 5BN (8960 4600, www.mgca.f2s.com). Open 24hrs daily.

❸ Dock Kitchen
Portobello Docks, 342-344 Ladbroke Grove, Kensal Road, W10 5BU (8962 1610, www.dockkitchen.co.uk). Lunch served noon-2.30pm Mon-Sat; noon-3.30pm Sun. Dinner served 7-9.30pm Mon-Sat.

❹ Kensal Green Cemetery
Harrow Road, W10 4RA (8969 0152, www. kensalgreencemetery.com, 07904 495012). Open Apr-Sept 9am-6pm Mon-Sat; 10am-6pm Sun. Oct-Mar 9am-5pm Mon-Sat; 10am-5pm Sun. All year 10am-1pm bank hols. Tours 2pm Sun. Admission free.

❺ Ace Café
Ace Corner, North Circular Road, Stonebridge, NW10 7UD (8961 1000, www.ace-cafe-london.com). Open 7am-11pm Mon-Sat; 7am-10.30pm Sun.

❻ Black Horse
425 Oldfield Lane, Greenford, Middlesex UB6 0AS (8578 1384, www.fullers.co.uk). Open 11.30am-11pm Mon, Tue; 11.30am-midnight Wed-Sat; noon-11pm Sun. Food served noon-9pm Mon-Sat; noon-8pm Sun.

❼ Mirch Masala
171-173 The Broadway, Southall, Middlesex UB1 1LX (8867 9222, www.mirchmasalarestaurant.co.uk). Food served noon-11pm daily.

❽ Shahi Nan Kabab
59 High Street, Southall, Middlesex UB1 3HF (8571 0777). Open noon-midnight daily.

❾ Brent Meadow
Southall, Middlesex UB1 3ER (8813 9232, www2.ealing.gov.uk). Open 24hrs daily. Admission free.

Kit Bag

Helmet? Check. Puncture repair kit, tyre levers and pump? Check. Strong legs? Getting there.

Inner tube? No? A spare one could be your best friend in the relatively unlikely event of a puncture as you venture a little farther from home.

Round and about

Tyres, with the additional help of barriers like Kevlar now waging war against all things nasty, pointy and sharp, have come on in leaps and bounds in recent years, so a sudden bang followed by disheartening hiss is becoming an ever-decreasing occurrence. But when it does happen – and it will at some point – just replacing a punctured tube with a new one is a lot quicker than fixing a puncture by the side of the road. In the rain. You can then fix that punctured tube back in the comfort of your own home. Or, if you're feeling particularly lazy and reckless, not to mention flush, just throw the punctured one away and buy a new spare.

Replacing old tyres can be an expensive but necessary upgrade. Worn, paper-thin rubber isn't going to stand up for one minute against a wet, grit- and glass-strewn gutter.

A fresh pair of tyres will serve you well, but consider the kind of terrain you're going to be riding on before buying the first pair that you see. Knobbly mountain bike-type tyres are perfect for all surfaces, but consider some slick – or at least less knobbly – tyres for your mountain bike if you're mainly going to be using it on the road, as your bike will roll much more easily and freely.

Soft seat

Sitting on a bike is never going to be as comfortable as lounging on your sofa in front of the television, so you might want to consider upgrading your saddle, too. Many shops will let you try before you buy, as we're all different shapes. Women's saddles also tend to be wider than men's due to the shape of the sit-bones, so there's no need to feel offended. Sitting comfortably could make the difference between only using your bike to nip to the shops and heading out for a day of relative comfort.

Taking the weather with you

Lastly, as British summers are as predictable as British winters, a waterproof jacket that packs up nice and small should be something to keep with you at all times. Many are small enough to scrunch up into a saddlebag (which is also a useful place to keep your puncture repair kit). You can quickly get cold when stopping for a break, so you'll be pleased to have the option of an extra layer.

A jacket could be the one piece of kit you'll want to spend a bit of money on. Cycling-specific options offer a longer back to help keep your bum dry, and longer arms for a better fit on the bike. And while cheaper ones will ward off a shower, they're also likely to quickly have you feeling clammy due to trapped sweat, so consider more expensive models that incorporate the material Gore-Tex, a waterproof and breathable fabric. It will pay you back for years to come in warmer, more comfortable rides when the heavens open.

AT YOUR LEISURE

Twin Peaks

London is a predominantly flat city, with the nearest climbs to the centre being the approaches to the hilltop villages of Hampstead and Highgate, and the sprawling parkland of Hampstead Heath in between. The Heath offers a host of enjoyments, including swimming in the lido or freshwater ponds, kite-flying on Parliament Hill, and open-air concerts at Kenwood House. Add to this touristic itinerary the delights of Primrose Hill, Regent's Park, Camden Town, Islington, Finsbury Park and the lovely Parkland Walk, and you have a fine selection from north London's wealth of attractions rolling past your wheels.

START Finsbury Park stands at the junction of three present-day boroughs, Islington, Haringey and Hackney. Opened in 1869 on the site of Hornsey Woods, it was named to placate the Finsbury electorate; they were probably after an open space a little closer to home, but at least the new amenity assured them of somewhere to go on their days out. The park contains a ❶ café, a boating lake, a small skate park and, opposite Finsbury Park tube/rail station on Stroud Green Road, a purpose-built, supervised, secure, indoor ❷ bike-parking facility. The station, which pre-dates the park and was originally know as Seven Sisters, has good connections, including an overground service, to King's Cross and out into Hertfordshire.

The 1.4-mile road circuit inside the park makes it a useful venue for fitness training, although, as part of this circuit is used for car parking and it's all subject to flying footballs, wandering dogs, toddlers and drunks, you can't go too mad rehearsing sprint finishes; but it has varying gradients and a long, broad, sloping straight. The southern part of the circuit is subject to random closure for funfairs, festivals and outdoor concerts, so keep an eye on the event listings or you may find your training schedule unexpectedly disrupted by a Stone Roses reunion.

The Parkland Walk (❶ 0.4 miles) begins just across the footbridge over the East Coast Mainline tracks. The gentle, even gradient is a very smooth way of gaining significant height, and the overgrown platforms of abandoned stations add atmosphere. At some points, you're above the surrounding streets, looking down over the rooftops; at others, down into a wooded vale. The unmade surface is rough in places and the upper sections used to be ill-drained and muddy after rain, but current management of the path strikes a good balance between

Start & finish Finsbury Park tube/rail, N4 2DF
Time 3 hours minimum
Distance 13 miles
Connects with ❸ ⓭
Traffic & safety Mostly on paths, which may be lonely after dark, or quiet roads, but there are some busy high streets
Terrain Parkland walk and canal path. Hilly
Transport Finsbury Park tube/rail
Good for Urban hillbillies

Route Directions

START Enter Finsbury Park from the Finsbury Park Gate on Seven Sisters Road opposite Finsbury Park Road. (When the park is closed, access the Parkland Walk by turning left on Seven Sisters Road, right on Stroud Green Road, right on Woodstock Road and right on Oxford Road.)

Keep left to follow the road up the hill past the tennis courts

Left to leave the park at Oxford Gate, using the narrow metal bridge across the railway tracks

❶ **0.4 miles Right**, once over the bridge, on to Parkland Walk

Left to exit Parkland Walk, at its terminus

❷ **2.1 miles T-junction: right** on to Holmesdale Road

T-junction: right on to Archway Road.

Traffic lights: second left into Jacksons Lane

T-junction: left Southwood Lane

Mini roundabout: second exit (right) Highgate High Street

Mini roundabout: second exit (straight over)

Mini roundabout: first exit (left) Hampstead Lane (second exit on to North Road for pubs)

Left into The Grove

❸ **3.5 miles Right** into Fitzroy Park – Millfield Lane

Right into Hampstead Heath on shared-use route (second entrance after emerging from Millfield Lane)

Straight over uphill on earth path

Straight over crossroads into wooded area

Fork right then **turn right** shortly after

Straight over Viaduct Bridge

❹ **4.7 miles T-junction: left** (rejoin Spaniards Road)

Roundabout: first exit (Whitestone Pond) into Heath Street

Traffic lights: left into East Heath Road – South End Road – Constantine Road

❺ **6 miles Right** into Agincourt Road

Traffic lights: straight on into Southampton Road – Malden Road

Right into Queens Crescent

T-junction: left into Prince of Wales Road

Right into Crogsland Road

Traffic lights: straight on into Regent's Park Road

Left on to painted railway bridge

Straight on continuing on Regent's Park Road

Right into Primrose Hill, enter park and walk to the summit

❻ **7.4 miles Continue** to south-western gate of park

Cross Prince Albert Road on to footbridge

Left down on to Regent's Canal towpath heading east

T junction: left follow towpath to Camden Lock

❼ **8.4 miles Walk** through the market to continue under Camden High Street

Continue along the towpath to Battle Bridge Basin

   To visit the Canal Museum
   Exit via the ramp just under Thornhill Bridge
   Cross canal on bridge
   T-junction: right into All Saints Street
   T-junction: left into New Wharf Road
   Return to towpath and continue to tunnel exit ramp

❽ **10 miles T-junction: right** on to Muriel Street

Immediate left on to estate path (walking may be necessary – take care)

Straight on into Maygood Street

Right into Barnsbury Road

Immediate left into Dewey Road

Continue straight through small park at end of Dewey Road (walking may be necessary)

Left, immediate right into Ritchie Street

Straight over into Broomfield Street

T-junction: left into Parkfield Street – Berners Street

Traffic lights: left into Upper Street

Roundabout (Highbury Corner): first exit Holloway Road

Immediate right into Highbury Place

⓿ **11.3 miles Enter park** on dual-use path

> **Alternative route when Arsenal are playing**
>
> *T-junction: right into Highbury Hill*
> *T-junction: right into Leigh Road*
> *Immediate T-junction: left into Highbury Park*
> *Right into Riverdale Road*
> *Left into Canning Road*
> *T-junction: right into Mountgrove Road*
> *Immediate left into Finsbury Park Road*
> *Straight on into Finsbury Park*

T-junction: left into Highbury Hill (Clock Tower)

Left into Martineau Road

T-junction: right into Drayton Park

Left into Gillespie Park (Islington Ecology Centre)

Right to follow dirt path through the reserve

Down steps

T-junction: right into Seven Sisters Road

END **12.9 miles Left** into Finsbury Park

---

comfortable travel and slightly scruffy wildness. Never a place to hurry, the path may get too busy for easy riding on summer weekends, but, usually, the surprise is how quiet it is.

You can't really overshoot the exit from the Parkland Walk as there is a blocked tunnel just beyond the steep exit climb to Holmesdale Road, which begins another steep climb, up Highgate Hill (❷ 2.1 miles). ❸ Jacksons Lane arts centre – in a converted red-brick church on the corner of Archway Road and Jacksons Lane – was established in 1976, around the time when Archway Road was blighted by (thankfully defeated) plans for an urban motorway. It has a café.

Top of the hill

At the top of Jacksons Lane, there's a long chicane just wide enough for a single car; it's just the place for inexperienced riders to get the feel of 'taking the lane' (riding in the centre of a traffic lane to claim a safe space) – an invaluable skill for city cyclists. As you ride down Southwood Lane, glimpses down alleys and between houses on your left give you a sense of how high you've climbed. You soon arrive at the hilltop village of Highgate. There are two pleasant pubs with gardens – the ❹ Red Lion & Sun in North Road, and the ❺ Wrestlers in its continuation, North Hill. If you want to explore the village with its combination of quaint corner shops and gift stores, turn left into Highgate High Street and walk the no-right-turn into South Grove. This route takes you past the end of Swain's – formerly Swine's – Lane, which leads down to the famous ❻ Highgate Cemetery. Unfortunately it's one-way uphill, so you have to walk if you want to visit the cemetery without going a long way round and down.

Fitzroy Park (❼ 3.5 miles) is a gated private road classed as a bridleway, legal for public cycling. The steep descent passes numerous very exclusive

En Route

The Parkland Walk corridor used to carry a railway line (opened 1867) from Finsbury Park to Edgware. Its gradient – steep by railway standards – made trains expensive to run, and the passenger service closed in 1954. The line persisted for another ten years carrying freight and, finally, just to move empty Underground trains between Drayton Park and Highgate. It closed for good in 1970. The tracks and most of the buildings were removed and ownership passed to Haringey Council, whose initial idea was to build houses wherever access allowed. Public opposition to the plan led to an inquiry. The result was the Parkland Walk, which opened in 1984. Five years later, it was identified as one of many potential lines for new road construction through London, but the wave of public protest consolidated the path's status as a valuable local resource, and it was declared a local nature reserve – London's longest – in 1990.

properties before emerging, as Millfield Lane, beside a flight of ornamental ponds on Hampstead Heath. While it's tempting to freewheel down, no-holds barred, watch out for potholes, oncoming traffic and some sneaky speed bumps that take you by surprise as you merge into Millfield Lane.

London Bowling Club is straight ahead of you as you descend, but the road veers round to the left until you emerge with Hampstead Heath on your right. Continue to the second turning into the park, signposted 'Shared use route' and take the path that runs between two lakes. The ❼ Men's Pond, on your left, and the Ladies' Pond, higher up, with a nicer wooded aspect, are open for swimming all year round. The smaller Mixed Pond on the other side of the Heath is open only in summer. Cycling on the Heath is restricted to certain paths which have an 8mph speed limit, so, if you like to push the pedals, it's more practical to use the Heath for going uphill. The designated cycle paths are generally wider and flatter than their walking counterparts, and have yellow bicycle plaques placed at sporadic intervals.

All these ponds feed the River Fleet whose source is in the marshy valley higher up. The upper Fleet is known as Ken Ditch (Ken Woods and Kenwood House are features of the Heath), hence the first village downstream is Kentish (Ken Ditch) Town. Just before you leave the park on to Spaniards Road, stop for a minute to take in the views on your left. From here, it seems like the whole of London is laid out before you.

Spaniards Road links Hampstead to Highgate and, along with Fitzroy Park and the cycle paths across the Heath, can be used as a hilly training circuit when the Heath is quieter – winter evenings or early mornings in summer. At other times you can make a road circuit going up Fitzroy Park, right into the Grove, right again down Highgate West Hill and right into Millfield Lane.

Primrose Hill.

Downhill all the way

From Whitestone Pond (❹ 4.7 miles), it's downhill to Chalk Farm, either through well-heeled Hampstead Village or beside the Heath via South End Green and Gospel Oak (❺ 6 miles). While Spurs players may favour Chigwell, Arsenal players prefer Hampstead; Patrick Vieira, born in Senegal and former player for France, Arsenal, Juventus and, most recently, Manchester City, once declared his intention to retire to Hampstead, where everybody speaks French.

❻ Marine Ices at Chalk Farm serves acceptable Italian food and exquisite ice-cream. As you cross Chalk Farm Road, look out for the Roundhouse on your left, recently reopened after a long, dark period. This 19th-century engine shed was a wine warehouse before becoming the leaky-roofed rock 'n' roll auditorium where the Clash met the Ramones.

Cycling is forbidden on Primrose Hill, but it's worth the walk to the summit (❻ 7.4 miles) for its views of London. In the 1960s, the attempts to close the hill's gates after dark were resisted by mass sit-ins, so today it remains open throughout the night. Southwark Cyclists organise a midsummer ride, starting at Greenwich, to the summit to watch the sunrise.

The towpath of the Regent's Canal, which opened in 1820 to connect the Grand Junction Canal at Paddington with the Thames at Limehouse, bisects the animal terraces and aviary of London Zoo.

Forty years ago, TE Dingwalls wood yard at Camden Lock (● 8.4 miles) closed down. Workshop space was rented out and, in 1973, a pub-rock bar called Dingwalls opened on the site. A small weekend craft market started and, as the goods sold diversified, the market spread into more redundant industrial buildings, including now-renovated stables that once housed the horses that hauled canal barges and made deliveries to and from the railway yards. As the market was on private land, it was exempt from the ban on Sunday trading. By 1985, three other markets had opened on or near Chalk Farm Road, and most of the businesses between Camden Town and Chalk Farm had changed hands and become shops and restaurants catering mainly to visitors rather than locals. The trading area has spread so far beyond the Lock that it's now simply known as Camden Market. At Camden Lock the towpath is interrupted, so you'll have to get off and walk through the cobbled market. It's always busy.

Camden Lock.

In the lands behind St Pancras and King's Cross stations most canalside property has turned its back on the water although Battle Bridge Basin, where cargoes were unloaded for north London, now houses the ❾ Canal Museum. You have to leave the canal path to reach it.

The canal runs under Islington in a 960-yard tunnel with no towpath (❽ 10 miles). The plaques marking the straight path through the Half Moon Crescent Housing Co-operative make navigation surprisingly easy. Upper Street, the start of the Great North Road just north of the Angel, is where (before the arrival of the railway) you transferred from local to national transport. The options were walking, riding a horse or donkey, a horse-drawn cart, cab, carriage or coach. Note the elevated pavements – transport-related pollution is not a recent problem.

Islington competes with Hampstead as the home of dinner party-throwing liberals and champagne socialists. And they don't want for entertainment; as well as a plethora of bars and restaurants on Upper Street, you pass – in less than a mile – the Screen on Green cinema, the Almeida theatre (on Almeida Street), the Little Angel Puppet theatre, the King's Head for dinner-theatre, the Hope & Anchor and Union Chapel for music, and the Hen & Chickens pub-theatre on Highbury Corner (❾ 11.3 miles).

❿ Arsenal FC's Emirates Stadium provides a useful circuit for gentle training. The broad paved oval around it is private, but nobody objects to cycling. There's a ramp, rising from Benwell Road, for hill sprints. Don't bother when there's a game on (unless you've got tickets). Free, secure, match-day bike parking is available at the entrance on Drayton Park. Gillespie Park – another ex-railway nature reserve, home to the ⓫ Islington Ecology Centre – offers a daytime shortcut to Seven Sisters Road, although you have to descend

En Route

Whitestone Pond houses what was once the highest pub in London: Jack Straw's Castle. Built in 1721, this former coaching inn is named after one of the leaders of the Peasants' Revolt of 1381. It is thought that Jack incited groups of peasants from a hay wagon (his 'castle') on Hampstead Heath, encouraging them to protest about their lot under the boy-king Richard II – a life of serfdom, tithes and ever-increasing taxes. Up to 60,000 peasants marched to London with a petition that demanded abolition of the first poll tax. Frustrated with the lack of progress in the negotiations, the rebels stormed the Tower of London and attacked and killed the Archbishop of Canterbury and the Lord Chancellor. Straw and many other rebels were duly executed, and so ended the first ever uprising of the 'common man'. Sadly, the grand building has now been converted into upmarket flats.

a flight of stairs, and it's locked on match days. If you don't do steps (or the Gunners are playing at home), using the streets north of Blackstock Road takes you past ⓬ Sargent & Co, a young shop catering to the new interest in old bikes to the **END** (12.9 miles).

❶ Finsbury Park café
Finsbury Park, N4 2NQ (8880 2681). Open 9am-6pm daily.
❷ Finsbury Park Bike Park
Parkland Walk, Stroud Green Road, N4 2DF (8211 8501, www.tfl.gov.uk/roadusers/cycling/11947. aspx#finsbury). Open 4-8pm Mon, Wed, Fri; 7am-10am Tue, Thur; 11am-1pm Sat. Smartcard needed.

Islington Green.

❸ Jacksons Lane Café
269A Archway Road, N6 5AA (8340 5226, www.jacksonslane.org.uk). Open 10am-6pm Mon-Sat.

❹ Red Lion & Sun
25 North Road, N6 4BE (8340 1780, www. theredlionandsun.com). Open noon-midnight Mon-Sat; noon-11pm Sun.

❺ Wrestlers
98 North Hill, N6 4AA (8340 4297). Open 4.30pm-midnight Mon-Thur; 4.30pm-1am Fri; noon-1am Sat; noon-midnight Sun.

❻ Highgate Cemetery
Swain's Lane, N6 6PJ (8340 1834, www.highgate-cemetery.org). Open East cemetery Apr-Oct 10am-5pm Mon-Fri; 11am-5pm Sat, Sun. Nov-Mar 10am-4pm Mon-Fri; 11am-4pm Sat, Sun. Admission charge.

❼ Men's Pond, Ladies' Pond, Mixed Pond
Hampstead Heath (7485 3873, www.cityoflondon. gov.uk/hampstead). Open varies. Admission charge.

❽ Marine Ices
8 Haverstock Hill, NW3 2BL (7482 9003, www.marineices.co.uk). Open 10.30am-11pm Tue-Sat; 11am-10pm Sun.

❾ Canal Museum
New Wharf Road, N1 9RT (7713 0836, www. canalmuseum.org.uk). Open 10am-4.30pm Tue-Sun; 10am-7.30pm 1st Thur of mth. Admission charge.

❿ Emirates Stadium
Ashburton Grove, N7 7AF (7619 5000, www.arsenal.com).

⓫ Islington Ecology Centre
Gillespie Park Nature Reserve, 191 Drayton Park, N5 1PH (7527 4374, islington.gov.uk). Open 10am-4pm Mon-Fri. Admission free.

⓬ Sargent & Co
74 Mountgrove Road, N5 2LT (7359 7642, www. sargentandco.com). Open 10.30am-6.30pm Wed-Sat.

At Your Service

Enjoyable cycling is the result of a ship-shape bicycle, so diagnose any problems you're experiencing by way of the handy check list below.

An annual, or even twice-yearly, service at your local bike shop will set you back around £50, depending on what may or may not need adjusting or replacing, but it's still cheaper (and safer) than letting your machine get into such a state of disrepair that the only option is a whole new bike.

A well-maintained bicycle should last for years, and with regular attention will serve you as well five years down the line as the day you bought it.

Symptom Frequent punctures
Diagnosis Tyre tread worn, hairline cracks in rubber
Fix Need new tyres
Urgency Look at straightaway; could be dangerous, especially in the rain
Cost ££
DIY or DSE (Done by Someone Else): DIY, definitely

Symptom Brakes don't work
Diagnosis Worn brake blocks or badly adjusted brakes
Fix New brake blocks or adjustment needed
Urgency Vital to remedy immediately – for obvious reasons
Cost £
DIY or DSE Replacing brake blocks: DIY. Brake adjustment: DSE, unless you're confident

Symptom Noisy gears, chain slipping
Diagnosis Badly adjusted gears
Fix Adjust gears
Urgency Noisy gears are simply annoying; a slipping chain is potentially dangerous
Cost £
DIY or DSE Gear adjustment requires a little experience, so DSE until someone shows you how

Symptom Sluggish, odd-feeling ride
Diagnosis Cracked frame or forks
Fix Older-style steel frames can be re-welded, while forks can be replaced separately
Urgency Stop riding your bike – a broken frame can prove fatal
Cost £££££
DIY or DSE One for the experts, this. It may be mendable, but, unfortunately, it may mean a whole new bike.

Symptom Loud bang, and a loss of control…
Diagnosis Flat tyre!
Fix Repair or replace inner tube
Urgency Not only does a puncture make it difficult to keep riding, but it also damages the tyre
Cost £
DIY or DSE DIY

Symptom Wobbly wheel
Diagnosis Damaged wheel, possible broken spoke
Fix Replace spoke, 'true' wheel
Urgency Relatively urgent: a weakened wheel may eventually fail entirely
Cost ££
DIY or DSE Quite a skill – DSE

⑩ Time, Tide & Towpaths

Sometimes the glorious simplicity of cycling really takes your breath away, and this ride is a good example. Starting from the depths of London, all you do is climb on your bike and follow the towpath of the Lee Navigation Canal out into the understated greenery of Hertfordshire. Along the way, you'll pass examples of history ancient (Rye House, where conspirators plotted to assassinate Charles II), recent (the old Big Brother house) and future (the Lee Valley White Water Centre, the Canoe Slalom venue for the London 2012 Olympic and Paralympic Games). What's more, since the route follows water, the only climbs are up ramps at locks and bridges, and there's a railway line running parallel most of the way, meaning that it's always easy to bail out should muscles fail or the weather turn nasty.

The Lea Valley follows the path of the meandering River Lea, from its source in Hertfordshire to the Thames. From Hertford, the river flows south, appearing as a reflecting ribbon of water under the radiating arterial roads of north London. This makes it easy to pick up the route from anywhere in north London – just ride east until you come to water and then turn left. But for ride completists, and until the plans to open the banks of the Lea below Bow Locks are realised, the starting point that gives the longest journey is on the banks of the Thames at the entrance to Limehouse Basin. The towpath is being renovated, but any diversions are well signposted and easily followed.

START The pub in Narrow Street at the Limehouse Basin entrance was renamed ❶ The Narrow; local old-timers still prefer the Barley Mow. It's now part of Gordon Ramsay's empire, so the menu is a cut above the normal run of pub fare, in quality and price. Its terrace overlooks the Thames on one side and the outflow of the Regent's Canal and the Limehouse Cut on the other. You can wheel a bike down to the pub and keep an eye on it while eating and drinking.

Limehouse Basin, on the other side of Narrow Street, is the terminus of the Regent's Canal; here, freight was transferred between narrow boats and sea-going vessels. It was originally known as the Regent's Canal Dock. Now it's used by pleasure craft, with a congenial mix of salt- and freshwater vessels.

Limehouse Cut, the other inflow into the Basin, pre-dates the Regent's Canal. Its original function was to bypass the tortuous meanderings of the last mile of

Start Thames entrance to Limehouse Basin, by the Narrow, 44 Narrow Street, E14 8DP
Finish Hertford East Railway Station, Hertford, SG14 1SB
Time 4 hours minimum
Distance 28 miles
Connects with ❸ ❹
Traffic & safety
Almost all the route is on the towpath of the Lee Navigation Canal, except for a short detour through Amwell and the last few hundred metres through Hertford to reach the train
Terrain Flat
Transport *Start* Limehouse DLR/rail. *End* Hertford East rail, Hertford North rail.
Good for Car-free cycling, industrial history and a train bail-out option

the Lea and to get boats sailing the Lea to London without the long haul around the Isle of Dogs. The Cut used to be tidal, so the path is some way above the water. This may make inexperienced riders nervous. The trick is to concentrate on the path ahead, not the wet alternative.

In the 1960s, when water-borne commercial traffic was almost finished and before waterways and towpaths became widely used for leisure, a new road bridge was built across the Cut, with no path beneath. This broken link was re-established in 2003 by the ingenious floating path that leads to Bow Locks (❶ 1.4 miles). It rises and falls on vertical runners as the water level fluctuates – a novel riding sensation.

The concrete bridge at Bow Locks was built when they were renewed in the 1930s. Modern material, but the rumble strips on the ramps weren't included to stop speeding cyclists, but to stop heavy horses from slipping. The picturesque Grade I-listed House Mill, from which Three Mills Island gets its name, is thought to be the largest in Britain still standing. The main product of the old tidal-powered mills used to be gin. Now it houses TV studios.

At Canning Town a second floating path passes under the busy A11. The Northern Outfall Sewer – the Greenway – passes over the Navigation, then there's Old Ford Lock (❷ 3 miles). The former lock keeper's house on the right hosted *The Big Breakfast* TV show for ten years until 2002. If you want to get a flavour of Camden Lock circa 1975, divert on to the arty enclave of Fish Island, where the ❷ Counter Café offers excellent coffee and cakes.

The Lee Navigation follows the western border of the Olympic Park site of the London 2012 Olympic and Paralympic Games, then the edge of the Wick Woodland, which was planted in the early 1990s up to Marshgate Bridge. The plain to your right is

The Narrow.

Hackney Marshes. On a winter weekend you can watch 50 simultaneous soccer matches, with cries of 'man-on' and 'on me 'ead' floating on the breeze.

Border lines

At the end of the marsh, the towpath on the east bank runs out and a bridge takes you over to the west. Just beyond, where the cycle track across South Millfields Recreation Ground joins the towpath, there's a discreet iron post. It marks the boundary of the old London County Council (LCC). Before the LCC was founded in 1889, this was the boundary of Middlesex and Essex. Then, until 1965, to the west of the post was London, to the east, Essex. Finally, the Greater London Council annexed inner Essex and the mark became the boundary between the boroughs of Hackney and Waltham Forest.

These modern boundaries are by no means the first time the Lea has served as a border. Some 1,500 years ago, the swamp lands of the Lea marked off the Saxons from the Danes. The historic discontinuity continues, with many Hackney people imagining Leyton is somewhere near Chelmsford, while some residents of Walthamstow are reluctant to venture into Hackney.

Beyond the Princess of Wales pub, Lea Bridge Road and North Millfields, you have the choice to recross to the east bank and blast along the rougher but quiet path on the Essex side of the Lea. The path on the west bank is smoother but narrower and busier, so consideration is required. In fact, past conflicts between pushy cyclists and drinkers outside the Anchor & Hope pub have led to chicanes being installed. Slow down and say hello, or stop for a beer. Springfield Park on your left contains Hackney's only hill and was once a day-trip destination for East Enders. Local author Iain Sinclair writes of its 'accessible obscurity' and the view from the top, across the marshes toward Epping Forest, is worth the climb if you've time. There's a café at the top and another by the rowing club at the park's northern limit.

The next park, Markfield, has a quirky BMX/skate-park, a café and the ❸ Markfield Beam Engine built in 1888 to pump sewage out of Tottenham and Wood Green. Peer through the window at the giant spanners hanging on the wall. Once a month, a team of enthusiasts get up steam; the flywheel, which is the size of a house, spins and you can go in and feel the wind from its awe-inspiring rotation. Beyond Tottenham Hale, the path crosses sides at Stonebridge Lock (❸ 8 miles). The reservoirs whose banks dominate the next few miles supply more than ten per cent of London's water and are apparently visible from space.

At Enfield Lock (❹ 13.2 miles), the former Royal Small Arms Factory dates from 1816. The Lee Navigation allowed easy dispatch of its finished products and the ready supply of raw materials. Although it might be hard to believe now, the site was chosen partly because it combined good transport links with rural isolation, thus ensuring secrecy, safety – occasional explosions were expected – and space for weapons testing. The Lee-Enfield .303 rifle – standard issue in the British army from the 1890s until 1957 – was made here, but 'Lee' actually refers to a Scots inventor, not the river. The factory site is now a housing estate. You can cut through it and across Sewardstone Marsh, then follow lanes to High Beach on ride ❶❾.

Out of the city

Enfield, formerly in Middlesex, gives way to the Borough of Broxbourne, and the Lea now roughly marks the boundaries of Hertfordshire and Essex. Within living memory, the rival youths of Waltham

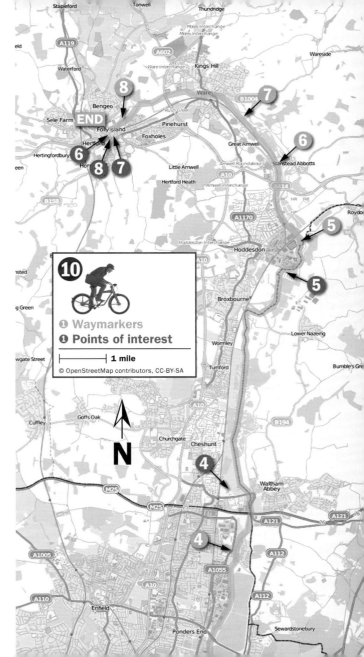

Route Directions

START Thames entrance to Limehouse Basin,
E14 8DP

Head north along the east side of the channel
(the right-hand bank facing away from the Thames)

Straight along the east side of Limehouse Basin

Right on to Limehouse Cut towpath; continue on
towpath

➊ **1.4 miles** **Continue** over floating towpath under
the A12

Continue on to concrete footbridge over Bow Locks

Cross the Lee Navigation using the bridge to Three
Mills Island

Right continuing on towpath on the west (left) bank
of Lee Navigation

Continue along the floating towpath under the A11
flyover

Continue under the Greenway (Northern
Outfall Sewer)

➋ **3 miles** **Cross bridge** to Old Ford Lock

Detour to Counter Café

*Cross to west side of Lee Navigation via Old
Ford Lock; straight into Dace Road; right into
Bream Street; T-junction: right into Stour Road;
T-junction: right into Beachy Road; Counter
Café is straight ahead. Retrace route to Old
Ford Lock*

Continue on towpath to end of Hackney Marshes

Cross Lee Navigation on footbridge

Continue on towpath on the west bank

Pass chicane outside Anchor & Hope pub (beware
of outdoor drinkers)

➌ **8 miles** **Cross** the bridge at Stonebridge Lock
to east bank of Lee Navigation

Lee Navigation at Broxbourne.

Continue on towpath

➍ **13.2 miles** **Left** to cross Lee Navigation, then

Immediate right into towpath on west bank

Continue on towpath under M25 and northwards

Cross Lee Navigation towards the Crown pub

Left on to towpath

Continue on east bank of Lee Navigation north

Cross Lee at Dobb's Weir by the Fish & Eel pub

Immediate right over the long steel and concrete
footbridge

Continue on towpath on west bank of
Lee Navigation

AT YOUR LEISURE

❺ 21 miles Continue on west bank past Feildes Weir Lock

❻ 23 miles Continue on towpath or...

Detour to shorten route

Left by Jolly Fisherman pub on to Station Road; cross level crossing; then turn right into Amwell Lane – Lower Road; turn right on to public footpath just before Lower Road crosses New River; cross the railway tracks with extreme caution; turn left to rejoin Lee Navigation towpath

❼ 24.7 miles Continue north on towpath

At Ware, leave towpath (it doesn't go under the bridge)

Right on to Viaduct Road

Cross Amwell End

Rejoin towpath on to Hertford

Cross via Bridge 71 (Mill Road)

Immediate left to rejoin towpath

Cross weir bridge

❽ 28 miles At the 'No Cycling' sign at the boundary of Hertford either...

Dismount and continue walking

Along the towpath, cross the bridge and then turn left into Bull Plain

Or to continue cycling

Turn right on to Frampton Street; first left on to Oldhall Street – The Folly – Bull Plain

Left into Salisbury Square – Railway Street

Roundabout first exit Railway Street

END 28.5 miles Continue to Hertford East station or Hertford North station

Cross and Waltham Abbey would square up on the bridge on Saturday afternoons to exchange words, stones or blows.

As you cycle, you'll see to the left the new **❹** Lee Valley White Water Centre, the venue for the Canoe Slalom at London 2012. Engineers have spent hundreds of years struggling to pacify the river, and now they've spent millions engineering the opposite: controlled white water.

The many lakes you'll see as you continue north of the Walthams are the result of gravel extraction. At Broxbourne, use the brick bridge to cross a side channel and then cross the Lee Navigation towards the Crown pub, which has a beer garden, and continue on the east bank. By the **❺** Fish & Eels pub in Hoddesdon, which serves serviceable chain-pub food all day in a great location, cross back to the west bank on the road bridge, and then use the long steel and concrete footbridge to cross the weir. If you're lucky enough to be cycling the route after heavy rain, the sound and sight of thousands of gallons of water flowing beneath you make for a thrilling ride.

At Feildes Weir Lock (**❺** 21 miles), the Stort Navigation, a rougher, more rural ride, breaks off east for Harlow and Stortford. It also has a shadowing train line. The Lee continues past Rye House, a manor where a plot to assassinate Charles II on his way home from Newmarket Races was supposedly planned in 1683. Only the gatehouse remains.

In St Margarets (**❻** 23 miles), you have the choice of continuing on the Lee Navigation or shaving off a corner by following the New River. The New River's shallow gradient means that, although in Islington it's high above the Lea, here they're almost on a level. If you take the New River option, you'll find Amwell Lane rising gently to pass the island monument inscribed: 'Sacred to the memory of Hugh Myddelton, Baronet,

Lea Valley, Tottenham Hale.

whose successful care assisted by the patronage of the King, conveyed this stream to London. An immortal work: since men cannot more nearly imitate Deity, than in bestowing Health.'

Having passed Myddelton's memorial, the route back to the Navigation involves crossing the railway line on an unguarded foot crossing. Look both ways twice and don't hurry, the sightlines are good. You also need to swing your bike over a stile, so if this all sounds too stressful, stay on the Navigation. The two routes rejoin at Hardmead Lock (❼ 24.7 miles).

Beyond the punster's favourite town of Ware (where?), there are more spectacular weirs as the natural Lea, which rises near Luton, and tributaries the Rib, the Beane and the Mimram collect and wash through the Navigation's upper levels. The old Intake House allows water from the Navigation into the New River near the latter's original source at Chadwell Springs, just beyond the high-level A10 Ware by-pass.

The 'No Cycling' sign as the Navigation enters Hertford (❽ 28 miles) forces a diversion. The ❻ Old Barge snuggled beside the Navigation offers free Wi-Fi; if you've ridden all the way from Limehouse, the varied menu may be more welcome. The ❼ Rose Café in Railway Street provides simpler food in big portions.

If you want to keep cycling, there's an ex-railway path – the Cole Green Way – to Welwyn Garden City, but, for obvious reasons, you'll no longer have the security of a parallel train. If you want amusement, the small but varied collection at ❽ Hertford Museum is free.

You're spoiled for choice for getting back to London. Trains to Liverpool Street leave from Hertford East (END 28.5 miles), while the Hertford North line runs to Moorgate during the week and King's Cross at weekends. Should this spirit-level flat ride have left you hungry for hills, you can ride back to Cheshunt via Essendon, Brickendon and Cuffley.

❶ The Narrow
44 Narrow Street, E14 8DP (7592 7950, www.gordonramsay.com/thenarrow). Open noon-11pm Mon-Sat; noon-10.30pm Sun. Food served 11.30am-3pm, 6-11pm Mon-Fri; noon-4pm, 5.30-11pm Sat; noon-4pm, 5.30-10.30pm Sun.

❷ Counter Café
7 Roach Road, E3 2PA (mobile 07834 275 920, www.thecountercafe.co.uk). Open 7.30am-5pm Mon-Fri; 9am-5pm Sat, Sun.

❸ Markfield Beam Engine
Markfield Road, N15 4RB (01707 873628, www.mbeam.org). Open 11am-4pm 2nd Sun of mth. Admission free.

❹ Lee Valley White Water Centre
Station Road, Waltham Cross, Herts EN9 1AB (08456 770 606, www.leevalleypark.org.uk/whitewaterrafting). Open 10am-7pm Wed-Fri; 10am-5pm Sat, Sun. Admission charge.

❺ Fish & Eels
Dobbs Weir Road, Hoddesdon, Herts EN11 0AY (01992 466073, www.vintageinn.co.uk/thefish andeelshoddesdon). Open noon-11pm Mon-Sat; noon-10.30pm Sun.

❻ The Old Barge
The Folly, Hertford, Herts SG14 1QD (01992 581871, www.theoldbarge.co.uk). Open 11am-11pm Mon-Thur; 11am-midnight Fri, Sat; noon-11pm Sun. Food served noon-3pm, 7-9pm Mon-Fri; noon-9pm Sat; noon-4pm Sun.

❼ Rose Café
33 Railway Street, Hertford, Herts SG14 1BA (01992 553524). Open 6.30am-5pm Mon-Sat; 8am-4pm Sun.

❽ Hertford Museum
18 Bull Plain, Hertford, Herts SG14 1DT (01992 582686, www.hertfordmuseum.org). Open 10am-5pm Tue-Sat. Admission free.

AT YOUR LEISURE

Pimp Your Ride

You've got your urban dream machine, so how about really making it your own, taking some pointers from those achingly cool bike couriers zipping around town?

❶ Wrap star

We've all got to start somewhere, right? And if your current steed's doing the job for you mechanically, then all it needs is a few tweaks to make it truly original. Easy, relatively cheap DIY 'pimping' starts with swapping your handlebar grips or bar tape for something a little more special – the cycling equivalent of changing the colour of your shoe laces, and just as easy to do. Go for some genuine leather bar tape from Brooks, available in a plethora of colours (pictured), or take the cheaper route via Fi'zi:k's superb Microtex tape in antique or honey brown.
www.extrauk.co.uk
Pimp-o-meter ★

❷ DIY from the ground up

Building your bike from scratch is the route that most bike couriers go down, and begging, borrowing or stealing – OK, not stealing – components from friends, colleagues and bike shops is the way to go. If this is too drastic, an effective and affordable cheat is to replace the tyres with a funkier set: go for the excellent Continental Grand Prix 4000 tyres, available in a conti-mental array of colour choices.
www.conti-tyres.co.uk/conticycle
Pimp-o-meter ★★

❸ Colour me bad

If colours are your game, look no further than bike-messenger favourite Brick Lane Bikes for pedals, handlebars, chainsets and even sprockets in every colour of the rainbow to customise your bike, without the vast cost of replacing or respraying the frame itself.
http://bricklanebikes.co.uk
Pimp-o-meter ★★★

❹ Armoured bikes

Whether you're looking for an individual paint job or if it's just time to spruce up your bike frame, Hackney-based Armourtex has built an enviable reputation for delivering high-quality, powder-coated frame resprays at very competitive prices. They can often turn your frame around in just a few days too.
www.armourtexltd.co.uk
Pimp-o-meter ★★★★

❺ Bespoke to suit

Get the whole kit and caboodle exactly how you want it, thanks to 14 Bike Co, based at the Truman Brewery in Brick Lane. All their frames are built using British Reynolds steel, and

can be painted and kitted out to your desired specifications. Savile Row, eat your heart out.
www.14bikeco.com
Pimp-o-meter ★★★★★

❻ Material boy

For those in need of real decadence, why not see if you can persuade British design company Tom Dixon (www.tomdixon.net) to copperplate your pride and joy – just as they did on a special limited-edition run of Bromptons as part of a recent collaboration with the British folding-bike company (www.brompton.co.uk)? The result was so stunning that it won the Best Use of Material award at the 2011 *Wallpaper** magazine design awards.
Pimp-o-meter ★★★★★★★★★★

What Goes In Must Come Out

In the capital, the usual choice is between getting somewhere fast by following straight lines on busy streets and dealing with the selfish temper of city traffic, or pootling gently along winding paths, giving way to dawdlers and taking care not to infringe their quiet enjoyment. The Greenway provides a middle way; it's shared with joggers, dog walkers and slow-moving family groups, but it's wide enough, with uninterrupted sightlines, that you can usually travel as fast as you want without being rude, threatening or dangerous. What's more, it provides a heady sense of exploration. The route slices directly through the villages of Newham on an embankment. The Royal Docks have the redundant grandeur of a lost civilisation – maybe not as old as Stonehenge or the Pyramids, but almost as mysterious. The Woolwich Ferry provides an entertaining parody of a sea journey and the woodlands on Shooters Hill are well worth the climb.

START You can begin this ride from the ❶ Container Café in the ground floor of the View Tube, which stands on the Greenway, or pick up the route where the Greenway crosses Stratford High Street (❶ 0.7 miles).

The Greenway is a useful corridor, but carrying people, on bikes or on foot, has never been its primary function. What it actually is for is not revealed by its name, but passing one of its vents in warm weather you may detect the faint whiff of a clue. You are travelling above the Northern Outfall Sewer, a limb of the network of brick tunnels constructed between 1859 and 1875 that remain a central part of the drainage system that keeps London habitable.

This section of the Greenway path ends at High Street South, where it's necessary to cross under the elevated A13 (❷ 3.8 miles) to reach the area's most prominent landmark. The Beckton Alp stands in splendid isolation, like a mysterious prehistoric barrow, the Ventoux of Newham. In fact, it's a slag heap made of waste from the gigantic Gas Light and Coke Company works, which dominated the area, from its establishment in 1867 until town gas was replaced by natural gas in the 1970s. The cheap marshland allowed an extensive state-of-the-art plant to be constructed, and the downriver waterfront location reduced the price of coal deliveries; the combination enabled the company to undercut all competitors. Beckton Gas Works, named after the company's governor Simon

Start Greenway, Stratford, E15 2PJ
Finish Castle Woods, Shooters Hill, SE18 3JA
Time 1.5 hours minimum
Distance 11 miles
Connects with ❸ ⑩
Traffic & safety First half is motor-free; uphill section from Woolwich is on residential side streets.
Terrain Flat to Woolwich (with a steep detour up and down Beckton Alp), then 432 feet of climbing up Shooters Hill
Transport *Start* Stratford tube/rail or Hackney Wick rail or Pudding Mill Lane DLR (folding bikes only). *End* Woolwich Arsenal rail/DLR or Eltham rail
Good for Industrial archaeologists and frustrated mountaineers

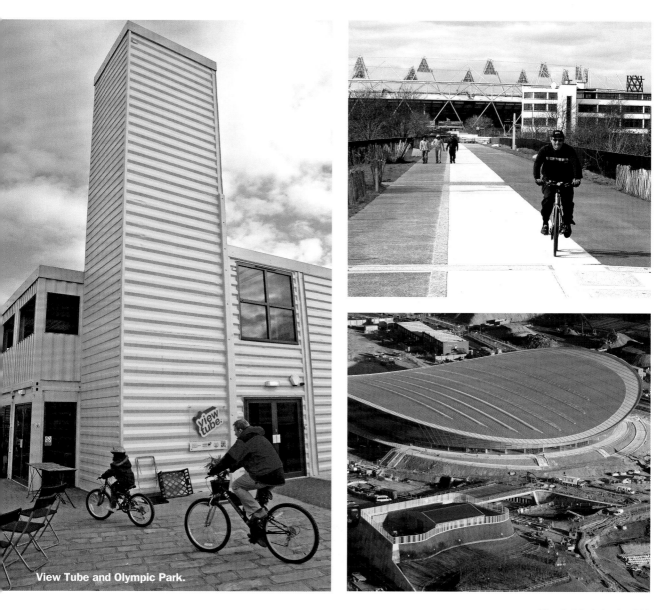

View Tube and Olympic Park.

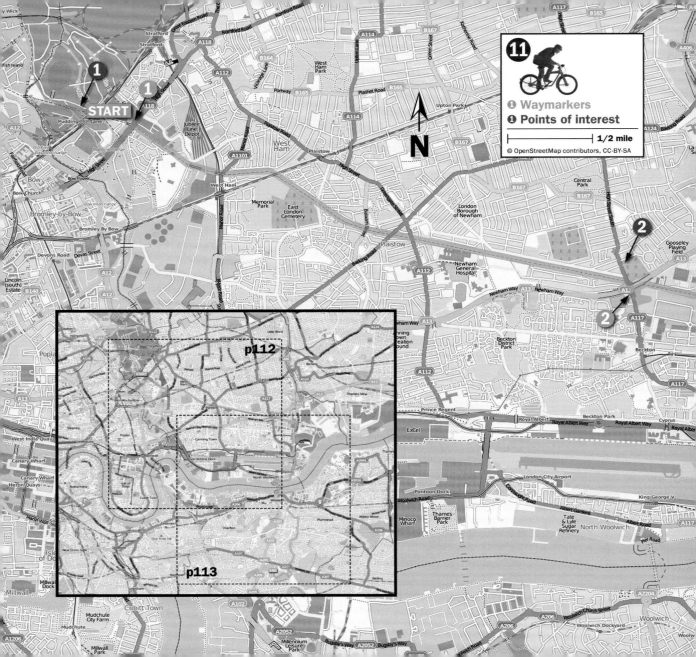

Route Directions

START View Tube. (The Greenway is interrupted between the View Tube, on the boundary of the Olympic Park, and Stratford High Street, so descend the ramp from the embankment just before you reach the View Tube. Follow the diversion signs with care under the mainline train tracks to reach Stratford High Street at the end of Pudding Mill Lane)

Traffic lights; T-junction: left into Stratford High Street

Traffic lights: right into Abbey Lane

Immediate left on to footway

❶ **0.7 miles Right** to rejoin the Greenway

Continue to East Ham Church

Cross High Street South

❷ **3.8 miles T-junction: right** under flyover

Left through galvanised steel fence to the summit of the Beckton Alp

Retrace to gate

Right on to CS3 Cycle Superhighway

Right on to the Greenway

Right at the end of the Greenway

Follow cycle track in the trees, keeping left to stay beside Royal Docks Road

Continue on cycle track to pass Gallions Reach Shopping Park Centre on your left and a housing estate on your right

Follow the cycle path under the flyover and around the spiral ramp to emerge on top of the flyover

T-junction: left on to flyover to reach roundabout on Woolwich Manor Way

Roundabout: first exit (south) on to Woolwich Manor Way

Gallions roundabout: second exit Atlantis Avenue

Traffic lights: right to walk over wooden boards on to the access road towards the brick chimneys of Gallions Hotel

Right (east) along the dockside under the road bridge

Right on cycle path up to rejoin Woolwich Manor Way, heading south over the Albert Basin

Continue over Sir Steve Redgrave Bridge (footway cycling allowed) – Woolwich Manor Way – Albert Road

❸ **6.7 miles Left** into Woolwich Manor Way

Right along river wall through Royal Victoria Gardens

Continue past rusty iron jetty

Right on to hairpin ramp to exit river wall. Use the foot tunnel (entry via brick rotunda on your right) or catch the free ferry to cross the river

Exit ferry first left through leisure complex, following the signs to the Thames Path, passing in front of the tunnel exit

Follow riverfront east (downstream) to Royal Arsenal, past the large wooden posts

❹ **8.1 miles Right** at the group of iron Antony Gormley figures, signposted Woolwich Arsenal Station

T-junction: left out of Royal Arsenal on to Beresford Street/Plumstead Road

Turn right at the crossing to enter Woolwich New Road

Pass on the left of the Royal Arsenal Gatehouse and O'Connors pub. (Take care here; walking may be necessary)

Left at Anglesea Arms pub into Anglesea Road –

Conduit Road – Raglan Road
Right into Burrage Road
T-junction: left into Plumstead Common Road
Immediate right into Wrottesley Road
T-junction: right into Genesta Road
T-junction: left into Eglinton Hill
T-junction: right into Plum Lane
Immediate left into Eaglesfield Road
Right into Cleanthus Road

🄯 10.3 miles **Through gap** at the end of the
road to pass the water tower on your left
T-junction: right on to Dover Road
Immediate left into Kenilworth Gardens
Left into Crown Wood Lane
END 11.1 miles **Bear right** at the Terrace
Café and follow the path round the hill to reach
Severndroog Castle in Castle Woods; you can
continue past the castle to rejoin the Dover Road

Woolwich Ferry.

En Route

As well as modernising the sewage system, the Buildings Act of 1844 restricted the practice of 'noxious trades' within London. As these works moved east across the Lea Valley, West Ham grew rapidly while its neighbour East Ham remained a rural Essex village; in 1851 there were 300 houses in East Ham, while West Ham had 3,300.

To the north-east, on the Barking Road (closer to East than West Ham) you can see the stands and floodlights of Upton Park (current home of West Ham United FC). West Ham was originally a works team at the Thames Iron Works, a great shipyard close to Leamouth. The nickname the 'Hammers' (crossed hammers feature on the club badge) or, more colloquially, the 'Irons', derives from this past.

Adam Beck, eventually delivered gas to London in a famous mains pipe that was 48 inches in diameter. Beckton Gas Works closed in 1976 and stood rusting for another ten years. During this period it served as a location for major film shoots including *Full Metal Jacket*, *For Your Eyes Only* and *1984*. Blowing up or burning down the rusting, redundant buildings was a speciality.

The scrubby trees now well established on the Alp must be stabilising the hill, but beware of the deep fissures in the tarmac path that winds to the peak. In the 1980s, an incongruous dry ski slope was laid on its southern slopes. From the summit you can clearly see the line of concrete footings that held the pylons of the drag lift waiting to confound the industrial archaeologists of the future. To the north, just across the A13, the church of St Mary Magdalene harks back to village days; it is supposedly London's oldest parish church still in use, and parts of the flint structure date from the 12th century. The churchyard is now a seven-acre ❷ nature reserve with marked trails and a visitor centre. Further north stands the bold Edwardian edifice of East Ham Town Hall and the distant heights of Epping. To the east is the mouth of the River Roding where, in Kipling's *The River's Tale*, '...Norseman and Negro and Gaul and Greek, drank with the Britons in Barking Creek'.

Docking in

South-east of here are the Royal Docks. The soil dug from the first dock (the Royal Victoria, which opened in 1855) was taken upstream to consolidate the marshy area that would become Battersea Park. London City Airport, the ExCeL (Exhibition Centre London) and the University of East London have replaced the cranes, wharves and railway sidings that serviced what was once the largest area of impounded water in the world. The high ground to the south is on the other side of the Thames, and the pointed water tower of Shooters Hill is this ride's high point. The sugar refinery at Silvertown marks the riverfront. Silvertown is named after a long-gone factory owned by Mr Silver, not, as is often assumed, Tate & Lyle's retail brand of sugar, 'Silverspoon'. Looking west, the towers of the City, the new Olympic Park and the heights of north London complete the panorama.

The Greenway terminates at Royal Docks Road, while the Northern Outfall Sewer continues a few hundred feet to reach the treatment works where its discharge is cleaned and released into the Thames. The residue sludge used to be loaded on to delightfully named 'Bovril Boats' and dumped in the North Sea until this practice was forbidden by the

European Union. Since 1998, it's been incinerated. The route south through Beckton traces the current margins of new suburban development, with wide roads and bridges ending abruptly.

The Royal Docks closed to commercial traffic in 1981. The Gallions Hotel, newly refurbished and due to reopen as a sports facility, restaurant and offices, is a rare survivor from their imperial heyday. Standing at a railway terminus and connected by a subway to the quay, the faux-Jacobean hotel with its elaborate classical friezes once allowed Pacific & Orient passengers to await embarcation in luxury. In Kipling's novel, *The Light that Failed*, artist Dick Heldar is setting off for Egypt and enquires: 'Is it Tilbury and a tender, or Gallions and the docks?'

Until its incorporation with the London Borough of Newham in 1965, North Woolwich was administered as part of Woolwich on the south shore. The administrative anomaly of 'Kent in Essex' is supposedly the responsibility of an 11th-century Sheriff of Kent whose manorial lands fell on both sides of the river. The medieval hamlet may have been destroyed by floods, as there was nothing there when the railway arrived in 1847. The Royal Victoria Gardens (❸ 6.7 miles) – privately run pleasure gardens famous for lavish outdoor entertainment – were originally opened in 1851 to try to generate traffic on the line. A foot tunnel runs to Woolwich proper, but the preferred option is a short cruise on the Woolwich Ferry. Originally, a ferry crossing was provided to complement the train service, but a parallel free municipal service opened in 1889. Paddle steamers ran until 1963, when they were replaced by the current fleet and their monumental hydraulic loading ramps.

The original Gunners
It's possible to follow the southern riverbank all the way to Crossness Pumping Station (Abbey Mills' south-side twin) but first comes the Woolwich Arsenal. There's a group of Antony Gormley figures (❹ 8.1 miles) marking the point to turn off the river. Only as you get close, do you realise they're open and hollow, like sarcophagi. Originally known as 'the Warren', the

Severndroog Castle in Oxleas Woods.

Make your London day out even better

With great London 2012 clothes and accessories available at the London 2012 Shops, conveniently located at Paddington Station, Heathrow Terminal 5, St Pancras International, Liverpool Street Station and John Lewis Oxford Street.

london2012.com/shop

Arsenal was a centre for the manufacture and testing of arms from Tudor times. George III renamed it the Royal Arsenal. During the 20th century, 40,000 people worked here, but now much of the site has been redeveloped for housing. The ❸ Royal Artillery Museum to your left took over some of the remaining historic buildings in 2001, rebranding itself 'Firepower'. It was here that migrant workers founded the soccer team currently resident in N5. In 1886, before they became 'the Arsenal', the team were called Dial Square after their workshop built by John Vanbrugh in 1720. All that remains of the building today is the Dial Arch, also commemorated in a ❹ gastropub of the same name; you pass it as you bump over a small patch of cobblestone.

Woolwich town centre and market are currently being redeveloped; the area is still recovering from the long decline of the munition works and other local industry. The redevelopment of the Arsenal and the opening of a new Docklands Light Rail station have given the area a boost.

The climb from Woolwich is steep in places. Stop and turn back for views of the sweeping river and the lands just crossed. If you don't like riding uphill, then passing a water tower is always a relief; they're sited at high points, and thus indicate that you don't have to climb any higher. The Gothic example on Shooters Hill (❺ 10.3 miles) is additionally pleasing since it's a landmark previously espied from afar. The Dover Road is Roman and was the major route for Canterbury, Dover, Rome and Jerusalem until the opening of the Rochester Way Relief Road in 1988.

Crown Woods Lane runs gently down into Oxleas Woods, a section of the ancient woodlands that cover much of Shooters Hill and the heights above Thamesmead. These woods were once threatened by a new motorway access road for a proposed East London River Crossing (a bridge replacement for the Woolwich Ferry). In 1993, the planning enquiries had been held and the paperwork was all in place, but, at the eleventh hour, fearing a repeat of the aggravation on Twyford Down (the Winchester bypass), the government relented and the plan was abandoned.

The homely ❺ Oxlea Wood Café stands above a long green meadow where the view gives the impression that north-west Kent is a forest (albeit one filled with rumbling motor traffic). Working round the hillside to the right, you can climb back into Castle Woods. Hiding in the trees is Severndroog Castle (END 11.1 miles), an odd three-sided folly built in 1784 by the grieving widow of Sir William James in honour of his heroics on the Malabar coasts of south India. Enjoy the shade, London is downhill from here.

❶ Container Café
The View Tube, The Greenway, Marshgate Lane, E15 2PJ (07702 125081, www.theviewtube.co.uk). Open 9am-5pm Mon-Fri; 10am-6pm Sat, Sun.
❷ East Ham Nature Reserve
Norman Road, E6 4HN (8470 4525). Open call for details. Admission free.
❸ Firepower Royal Artillery Museum
Royal Arsenal, SE18 6ST (8855 7755, www.firepower.org.uk). Open 10.30am-5pm Wed-Sun & daily during school hols. Last entry 4pm. Admission charge.
❹ Dial Arch
Dial Arch Buildings, The Warren, Royal Arsenal Riverside, SE18 6GH (3130 0700, www.dialarch.com). Open 7.30am-midnight Mon-Fri; 10am-midnight Sat; noon-11pm Sun.
❺ Oxlea Wood Café
Shooters Hill, SE18 3JA (8856 4276, http://oxlea woodcafe.info). Food served 8.30am-3.30pm daily.

Bike Polo

When it comes to cycling for pleasure, it's not only a choice between days out in the countryside, commuting to work or out-and-out, hell-for-leather road racing: bike polo gives you a different way to see life from the saddle.

A history of bike polo
Bike polo was invented by Irishman Richard J Mecredy in 1891 – only 20 years after the equestrian version of the game. The rules were, and remain, pretty simple, with the basic aim being to score goals. But, as you might have guessed, putting your feet down is the big no-no, and results in a penalty.

Bike polo first appeared at the London 1908 Olympic Games as a demonstration sport, where Ireland quite rightly – as the inventors of the game – beat Germany in the final.

Bike polo in Brick Lane.

Today's game

Although the more traditional, on-grass version still exists, since the late 1990s, hardcourt bike polo has taken over as the fastest-growing form of the sport thanks to the ready availability of tennis courts as match venues.

Teams of three play what is a fast-paced and sometimes physical game. Putting a foot down is penalised with a 'tap-out', whereby the guilty player is required to touch an area to the side of the middle of the court before resuming play.

Players ride fixed-wheel bikes, often with spoke-protectors fashioned from house-for-sale or street signs. They control the bike skilfully with one hand and the pedals, often using the mallet held in the other hand as a third 'tripod leg' – in addition to the two wheels – to help them keep their balance. It's an impressive sight.

Bike polo is played all over the UK, and in London is under the guidance of the London Hardcourt Bike Polo Association (www.lhbpa.org). New players are very much encouraged to get in touch and go along to a practice session, and will quickly be persuaded to play in the London Bike Polo League (www.londonbikepololeague.com).

The game is practised and played at a variety of venues around town, including Mitchison Road near Dalston in north London, Brick Lane in east London and Hurlingham Park in Fulham, where the equestrian version of the game was invented.

AT YOUR LEISURE

The World's Clock

This route starts at a symbol of the self-confidence of the Victorian era (Tower Bridge), runs past the result of Victorian domination (the Greenwich Meridian) and finishes at a Jacobean mansion (Charlton House). Along the way it passes many signs of the restless energy that marks the capital. Areas once abandoned to artistic squatters and TV crews shooting car chases are now full of galleria shops and bistros. Maritime history is ever-present. It's a ride that bears repetition, as it's constantly changing. By the time all the current derelict sites are developed, the oldest of the new buildings will probably be ready for remodelling.

START Tower Bridge leaves the City of London from its south-eastern corner. From the control room at the foot of the southern tower a uniformed mannequin mutely scans downstream, but the rarity of tall craft this far upriver means that there is rarely any need for his animated overseers to raise the roadway. ❶ Tower Bridge, completed in 1894, is a lovely metaphor. The fairy-tale Gothic stonework is just a façade; the bridge is really made of steel. Below Tower Bridge, in the narrow cobbled canyons of north Bermondsey, the process of cleaning up and converting warehouses into exclusive apartments has eliminated the scent of spices that permeated their bricks up to the 1980s. At the eastern end of Shad Thames, the ❷ Design Museum offers a café stop for the aesthetically minded. A new footbridge across the mouth of St Saviour's Dock enables riverside passage beyond the museum. The short bridge is too narrow for riding and not a public right of way, but it is open from 7am until 10pm (winter) or 11pm (summer).

A couple more blocks of exclusive warehouse conversions take you briefly beyond the breaking wave of gentrification to Chambers Wharf, a large site where development was stalled by the economic readjustment of 2008.

King's Stairs Gardens (❶ 0.9 miles) are under threat; at times of heavy rain the existing 19th-century drainage system can't cope and overflow rainwater contaminated with sewage is discharged into the Thames. To prevent this, a new 'super sewer' (the Thames Tideway Tunnel) is to be sunk 245 feet from and roughly parallel to the river. King's Stairs Gardens is currently identified as a construction site, with large access and ventilation buildings left behind when the work is done. A dynamic local campaign has opposed this and in response

Start Tower Bridge, SE1 2UP
Finish Charlton House, SE7 8RE
Time 2 hours minimum
Distance 12 miles
Connects with ❶ ❹
Traffic & safety Mostly motor-free, with sections on quiet roads in Deptford and Charlton
Terrain Flat to the Thames Barrier, then a short climb up Charlton Lane
Transport *Start* Liverpool Street or London Bridge tube/rail, Fenchurch Street rail. *End* Charlton rail
Good for Beachcombers, outdoor drinkers

AT YOUR LEISURE

Thames Water has bought land at Chambers Wharf that may be used as an alternative.

Bumping over the old cobbles of Rotherhithe Street, you soon pass the Mayflower Inn and St Mary's Rotherhithe, where the feel of the waterside village of long ago, swamped by docks and housing, can just about be divined. The old pumping house for Marc (father of Isambard Kingdom) Brunel's Thames Tunnel now functions as the ❸ Brunel Museum. The tunnel opened in 1843, after 18 years of construction work. The world's first subaqueous tunnel is still in use, carrying trains. Housing developments bar the riverfront along Rotherhithe Street. Surrey Docks and Thames Docks have been mostly filled in, but steel bridges and derricks remain. The small park of Durand's Wharf allows access back up to the shore. A new fence is planned for ❹ Surrey Docks City Farm, so that the Thames Path here may soon stay open day and night, but currently it can only be used while the farm is open. Access to the farm (and café) are through the gardens.

Beyond the farm, you're forced back to Odessa Street – the current route when the farm is closed – to regain the river (with care) up the narrow alley of Randall's Rents (❷ 2.9 miles). Greenland Dock gate has a gangway that enables the crossing of its entrance. This is London's oldest wet dock; before it was finished in 1699, all shipping simply tied up in the river. It once served the whaling and timber trade, but is now used exclusively by pleasure craft and houseboats. Deptford Strand is where Samuel Pepys – as Clerk to the Navy Board – supervised the Royal Navy's storehouses in the 17th century. From here it's necessary to turn inland almost to Evelyn Street (named after Pepys' contemporary and fellow diarist, John Evelyn, who lived in Deptford), the direct line from Tower Bridge to Greenwich. Not long ago, the area between Deptford Green and Deptford Creek – the mouth of the River Ravensbourne, whose deep ford gave the village its name – was characterised by dirty lanes between scrapyards; now there are new

Surrey Docks City Farm.

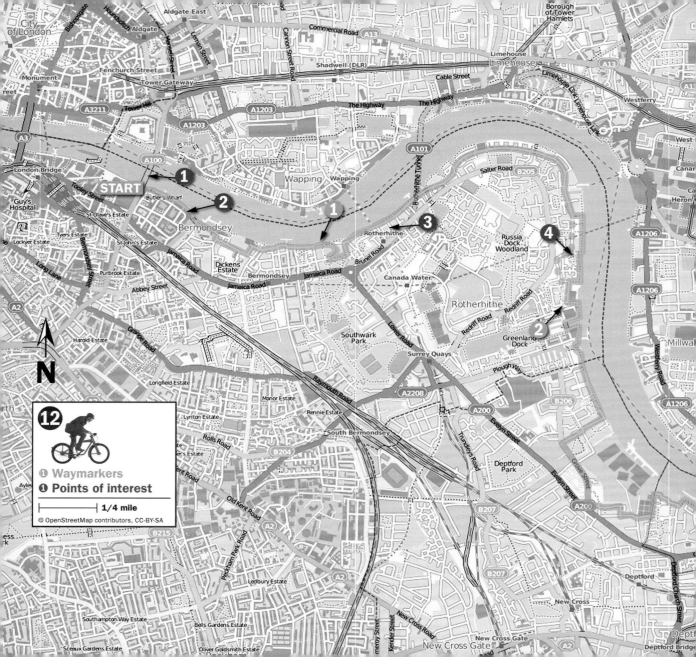

START

① ② ③ ④

① ②

12

① Waymarkers
① Points of interest

1/4 mile

N

Route Directions

START under Tower Bridge on the South Bank
Head east (river on your left) along Shad Thames
– Maguire Street (walking may be necessary)
T-junction: left through the bollards just before
the Design Museum
Riverside: pass in front of the Design Museum
Cross St Saviour's Dock on private footbridge
Right into Bermondsey Wall West
T-junction: right into East Lane
T-junction: left into Chambers Street
T-junction: left into Bevington Street (following
the 'Thames Path' signs)
T-junction: right Bermondsey Wall East
❶ 0.9 miles Straight on into King's Stairs Gardens
Follow the path away from the river
First left at playground to exit the park
T-junction: left into Elephant Lane
T-junction: right into Rotherhithe Street
Continue on Rotherhithe Street past Hilton Hotel
Left to riverside through Durand's Wharf park
(marked by the large concrete structure).

    If Surrey Docks City Farm is open:
     Follow riverside to old red crane; turn right,
     down the ramp, to turn left into Odessa Street
    If Surrey Docks City Farm is closed:
     Continue straight on to rejoin Rotherhithe
     Street; at T-junction, turn left (still Rotherhithe
     Street); at T-junction, turn right into Odessa
     Street (at Aardvark pub)
❷ 2.9 miles Left into Randall's Rents (take care,
walking may be necessary)
Follow the Thames Path
Cross the dock gates of Greenland Dock

At Deptford Strand (the end of the riverside path)
turn left through the park, down the steps
and through the second park
T-junction: left into Grove Street
Left just before you reach Evelyn Street
T-junction: right into cobbled Sayes Court Street
Left into Dacca Street
Right still Dacca Street
T-junction: left into Prince Street
Left into Watergate Street

Tower Bridge.

Right into Borthwick Street (around Twinkle Park)
Slight left through bollards, turn right on waterfront
❸ 4.7 miles Follow Thames Path by Deptford Creek
T-junction: left into Stowage
T-junction: left into Creek Road
Left into Norway Street
Right into Thames Street
Left into Horseferry Place
Right into Thames Path to Greenwich Pier
   If Old Naval College is open
    Use path through grounds
   If Old Naval College is closed
    Walk along the narrow riverfront path
Join Crane Street beside the Trafalgar Tavern
❹ 5.7 miles Follow Thames Path past Trinity Hospital to Ballast Quay (by Cutty Sark Tavern) – Pelton Road
Left into Banning Street
From here there are variable diversions operating during construction, but the rule is to...
Follow 'Thames Path' signs. Keep the river on your left and Blackwall Tunnel Approach on your right
❺ 7.4 miles Follow Thames Path past the O2 to the Thames Barrier. Construction diversions may also be operating here, so follow signs
Turn inland on Eastmoor Street or on parallel cycle path through park
Cross Woolwich Road and turn right on to dual-use footway, parallel to Maryon Wilson Park
❻ 9.9 miles Left into Charlton Lane
Roundabout: second exit Charlton Lane
T-junction: right Charlton Park Road – The Village
END 10.8 miles Charlton House on the left

houses and an odd monument (**❸** 4.7 miles) celebrating Peter the Great's visit here in the 1690s to learn the secrets of British naval power. Peter, the modernising Russian tsar, might be disappointed that his monument is bilingual in English and Russian, as he insisted that his courtiers spoke French (and supposedly shaved off their beards by force).

Of bikes and barques

Greenwich, London's gateway to the sea, has a sense of place that no amount of motor traffic can swamp. The covered market in the centre of town is encircled by pubs and cafés. The **❺** National Maritime Museum holds lots of interesting nautical items and runs a varied programme of temporary exhibitions and visitor events. Flamsteed House (the Old Royal Observatory), topped with a signal ball by which ships' officers in the tideway can set their clocks, is nearby in the steep park. The *Cutty Sark*, a sleek tea clipper preserved as a museum in dry dock, caught fire in 2008, when an industrial vacuum cleaner was left on all night. Most of the superstructure was undamaged as it had been removed while renovation work was undertaken, and the hull has an iron frame. Restoration was originally due to finish early in 2010, but in spring 2011 the hull was still shrouded. Even after the advent of maritime steam power, sailing clippers were the fastest craft afloat. There were big premiums for the first crop of China tea landed in London each year, and clipper ships would race for profit and glory.

When Queen Mary saw the wounded of La Hogue (a sea fight off Normandy in 1692), she was so moved that she demanded a naval hospital be built in which they could be tended. In 1694, under the direction of Christopher Wren (who waived his fee), plans were made to demolish the neglected Greenwich Palace, favourite of the Tudor monarchs, with grounds

AT YOUR LEISURE

stretching from the waterfront to a watch tower on top of the hill; thus the Royal Naval Hospital was born. The plans were amended so that the Queen's House, an earlier classical building, would retain its view of the river. During the *Pax Britannica* of the 19th century, the numbers of wounded ex-seamen and their dependants declined, and the hospital closed in 1869. From 1873 until 1998, the buildings housed a training school for naval officers and the complex (parts of which, including the Painted Hall, are open to the public) is now known as the Old Royal Naval College. The Thames Path between the college and the river is too narrow for riding, but there's a bypass through the college grounds (open 8am to 6pm).

The ❻ Trafalgar next to the Old Naval College and the ❼ Cutty Sark on Ballast Quay are fine pubs for outdoor drinking or enjoying a whitebait supper seated in an upstairs bow window, where only the dearth of river traffic and absence of cigar smoke would surprise Dickens or Gladstone. Trinity Hospital (❹ 5.7 miles) nestles under Greenwich power station between the two taverns; it was established in 1613 (though the current building dates from 1812) as a home for 21 pensioners. Riverside housing is going up on brownfield land between Ballast Quay and the end of the Greenwich Peninsula, and, eventually, this will improve access to the waterfront, but for the moment it's necessary to follow diversion signs. Navigation isn't too problematic; just keep the river on your left and don't cross the dual carriageway.

Lining up the world

An ornamental sign marks the Greenwich Meridian (❺ 7.4 miles) and passage from western hemisphere into east. Before satellites, navigation relied on astronomy and measuring time; hence the red ball on the Observatory that drops at 1pm. Before the advent of the railway, every settlement kept its own time; midday was the sun's zenith wherever you were. But British mariners estimated their position east or west (longitude) by the discrepancy between time at Greenwich, kept by the ship's chronometer, and local solar time. British naval hegemony and the coincidence that the exact opposite side of the world is mostly ocean, a convenient place to put the line where today becomes tomorrow, meant that the zero longitude of Greenwich – as opposed to Paris or Lisbon – was adopted as a global maritime standard in 1884.

Downstream from Blackwall Point – the stretch known as Bugsby's Reach – is dominated by the ❽ Thames Barrier, a moveable dam built to protect London from floods. Its main function is to stop exceptionally high tides coming upstream, but it may also be raised at low tide to keep the river above empty to accommodate freshwater surges from heavy rains in the Thames Basin. It was planned in response to floods in 1953 that drowned 309 people; it opened in 1984. There are two nice pubs here: the ❾ Pilot Inn, set back from the river, which does gourmet food, and the more traditional ❿ Anchor & Hope.

Turning inland from the Barrier, you can use the road or the parallel cycle track. The Thames Path is broken here, so if you want to progress to the Woolwich Ferry, the only practical route is left on to the dual carriageway, Woolwich Road. Across the road is steep, wooded and mysterious Maryon Wilson Park, the location for the pivotal scene in Antonioni's 1966 mod classic *Blow-Up*. Charlton Lane (❻ 9.9 miles) marks the park's western border and climbs steeply to the main road running through Charlton – The Village. Charlton Athletic FC's home ground, the Valley, is nearby, quaintly set into the hillside. Charlton is a rarity: an inner London village that retains old pubs, church and remnants of a village

Greenwich Park.

green yet remains relatively ungentrified; the windswept adjacent open spaces of Charlton Park, Horn Fair Park and Woolwich Common are more playing fields than parks. The manor house, ⑪ Charlton House (END 10.8 miles), is an unsung gem: a well-preserved Jacobean mansion completed in 1612. The building, which currently houses a library and municipal offices, has a café open during the week and a small exhibition on the building's history. Until 1872, Charlton hosted the notorious Horn Fair. Today things are more sedate.

❶ Tower Bridge
Tower Bridge, SE1 2UP (7403 3761, www.tower bridge.org.uk). Open Apr-Sept 10am-6.30pm daily. Oct-Mar 9.30am-6pm daily. Admission charge.

❷ Design Museum
Shad Thames, SE1 2YD (7940 8790, www.design museum.org). Open 10am-5.45pm daily. Charge.

❸ Brunel Museum
Brunel Engine House, Railway Avenue, SE16 4LF (7231 3840, www.brunel-museum.org.uk). Open 10am-5pm daily. Admission charge.

Thames Barrier.

❹ Surrey Docks City Farm
*South Wharf, Rotherhithe Street, SE16 5ET
(7231 1010, www.surreydocksfarm.org.uk).
Open 10am-5pm Tue-Sun. Admission free.*

❺ National Maritime Museum
*Romney Road, SE10 9NF (8858 4422, www.
nmm.ac.uk). Open 10am-5pm daily. Admission free.*

❻ Trafalgar Tavern
*Park Row, SE10 9NW (8858 2909, www.trafalgar
tavern.co.uk). Open noon-11pm Mon-Thur, Sun;
noon-1am Fri, Sat. Food served noon-10pm
Mon-Sat; noon-5pm Sun.*

❼ Cutty Sark Tavern
*4-6 Ballast Quay, SE10 9PD (8858 3146,
www.cuttysarktavern.co.uk). Open 11am-11pm
Mon-Sat; noon-10.30pm Sun. Food served
noon-9pm Mon-Fri, Sun; noon-10pm Sat.*

❽ Thames Barrier
*1 Unity Way, SE18 5NJ (8305 4188, www.
environment-agency.gov.uk/homeandleisure/
floods/38353.aspx. Open 10.30am-5pm Thur-Sun.
Admission charge.*

❾ Pilot Inn
*68 River Way, SE10 0BE (8858 5910, www.
fullershotels.com). Open 11am-11pm Mon-Sat;
noon-10.30pm Sun. Food served noon-2.30pm 6-
9pm Mon-Thur; noon-10pm Fri, Sat; noon-6pm Sun.*

❿ Anchor & Hope
*2 Riverside Walk, Anchor and Hope Lane, SE7 7SS
(8858 0382). Open 11am-11pm Mon-Sat; noon-
11pm Sun. Food served 11am-3pm Mon, Wed;
11am-3pm, 6-9.30pm Tue, Thur-Sat; 1-4pm Sun.*

⓫ Charlton House
*Charlton Road, SE7 8RE (8856 3951, www.
greenwich.gov.uk). Open Library 2-7pm Mon, Thur;
9.30am-12.30pm, 1.30-5.30pm Tue, Fri; 9.30am-
12.30pm, 1.30-5pm Sat. Admission free.*

Wandling Free

This ride provides a serious selection of urban wild places for the metropolitan naturalist. Picking your way south from the Thames on the banks of the mighty Wandle, climbing over the heaths of Wimbledon Common to Beverley Brook, then knocking out a warm-up lap around the verdant expanses of Richmond Park, you'll see some of the last vestiges of the rough old countryside that once covered this part of the country. The bumpy road down Wimbledon Common to Beverley Brook requires a little concentration, but it can easily be ridden on a touring bike, hybrid or roadster. The lap of Richmond Park is on the road, but you could also use the alternative off-road parallel circuit.

START Emerging, blinking, from Wandsworth Town railway station and wheeling your bike down Old York Road, you'll find this part of Wandsworth has more of a sense of place than the rest of the area, even though it has been similarly sacrificed to the circulation patterns of slow-moving streams of traffic. Thanks in part to bars and cafés such as ❶ Doukan Moroccan and ❷ the Pantry, you realise you are actually somewhere, rather than anywheresville.

This latent sense of place has deep roots. Wandsworth was once an industrial powerhouse. The River Wandle rises near Croydon and, along its 11-mile length, falls 100 feet. Such a steep drop meant that, in the early 18th century, the river was able to power 68 waterwheels. The last major industrial site on the Wandle, Young's Ram Brewery – on your right as you ride down Ram Street – closed in 2008. The site is awaiting a redevelopment that promises a new public square framed by the old brewery buildings. King George Park (❶ 0.74 miles) follows the Wandle for a mile and provides a quick escape from Wandsworth Town out towards Earlsfield (❷ 1.7 miles), where topography and a young-family demographic have earned it the nickname 'Nappy Valley'.

Wimbledon Park Road runs into Church Road, once part of a romantic, winding, tree-lined drive leading to Wimbledon House. Continue riding up Church Road if you want to visit the All England Lawn Tennis & Croquet Club, which makes Wimbledon – for two weeks of the year at least – London's most famous village. The grass courts here are only used during the annual Grand Slam championship, so you won't see play at any other time, but there's a ❸ museum that is open

Start Wandsworth Town rail, SW18 1SU
Finish Richmond Park, SW15 3RS
Time 2 hours minimum
Distance 13 miles
Connects with ⑭ ⑮
Traffic & safety Some busy roads and some slightly technical dirt roads, but mostly backstreets and park roads
Terrain Hilly
Transport *Start* Wandsworth Town rail. *End* Richmond rail
Good for Nature lovers marooned in town

Route Directions

START From Wandsworth Town rail, turn right into Old York Road

Traffic lights: cross on to dual-use pavement on the north (right) side of Armoury Way

Left at light-controlled crossing into Ram Street

Traffic lights: straight on into Garratt Lane

Traffic lights: right into Mapleton Road. At 'No Entry', use contra-flow bike lane over the bridge

❶ **0.74 miles** King George Park

Left along the edge of the park, bear left up ramp

Exit King George Park, cross Kimber Road

Enter the next section of park path by the adventure playground

Stay on the west (right) side of the river, follow the path when it diverts away from the river

Exit the park, straight on into Acuba Road

❷ **1.7 miles Crossroads: right** into Ravensbury Road

Crossroads: straight on, over Durnsford Road into Revelstoke Road

Pass under railway bridge, enter Wimbledon Park

Right to follow path around the edge of the park

Exit the park

Left into Wimbledon Park Road

Right into Bathgate Road

T-junction: right into Somerset Road

T-junction: right into Parkside Avenue

❸ **3.6 miles Left** into Windmill Road

Left (through a green gate just before the windmill) on to dirt track, still Windmill Road

Fork right (on surfaced road), past white gates and on to cycle track

Continue down hill on track – Robin Hood Ride

At the bottom of the hill...

Right at crossroads before the old brick bridge

Continue past the rusty steel bridge

Left over new brick bridge just before the pavilion

Cross Kingston Vale at light-controlled crossing

❹ **6.2 miles Straight on** through Robin Hood Gate into Richmond Park

Mini-roundabout: first exit into Broomfield Hill

Mini-roundabout: second exit into Queen's Road

❺ **10 miles Mini-roundabout: second exit** into Sawyer's Hill

Mini-roundabout: second exit into Priory Lane

END 13 miles Finish lap at Robin Hood Gate

Wimbledon Common.

all year. Otherwise, turn right into leafy Bathgate Road and begin the gradual climb up to the acid heathland of Wimbledon Common.

Wombling along on a bicycle

The Common remains unenclosed; a short run along its border on busy Parkside Avenue and you can turn left into Windmill Road (❸ 3.6 miles) and on to the Common's windswept open spaces. Wimbledon Common and adjacent Putney Heath (across the Kingston Road) are rare examples of genuine heathland in greater London. Most other heaths – Hampstead, Hounslow, Blackheath – have long since been 'improved': their fertility boosted by displacing heather and gorse with garden, meadow and woodland plants. Wimbledon Common is actively managed to preserve and increase heathland habitat. The ❹ Wimbledon Windmill dates from 1817 and is the best preserved in London. It fell into disuse around 1865 and was the subject of a preservation campaign in 1893. A museum and popular ❺ tearoom are part of the same complex.

While crossing the Common, watch out for pedestrians, horse riders and dog-walkers, and be prepared to reduce your speed. As you approach riders on horseback, the best practice is to slow down and have an exchange; horses are powerful but also nervous creatures, so engaging the rider with pleasantries such as 'Good morning' or 'Good afternoon' reassures the animal that you're not a threat. Never ring a bell at a horse.

The road gets rougher and is mildly – to use mountain bike terminology – 'technical', meaning that you have to look where you're riding, rather than just gaze at the trees as you descend into Beverley Brook. This small stream runs from Sutton to join the Thames near Putney Bridge. The beavers (Old English

Richmond Park.

En Route

Wimbledon Park is a remnant of the grounds of Wimbledon House that stood on high ground to the south. The grounds once stretched back to Durnsford Road, up to Wimbledon Common and north as far as the London–Kingston Road. The first mansion on the site was Elizabethan. A replacement house was built in 1732 with formal gardens; these were remodelled in the new 'natural' serpentine style later in the century. As railways spread over south London, humbler housing encroached on the lands. There's a lake at the south end of the park that is big enough to accommodate a sailing club.

'beofor') that once gave the brook its name were hunted out years ago, and there are currently no plans to reintroduce them. The light-controlled crossing of the Portsmouth Road at Kingston Vale is almost comically massive, with segregated channels and pens for bike riders and equestrian traffic, but it makes for a stress-free crossing of this busy corridor into the last and largest green space of the ride.

Deerly beloved

Richmond Park (❹ 6.2 miles) has been a honeypot destination for bikers ever since cycling's 'golden age' in the 1890s. As evidence of this, in 1896, the elderly Duke of Cambridge, who held the rather lofty office of Ranger of Richmond Park, forwarded a letter to the Home Secretary complaining of '2,000 to 3,000 bicycles… not as if guided by thoughtful people, but by maniacs, persons in a state of madness… many groups, actually abreast, of ten to 20 or more, formed of roughs and others apparently members of bicycle clubs'.

The Cycling Road Race of the London 2012 Olympic Games will be passing through in 2012, but the park is a useful and popular training circuit for riders of all standards who enjoy the perimeter road's rolling hills. Three laps is roughly equivalent to 20 miles. A speed limit of 20mph is infrequently enforced on motor traffic, and cyclists are occasionally warned, but there are no records of riders receiving any paperwork to take home and frame. In practice, if you ride with 'due care and consideration', and don't pedal too hard downhill, your maximum speed doesn't seem to be a problem.

The Tamsin Trail is a continuous dirt cycle path around the outside of the park; it is shared with pedestrian traffic and has a notional speed limit of 10mph, which translates as 'Don't be a nuisance'. A clockwise circuit takes you past Kingston Gate, then Ham Gate (which offers the easiest route down to the Thames Path if you want to keep travelling west).

Richmond Park is beautiful, with herds of fallow and red deer, ancient trees and ponds. Although there are opening and closing times, the pedestrian gates (for walkers and cyclists) remain open 24 hours a day, except in autumn and early spring when the deer are culled; at this time the pedestrian gates close along with those for motor traffic (which usually shut at dusk). The park is a lovely place to picnic; otherwise there are a few cafés worth visiting. The first of these is at Pembroke Lodge (the park's highest point, on the left after Ham Gate). The gardens here have some of the finest views in London; to the north-east you can see the dome of St Paul's, to the west Windsor Castle and the Thames Valley. An exit through Richmond Gate (❺ 10 miles) will take you down to Richmond town centre and trains for central or north

London; take the next (Roehampton Gate) if you plan to ride back towards central London through Barnes or Putney. There's a café next to Roehampton Gate, along with a ❻ bicycle hire location. The last leg back to Robin Hood Gate (**END** 13 miles) is pretty flat, which might just inspire you to start another circuit.

❶ Doukan Moroccan
350 Old York Road, SW18 1SS (8870 8280, www.doukan.co.uk). Open 8.30am-10pm Tue-Fri; 10am-10.30pm Sat; 10am-5pm Sun.

❷ The Pantry
342 Old York Road, SW18 1SS (8871 0713, www.thepantrylondon.com). Open 8am-4.30pm Mon-Fri; 8.30am-5pm Sat; 9.30am-3.30pm Sun.

❸ Wimbledon Lawn Tennis Museum
All England Lawn Tennis Club, Church Road, SW19 5AE (8946 6131, www.wimbledon.org/museum).

Open 10am-5pm daily. Spectators only during championships. Tours phone for details. Admission charge.

❹ Wimbledon Windmill Museum
Windmill Road, Wimbledon Common, SW19 5NR (8947 2825, www.wimbledonwindmill.org.uk). Open Apr-Oct 2-5pm Sat; 11am-5pm Sun, bank holiday Mon (but not bank holidays on other days). Admission charge.

❺ Wimbledon Common Tea Rooms
Windmill Road, Wimbledon Common, SW19 5NQ (8788 2910, www.windmilltearooms.com). Open 9am-5.30pm Mon-Fri; 9am-6pm Sat; 9am-6.30pm Sun.

❻ Parkcycle
Next to Roehampton Gate, Richmond Park, SW15 5JR (07050 209 249, www.parkcycle.co.uk). Open 10am-6pm Mon-Fri; 10am-7pm Sat, Sun.

All England Lawn Tennis Club.

Wimbledon Lawn Tennis Museum.

AT YOUR LEISURE

Country Pleasures

For open-roaders

You don't have to travel far out of town to discover quiet roads through beautiful countryside. These nine train-accessible rides ring the city and offer a variety of distance (18-43 miles), difficulty and scenery – plus attractions to visit and great refuelling stops.

There...

There aren't many sports where you can test your skills on the same course as the elite competitors, but cycling is one of them. This ride covers the first section of the Cycling Road Race of the London 2012 Olympic and Paralympic Games. The course runs from the Mall in St James's Park via Fulham and Putney to Richmond Park, and then on through up-river suburbs to Weybridge, before heading south down the Wey Valley and over the North Downs into the gorgeous Surrey Hills. Most of the roads are classified as 'A' or 'B' roads, but in general they're high streets, not bypasses. You can ride this itinerary for various reasons: before the actual race to identify your preferred spectator spot or to enrich your appreciation of the spectacle later on live TV, or after the event to review the decisive moments – and to prove you can. However, the route is good enough to stand on its own merits as a grey-to-green breakout.

The riders will roll down **START** the Mall out of SW1 in a relatively relaxed manner. Competitors for whom an appearance in this event may be a lifetime highlight will take the chance to put in an early appearance at the front, but those with pretensions to victory, or hoping to put a teammate into a winning position, will be taking the chance to warm up gently and maybe catch up on gossip with their peers.

  Stand by the ❶ Michelin Building in the Fulham Road and witness the great caravan's passing. Bicycle racing has a long history. Cycling heroic distances was first undertaken to prove the technology practical; the secondary motive was to sell newspapers. It's still a sport that repays attention. Compare it with football. Watch a soccer game and your view is as valid as that of anyone else in the stadium, but the diffuse happenings of a road race are harder to pin down; even the main participants may not know exactly what happened or why. Properly seeing a bike race is less about understanding patterns and more to do with getting close to people testing their physical limits against physics. They pass, you gasp. On Fulham Broadway, by Stamford Bridge, home of Chelsea FC, there are many convivial bars and cafés. Some may show the whole race on television, so you can follow the action between the outward and inward progress, and then the final denouement.

COUNTRY PLEASURES

Start The Mall, SW1A 2WH
Finish Dorking Station, RH4 1TF
Time 4 hours
Distance 43 miles
Connects with ❷ ❻ ❼ ⓭ ⑮ ㉒
Traffic & safety Busy roads and country lanes
Terrain Except for Richmond Park, the first half of the ride is flat. The second half climbs from the River Wey over the South Downs and then rolls into the Mole Valley at Dorking
Transport *Start* Waterloo, Victoria or Paddington tube/rail. *End* Dorking rail
Good for Giants of the road

Box Hill.

The art of racing

Based on the simple premise that everyone starts together and the first rider to throw a wheel across the finish line wins, bicycle road racing – the queen of sports – is, perhaps surprisingly, a deceptively subtle and mysterious activity.

Atmospheric resistance rises exponentially with velocity. Riding a bike into a howling wind is hard work. At racing speeds, it's always windy, and small accelerations require big inputs of extra power. Riding in the turbulence produced by others makes travel easier. Two or more riders willing to work together can proceed with less effort than a soloist. The victor will stand alone on the top step, but nobody wins without the cooperation, support and sacrifice of dedicated teammates. Nor is it just co-équipiers who cooperate: rivals can choose to

work together in temporary alliance to eliminate others, before beginning to race against each other.

Putney Bridge (❶ 4.8 miles) is the first of six crossings of the Thames. Richmond Park and Richmond Bridge (❷ 10.5 miles) are photogenic; you have the choice to stop and wander by the river in Marble Hill Park, to visit the discreet Palladian splendour of ❷ Marble Hill House, or to check ❸ Orleans House Gallery for temporary exhibitions. The Olympians must concentrate on keeping fed and hydrated, riding efficiently to conserve energy. Their bodies carry no fat, so there are no reserves to fall back on. The formal straights and fountains of Bushey Park are another worthwhile photo opportunity, but the riverside run to Weybridge, which begins at the southern foot of Hampton Court Bridge (❸ 15.3 miles), is more suburban.

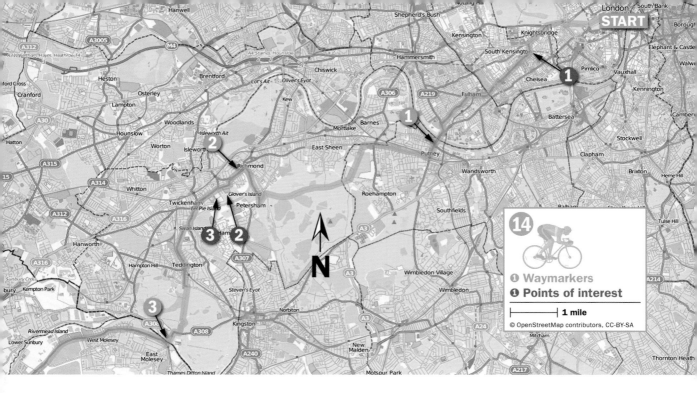

The end of the beginning

Weybridge Green (❹ 21 miles) has hosted cricket matches since the early 19th century. It will be a shame if games aren't scheduled for the days of road racing. Watch a ball or two as you roll past, or stop in the shade of a tree and spectate for a couple of overs. The subsequent turn away from the Thames is the end of the beginning. On Weybridge Heath, the route passes close to ❹ Brooklands Museum, a fascinating collection of bikes, aeroplanes, cars and motorcycles, in what remains of the world's first purpose-built motor-racing circuit. Bicycle racing's closest descendent now has a zero-tolerance attitude towards deadly danger. Most of the tactics of modern

motorsport are based on fuel and tyre conservation, while overtaking hardly ever happens. In contrast, bicycle racing remains loaded with hazards, many of them potentially mortal: flying downhill at 60mph in little more than a swimsuit can't be made safe. The unwritten rule remains: 'there must be blood'.

The Byfleet bypass – over the River Wey – is dull; divert through the village on the old road if you prefer. The route becomes countrified across the flat valley of the Wey. From here, the Wey Navigation towpath can take you via Guildford to Godalming, the south-west extreme of Surrey. The ❺ Seven Stars is a real country pub and a good rest stop, but there are similar establishments along the Portsmouth Road

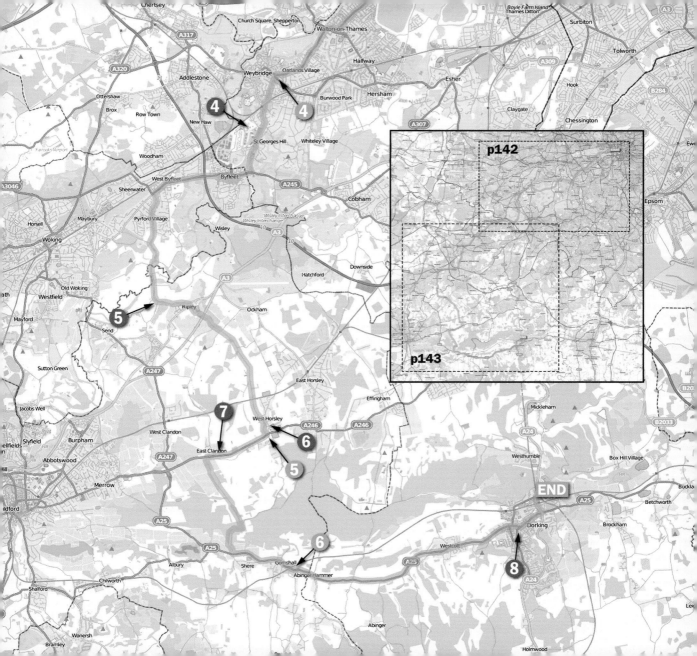

Route Directions

START West (away from Trafalgar Square) along the Mall
Traffic lights: bear right on Constitution Hill
Roundabout: 3rd exit (signpost Knightsbridge) into Knightsbridge
Traffic lights: fork left (signpost A4 The West) into Brompton Road
Traffic lights: fork left (signpost Fulham, opposite Brompton Oratory church) into Brompton Road
Traffic lights: bear right into Fulham Road – Fulham Broadway
Roundabout: 1st exit (signpost Putney) into Fulham Road
Roundabout: 1st exit (signpost Putney) into Fulham High Street
❶ **4.8 miles Cross** Putney Bridge
Continue on Putney High Street
Traffic lights: right into Upper Richmond Road (South Circular Road)
After Rosslyn Park RFC signs on left
Traffic lights: left into Priory Lane
Mini roundabout: 2nd exit still Priory Lane
Enter Richmond Park (via Roehampton Gate)
Mini roundabout: 2nd exit (physically straight on)
Mini roundabout: 2nd exit
Mini roundabout: 2nd exit
Exit Richmond Park (via Richmond Gate)
Mini roundabout: 1st exit into Star and Garter Hill
Traffic lights: right (signpost Richmond Bridge) into Petersham Road
Mini roundabout: 1st exit (signpost Twickenham)

❷ **10.5 miles Cross** Richmond Bridge
Traffic lights: left (signpost Twickenham) into Richmond Road – York Street – King Street
Traffic lights: left into Cross Deep
Mini roundabout: 2nd exit (signpost Teddington) into Waldegrave Road
Mini roundabout: 2nd exit into Broad Street
Mini roundabout: 1st exit into Park Road
Mini roundabout: 1st exit still Park Road
Right into Chestnut Avenue
Enter Bushey Park
Straight on at Diana Fountain
T-junction: right into Hampton Court Road
Roundabout: 1st exit (signpost Sandown Park) into Hampton Court Way
❸ **15.3 miles Cross** Hampton Court Bridge, then...
Immediate right (signpost Walton) into River Bank – Hurst Road
Roundabout: 2nd exit (signpost Walton) still Hurst Road
Mini roundabout: 1st exit (physically straight on) still Hurst Road
Traffic lights: straight on (signpost Weybridge) into Terrace Road – Church Street – Hepworth Way
Traffic lights: right immediate left (signpost Weybridge) into Oatlands Drive
Mini roundabout: 1st exit (signpost Hersham)
❹ **21 miles Roundabout: 2nd exit** (signpost Byfleet) into Hanger Hill
Roundabout: 1st exit (signpost Brooklands Museum) into Brooklands Road
Roundabout: 1st exit (signpost Byfleet) still Brooklands Road

Roundabout: 2nd exit (signpost Woking)
into Parvis Road
Cross River Wey
Left into High Road through village of Byfleet
Mini roundabout: 2nd exit High Road
Mini roundabout: 1st exit High Road
Mini roundabout: 2nd exit High Road
Roundabout: 1st exit (signpost Woking A345)
back on main road (Parvis Road)
Cross over M25
Bear left into Old Woking Road
Left (signpost Ripley) into Oakcroft Road –
Coldharbour Road – Upshott Lane
T-junction: left (signpost Ripley) into Church Hill
– Newark Lane
T-junction: left, immediate right (signpost
West Horsley) into Rose Lane
Over A3 bridge
Continue Rose Lane – Ripley Lane
T-junction: right into the Street
❺ 31.5 miles **Roundabout: 3rd exit**
(signpost Guildford) into Epsom Road (A246)
Left into Staple Lane (signpost Shere)
T-junction: right (signpost Shere) into
Combe Lane
T-junction: left (signpost Dorking A25) into
Shere Road – Station Road
❻ 36.7 miles **Under** railway bridge in Gomshall
Continue on Guildford Road (A25) to Dorking
Roundabout: 1st exit (signpost Leatherhead A24)
into Deepdene Avenue – London Road
Right into Station Approach (signpost Station)
END 43 miles Dorking railway station

in Ripley. The quality of the Portsmouth Road made
it a popular excursion for London-based cyclists from
the 1870s, the era of the high-wheeler. There's a
well-stocked convenience store – ❻ Charles Pain –
in East Horsley (❺ 31.5 miles) that is good for a
sugar boost, and then it's a short stretch on the
main Epsom–Guildford road before turning near
❼ Hatchlands Park at East Clandon to climb gradually
on to the North Downs. This is where the London
2012 Road Race is likely to begin in earnest.

Ten miles further on, the men make nine circuits of
Box Hill, the women two. The climb up Box Hill is short
and not steep, but it will be the place where 'rotten
wood is shaken from the tree'. As weaker riders fall
back, gaps will open. Riders will need to expend
energy to get back to the front group. The safest
place to ride Box Hill will be near the front. But when
everyone wants to ride there, something has to give.

The climb of the North Downs is through open fields.
The descent from West Hanger on steep wooded
Combe Lane will shock riders who haven't done their
reconnaissance or read the course manual carefully.
Those who survive the drop will turn on to the A25
for Dorking, which only has one sharp corner – under
the railway bridge at Gomshall (❻ 36.7 miles) – but is
never flat. Teams will be fighting to put their leading
riders at the front. The race will be on. The winner will
be among the first 50 through Dorking's narrow High
Street, ready for a last shuffle on the flat Mole Valley
road to Burford Bridge before the selections begin.

You can enjoy Dorking, and take on some well-
deserved fuel at ❽ Café Rialto, an unpretentious
Italian restaurant on South Street. Explore the lanes
beyond and break through into the Weald, jump
aboard a London train at Dorking railway station
(**END** 43 miles) or carry on down the Mole Valley
to test yourself on the shady slopes of Box Hill.

Brooklands Museum.

❶ Michelin Building
81 Fulham Road, SW3 6RD (7590 1189 café, 7581 5817 restaurant, www.bibendum.co.uk). Café 8.30am-5pm Mon-Fri; 9am-noon Sat. Restaurant Lunch served noon-2.30pm Mon-Fri; 12.30-3pm Sat, Sun. Dinner served 7-11pm Mon-Sat; 7-10.30pm Sun.

❷ Marble Hill House
Richmond Road, Twickenham, Middx TW1 2NL (8892 5115, www.english-heritage.org.uk). Open Apr-Oct 10am-2pm Sat; 10am-5pm Sun. Admission charge.

❸ Orleans House Gallery
Riverside, Twickenham, Middx TW1 3DJ (8831 6000, www.richmond.gov.uk/orleans_house_gallery). Open 1-5.30pm Tue-Sat; 2-5.30pm Sun, bank hols (Oct-Mar closes 4.30pm). Admission free.

❹ Brooklands Museum
Brooklands Road, Weybridge, Surrey KT13 0QN (01932 857381, www.brooklandsmuseum.com). Open 10am-4pm/5pm daily. Admission charge.

❺ Seven Stars
Newark Lane, Ripley, Surrey GU23 6DL (01483 225128, www.sevenstarsripley.co.uk). Open noon-3.30pm, 6-11pm Mon-Sat; noon-5pm Sun. Food served noon-2.30pm, 6-9.30pm Mon-Sat; noon, 2pm Sun.

❻ Charles Pain
10 The Street, West Horsley, Surrey KT24 6AX (01483 282090, www.charlespain.co.uk). Open 8am-7pm Mon-Fri; 9am-7pm Sat; 9am-1pm Sun.

❼ Hatchlands Park
East Clandon, Guildford, Surrey GU4 7RT (01483 222482, www.nationaltrust.org.uk). Open Apr-Oct 2-5.30pm Tue-Thur, Sun. Admission charge.

❽ Cafe Rialto
55 South Street, Dorking, Surrey RH4 2JX (01306 742885, www.caferialto.net). Open 11.30am-11pm daily.

What Bike?

Top tourers

You'll be looking to buy your perfect bike as your passion for cycling takes you further afield on longer rides. Racier types on their racing machines may be able to squeeze everything they need into their cycling jersey back pockets, but when you're looking for all-day comfort, that's where touring bikes come in: made-for-the-job bicycles designed to help carry all you need for a day out – or longer – in the country.

Proper touring-bike frames will include mounts for a luggage rack on the forks and seatstays. You can attach pannier bags to the rack, letting the bike carry the load, rather than spending all day wearing a rucksack. Tyres tend to be wider, and thus more comfortable, with drop handlebars allowing a variety of hand positions for riders who are going to spend all day in the saddle (Brooks, of course).

Best brands: there's only one name for the true British tourer to consider first, and that's Dawes. More specifically, the Dawes Galaxy. Versions have come and gone, but the heritage and name remain alive and well. Upgrades have appeared in the guise of the Super Galaxy and Ultra Galaxy – by way of components in the former's case, and frame material in the latter – but the Galaxy name, and Dawes, will forever be inextricably linked with bicycle touring on British shores.

Ridgeback also offers a good brace of touring bikes to suit different pockets, which have rightly attracted a loyal following.

Expect to pay: a Dawes Galaxy will set you back around £1,200, while the Super and Ultra versions come in at slightly more: in the region of £1,400 and £1,700, respectively. The Ridgeback tourers cost £800 for the Voyage and £1,250 for the flagship Panorama.

Getting the miles in

Comfort over speed is the priority for long hours in the saddle. If you're already complaining that your back, hands and neck are killing you after half a day, you might be on the wrong bike for the job. Consider what it is you want your bike to do for you, put in the research hours, and ask for learned opinions before you buy.

The influx of 'sportive' bikes into the market blur the boundaries between traditional, load-carrying, often heavy touring bikes and out-and-out racing bikes. They pair the slightly more upright position and greater gearing range of a tourer for those whose racing days are mainly behind them, with a more lightweight aluminium or carbon-fibre frame to help ease you through those epic rides in the Alps and the Pyrenees on your cyclosportive events.

Best brands: almost every respected racing bike manufacturer offers a sportive model, but those to take a closer look at are Specialized's Secteur series and Verenti's Rhigos carbon offering.

Expect to pay: Specialized's Secteur Elite Apex costs about £1,000, with the new Shimano 105-equipped Secteur Comp Compact at £1,350. The Verenti Rhigos, is priced according to the group set you choose, from £1,400 for the SRAM Rival-equipped Rhigos 03, to £2,900 for the top-of-the-range SRAM Red-equipped Rhigos 01.

COUNTRY PLEASURES

...And Back Again

This ride starts in Dorking, a commuter town with the feeling of a mountain resort, snuggled between the North Downs and the Greensand Ridge. It follows the second part of the Cycling Road Race of the London 2012 Olympic Games, which uses a repeating lap-within-a-lap to produce two courses. The women's Road Race covers a total of 87 miles, including two laps of the ten-mile Box Hill circuit; the men's event covers 156 miles and climbs Box Hill nine times. Once this repetition is over, the route runs – fairly directly – down the Mole Valley through Leatherhead to Hampton Court, then via Kingston, Richmond Park and up the Fulham Road to a grandstand finish in The Mall. Taking in one whole lap – climbing Box Hill twice – the route covers 42 miles. Once you've experienced how simple it is to link the Surrey Hills to the centre of London, your life in the city will be forever more restful.

The loop south via Weybridge, East Clandon and Shere (covered by Ride ⑭) will have taken the shine off the competitors, with the last ten miles to Dorking likely to have been raced at a frantic pace to put the leading contenders in a good position for the climbing interlude. The west face of Box Hill is so steep that, in places, it can't hold grass and shows white chalk to the London Road out of Dorking. The climb is neither long, nor steep. Zigzag Road sidles gently back and forth across the face at a fairly constant gradient that averages four per cent.

The damage will come from the narrowness of the road, which will make it hard to overtake failing riders, to close gaps and – particularly in the men's race – repeated applications. The climb is mostly shaded: the Hill's name comes from the box trees that cling to the slopes. This green tunnel will intensify the experience for spectators and riders. When it bursts into the open, height and views are dramatic. The summit has a ❶ National Trust café (❶ 2.2 miles and, after the repeated lap, ❸ 12.9 miles). There's a refuelling option at ❷ Rykas Café just before the start of the climb. The café is a favourite with bikers of the motorised variey, but it's popular with cyclists as well.

A rider who has lost a few yards on the climb may be able to make it up on the descent, which, after the drag from the café through Box Hill village up to Headley village, is almost all downhill. For the casual rider, Lodge Bottom Road, a left turn

Start Dorking rail, Dorking, Surrey RH4 1TF
Finish The Mall, SW1A 2WH
Time 4 hours minimum
Distance 41.6 miles
Connects with ❷ ❻ ❼ ⑬ ⑭ ㉒
Traffic & safety Busy 'A' and 'B' roads, town centres and city streets
Terrain Up and down Box Hill, then fairly flat
Transport *Start* Dorking rail. *Finish* Victoria, Waterloo or Paddington tube/rail
Good for Fantasists

Richmond Park.

Pembroke Lodge.

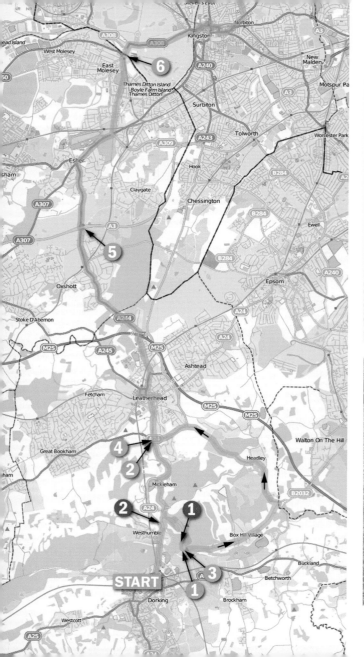

Kingston.

just below Headley, offers a quieter and more scenic descent. For people who like going downhill, it's one of the nicest lanes anywhere near London. The wider, faster loop that includes a section of the Leatherhead bypass (❷ 9.3 miles) is preferred for the Road Race because Lodge Bottom Road is too narrow for a convoy of team cars. If you elect to descend on Lodge Bottom Road, you rejoin the Road Race sub-lap at Mickleham. The bad part is that it gives you less time to recover before taking another dose of gravity.

When cycling uphill, even the professionals go slower. The effect of atmospheric resistance is reduced, which makes it easier for lone riders or small groups to 'attack' and break away. This is the other reason everybody wants to be near the front, to monitor the actions of others, but in a race with 145 riders, it's not possible to react to every rival's initiative. This reveals another layer of complexity. Mass-start cycle racing has a levelling, 'handicap' effect. The more dominant a racer, the less the other competitors are willing to let them go, or work with them in a breakaway. A young rider can break into an early escape, while every move made by, for example, Swiss cyclist Fabian Cancellara (silver medallist in the Road Race and gold medallist in the Time Trial at the Beijing 2008 Games) will be carefully monitored.

The shape of the race as it leaves the circuit is hard to predict. Some riders will have been eliminated by the repeated climbs, but as the race turns (❹ 16.4 miles) to flash through Leatherhead, with little more than 25 miles still to run, there are likely to be plenty of competitors still in contention.

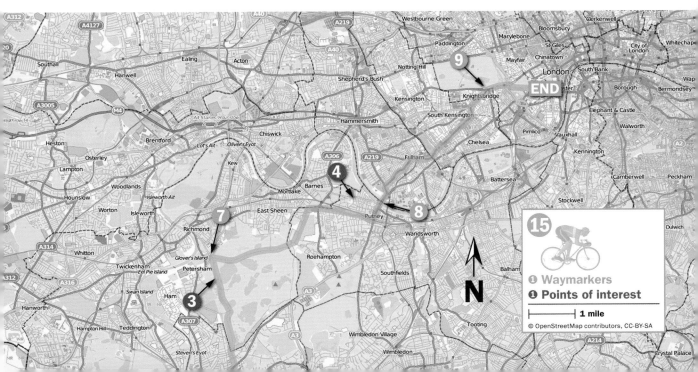

Route Directions

START Exit Dorking railway station

T-junction: left, immediate right to head north on London Road; use the dual-use pavement if you prefer

Roundabout: 2nd exit (physically straight on, signpost Leatherhead) still London Road

Roundabout: 2nd exit (signpost Box Hill) into Old London Road

Right (signpost Box Hill) into Zigzag Road

➊ **2.2 miles Continue** on Zigzag Road past the National Trust café

Continue on Zigzag Road – Boxhill Road

T-junction: left (signpost Headley) into Headley Common Road

Crossroads: left (signpost Leatherhead) into Leech Lane – Mill Way – Reigate Road (B2033)

Roundabout: 1st exit (signpost Dorking) into Leatherhead Bypass Road (A24)

To repeat the Box Hill lap:

➋ **9.3 miles Roundabout: 1st exit** (signpost Dorking) into Dorking Road (A24)

Left (signpost Mickleham) into Old London Road (B2209)

Left (signpost Box Hill) into Zigzag Road

➌ **12.9 miles Continue** on Zigzag Road past the National Trust café

Continue on Zigzag Road – Boxhill Road

T-junction: left (signpost Headley) into Headley Common Road

Crossroads: left (signpost Leatherhead) into Leech Lane – Mill Way – Reigate Road (B2033)

Roundabout: 1st exit (signpost Dorking) into Leatherhead Bypass Road (A24)

You can repeat the lap, as often as you like, or continue the ride:

➍ **16.4 miles Roundabout: 3rd exit** (signpost Town Centre) into Dorking Road – Church Street, into the middle of Leatherhead (B2450)

Traffic lights: right (signpost All Through Routes) into The Crescent

Traffic lights: bear left into Leret Way (signpost Crematorium)

Keep left on one-way system into Station Road

Under railway bridge

Immediate right (signpost Kingston)

Traffic lights: right back under railway (signpost Kingston)

T-junction: left (signpost Kingston) into Kingston Road (A245)

Roundabout: 1st exit (signpost Business Parks 6-7) still Kingston Road (B2430)

Roundabout: 2nd exit into Oxshott Road

Cross over M25

T-junction: left (signpost Esher) still Oxshott Road but now A244

Roundabout: 2nd exit Oxshott Road – Leatherhead Road – Warren Lane (A244)

➎ **22.2 miles Roundabout: 2nd exit** (signpost Esher) crossing A3 into Copsem Lane – Claremont Lane (A244)

Traffic lights: right (signpost London) into Portsmouth Road (A307)

Double roundabout: keep left (signpost Hampton Court)

Roundabout: 2nd exit (signpost Hampton Court) into Hampton Court Way (A309)

Sandown Park Racecourse.

Roundabout: 2nd exit still Hampton Court Way (A309)
ⓖ **26.6 miles Cross over** Hampton Court Bridge
Roundabout: 2nd exit (signpost Kingston) into Hampton Court Road (A308)
Roundabout: 2nd exit (signpost Kingston) over...
Cross Kingston Bridge
Bear left through underpass then...
Keep right (signpost Other Routes) under the railway
Traffic lights: bear left into Cromwell Road – Queen Elizabeth Road
Traffic lights: T-junction: left (signpost London) into London Road (A308)
Roundabout: 3rd exit into Kingston Hill (A308)

Traffic lights: left into Queen's Road (by the Albert Pub) (B351)
Enter Richmond Park through Kingston Gate
Mini roundabout: 1st exit still Queen's Road
ⓞ **32.6 miles Mini roundabout: 2nd exit** (physically right) into Sawyer's Hill
Mini roundabout: 2nd exit (physically straight on) still Sawyer's Hill
Mini roundabout: 1st exit through Roehampton Gate, leaving Richmond Park, into Priory Lane
Mini roundabout: 1st exit still Priory Lane
Traffic lights: right into Upper Richmond Road (A205)
Traffic lights: fork right (signpost Putney) still Upper Richmond Road (A205)
Traffic lights: left (signpost Fulham) into Putney Hill – Putney High Street (A219)
ⓞ **37 miles Cross** over Putney Bridge
Straight on into Fulham High Street (A219)
Roundabout: 2nd exit (signpost Fulham Broadway) into Fulham Road (A304)
Roundabout: 2nd exit (signpost Kensington) into Fulham Broadway – Fulham Road
Traffic lights: keep left into Fulham Road (A304, A308)
T-junction: right (signpost West End A4) into Brompton Road (A4)
ⓞ **40.5 miles T-junction: right** into Knightsbridge (A4)
Hyde Park Corner roundabout: 3rd exit into Constitution Hill
Traffic lights: keep left into The Mall
END 41.6 miles Arrive on The Mall

If there is a breakaway group, some will be fully committed, determined to hold their advantage all the way to the line. Others may be keeping one eye on the podium, while also staying ready to help teammates coming up from behind. In chasing groups, look for teams working together at the front, either to pull back escapees, or – if they have colleagues further up the road – to disrupt the pursuit by getting in the way.

Leatherhead is filleted for motor traffic, with a tricky one-way system that makes navigation troublesome. The racers' serpentine route through the town centre will make it easier for small groups to stay ahead. The wide straight roads running up to Esher, across Oxshott Heath (❺ 22.2 miles) and Esher Common, will favour large chasing groups. The route revisits the old Portsmouth Road past Sandown Park Racecourse before thundering down to the Thames on a broad flat carriageway for a fourth crossing of the river (❻ 26.6 miles), from East Molesey into Bushey Park.

Kingston is like Leatherhead, with plenty of bends to disrupt a chasing pack. The climb up and into Richmond Park (❼ 32.6 miles) is the last. The route through the park passes ❸ Pembroke Lodge, handy for snacks and larger meals.

Downhill all the way

From Richmond, it's all downhill, with the narrow roads tipping the balance back in favour of small groups. Going through Putney (❽ 37 miles), Fulham and Kensington, a larger pack will find it hard to get organised. (There are plenty of refuelling options on Putney High Street and, a short detour away, a fine gastropub, the ❹ Spencer Arms.) It's also where a final complication may come into play.

The small cadre of international professionals – from whom the gold medal winner will almost certainly be selected – race the other nine months of the season in trade teams. National teams only assemble for one race every year, the World Championships – except, of course, in Olympic Games years, when there are two such meetings. Riders from the premier road-racing nations are likely to be dedicated to a national win, but others may have half an eye on the fortunes of the leaders of their regular teams.

There will probably be crashes on the Fulham Road as the survivors push themselves to the limits. If British cyclist Mark Cavendish is in the leading group at Knightsbridge (❾ 40.5 miles), he will be the favourite. The racers will charge down Constitution Hill at 35mph, less than an hour since the leaders last climbed Box Hill. You don't have to run to such a tight schedule. Second place in a bike race is known as 'first loser', and almost all the Olympians will end the day with regrets. But as you freewheel past Buckingham Palace on to The Mall (**END** 41.6 miles), you'll be a winner.

❶ **National Trust café**
Old Fort, Box Hill Road, Box Hill, Surrey KT20 7LB (01306 885502, www.nationaltrust.org.uk). Open Apr-Oct 9am-5pm daily. Nov-Mar 10am-4pm daily.
❷ **Rykas Café**
Old London Road, Dorking, RH5 6BY (01306 884454, www.boxhill.co.uk). Open 8am-7.30pm daily.
❸ **Pembroke Lodge**
Between Ham & Richmond Gates, Richmond Park, Surrey TW10 5HX (8940 8207, www.royalparks. org.uk). Open 9am-5.30pm daily.
❹ **Spencer Arms**
237 Lower Richmond Road, SW15 1HJ (8788 0640, www.thespencerpub.co.uk). Open 10am-midnight Mon-Sat; 11am-11pm Sun.

Kit Bag

The long and short of it

A pair of real cycling shorts or tights, complete with padded insert 'down under', will quickly prove themselves to be one of the best purchases you've ever made – particularly if you already know what it is like to attempt to ride any distance of note without such support. Choose between a conventional pair, with an elasticated waistband, or the infinitely more comfortable 'bib' version.

It's true that bib shorts, in particular, will make you look like a wrestler, but, luckily, your cycling jersey (or whatever you decide to wear on top) will hide those braces, so you'll just look as normal as anyone can in a pair of Lycra bottoms.

The more self-conscious cyclist can steal a march from the mountain bike world, and wear baggy padded shorts instead. Or you can even cover your skin-tight cycling shorts with a pair of tracksuit bottoms. Whatever you choose, you'll be glad of the padding if you intend getting a few more miles under your belt. A wide variety of padded cycling garments are readily available from all bike shops and cycling websites.

Clunk, clip, every trip

Everyone has a mate who bought a pair of those special clip-in pedals, forgot he was clipped in and toppled over at the traffic lights. And now it's your turn. Without the falling over bit, preferably.

'Clipless' pedals are so called because they are different from the now outmoded toe-clips-and-straps combination, which used to hold a rider's feet securely to the pedals. Clipping yourself in –

which today requires a pair of special shoes with a cleat on the bottom and a specific pedal to click it into – makes for much more efficient pedal strokes. 'Mile-eaters' should seriously consider upgrading to a clipless system, in order to benefit from the stiff and efficient sole of a cycling-specific shoe, and the security of being attached to your bike.

When it comes to clipless pedals, you have two choices: road pedals or mountain-bike SPD pedals. Both must be married with the appropriate shoes.

If you're going to do much walking (say, from the bike park to your office, or up and down a lot of steps with a folding bike), then Shimano SPD pedals are the way to go, as the shoes that go with them have a thick 'off-road' sole with a recessed cleat that fits into the pedals.

Road shoes are not so easy to walk in, but are considerably stiffer and more efficient. As with the shoes available for use with SPDs, there's a big choice of road-shoe brands, but the pedals to look out for are Look or again Shimano.

Don't lose your bottle

Now is also the time to invest in that cycling water bottle. Examine your bike's frame to see if it has 'bottle bosses' on its downtube – Allen key bolts that secure a plastic, metal or sometimes even carbon-fibre cage to your bike. Many bicycles do. The cage holds a plastic, cycling water bottle securely in place, within easy reach for drinking on the move. On those hot, hard days in the saddle, this quickly becomes an essential purchase. Water cages and bottles are extremely cheap.

16 Far from the Madding Crowd

This turn around the juicy slice of Buckinghamshire slotted between the Bath Road and the road to Oxford starts and ends in the much-maligned Berkshire town of Slough. It soon shrugs off the sprawl, however, as you head off, via Thomas Gray's Monument, taking in quiet lanes and pretty villages before the climax of Burnham Beeches, an atmospheric ancient wood. There are a few good pubs too.

Slough was once a muddy hamlet on the Bath Road in the parish of Stoke Poges. The coming of the Great Western Railway boosted Slough's profile, and the modernisation of the Great West Road launched it as an industrial centre. A trading estate developed in the 1920s and workers flooded in. This rapid growth was denounced in mean, rather snobbish terms by John Betjeman, who, in 1937, as civilians were being blitzed in Spain, implored: 'Come friendly bombs and fall on Slough, it isn't fit for humans now'. Slough's contributions to humanity stretch from the creation of the Mars Bar in the 1930s to the development of the 'supermarionation' process by Gerry and Sylvia Anderson, who produced miniature masterpieces such as *Thunderbirds* and *Fireball XL5* from their Slough dream factory. We shouldn't be too hard on Sir John, though; he's the only Poet Laureate whose oeuvre includes a reference to the Sturmey Archer three-speed gear.

START Heading right from Slough station, there's ❶ Gaudio's delicatessen over the bridge if you want to buy supplies. Throughout Slough, along the left side of the road, are marginal kerb lanes marked with a dashed line and occasional bicycle logos. These encourage cyclists to ride closer to the edge of the road than is safe; if motor vehicles park on the verge, they can put you in the door zone. Drivers overtaking read the line as the edge of the road and pass cyclists with less room than they would if the lane wasn't there. The best policy is to use the dashed dividing line as your rough path; this forces traffic approaching from behind to look at you, rather than at the line.

The curfew tolls the knell of parting day

Crossing from Berkshire into Buckinghamshire, you'll come across ❷ St Giles' & St Andrew's Stoke Poges Church (❶ 2 miles), where Thomas Gray supposedly began *Elegy Written in a Country Churchyard*, better known as *Gray's Elegy*. Completed in

Start & finish Slough rail, Slough, Berkshire SL1 1XW
Time 3 hours
Distance 18.3 miles
Connects with ⑰
Traffic & safety Busy roads at the start and finish, otherwise mostly on quiet country and suburban roads, with one rough bridleway section and some tarmac forest paths
Terrain Gently rolling
Transport *Start & end* Slough rail
Good for Botanists

Route Directions

Start Exit right out of Slough railway station
Traffic light, T-junction: right (over railway) into William Street (B416)
Left into Belgrave Road (signpost Trading Estate)
Second mini roundabout: second exit into Stoke Poges Lane
Mini roundabout: second exit (straight on) still Stoke Poges Lane – Church Lane
① 2 miles Pass St Giles' & St Andrew's Stoke Poges Church (entrance by pond on left)
Second crossroads: left into Grays Park Road (B416)
Left into Rogers Lane
Continue on Rogers Lane
Left (by Dog & Pot pub) into Duffield Lane
② 3.5 miles T-junction: right into Templewood Lane
Cross B416 into Stoke Common Road
T-junction: left into Windmill Road – Fulmer Road
Continue through Fulmer village and over M40
③ 6.1 miles Left into Fulmer Drive
Traffic lights: right
Immediate left into Hedgerley Lane – over M40 – Village Lane
④ 9.4 miles At the bottom of the hill in Hedgerley, **right** into Kiln Lane
T-junction: straight on to join bridleway
Cross A355 into Harehatch Lane
⑤ 11.2 miles T-junction: left (no signpost) into Abbey Park Lane
T-junction: left (signpost Burnham Beeches) into Park Lane
⑥ 12.5 miles Sharp left into Morton Drive

Horlicks Factory.

(past green barrier on to forest path)
Keep right into Halse Drive
At car park, **right** into Lord Mayors Drive (past galvanised gates)
⑦ 13.9 miles T-junction: left into Hawthorn Lane (back on motor roads)
On left-hand bend, **right** into Thompkins Lane
Keep right into East Burnham Lane
T-junction: right into Crown Lane
T-junction: left into Farnham Lane
⑧ 15.5 miles Roundabout: second exit Farnham Road (past Dukes Head pub)
Roundabout: second exit (straight on) still Farnham Road
⑨ 17.3 miles Just after Farnham Road reverts to single carriage way, **traffic lights: left** into Sheffield Road – Oatlands Drive
Right into Stoke Poges Lane
Mini roundabout: first exit Belgrave Road
Right into William Street
END 18.3 miles Left into Slough railway station

White Horse, Hedgerley.

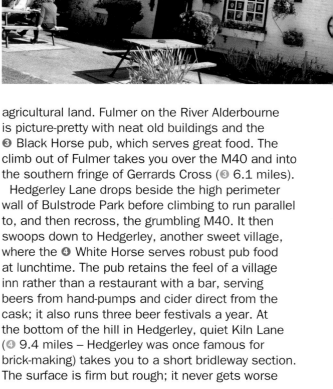

1751, this proto-romantic lament for the dead, no matter what their social station, is full of phrases that have been exploited as titles for other works and passed into cliché. It's said that self-conscious romantic hero James Wolfe declared he would rather have written the poem than succeed in conquering Canada for the British Crown. Wolfe is buried in Greenwich. Gray's tomb lies here, in the graveyard.

If the churchyard is busy (the church is popular for weddings), the meadow next door, owned by the National Trust and known as Gray's Field, is available for picnics, contemplation and composition. It is also home to a rather gross stone monument engraved with the much-quoted work.

Like Gray's churchyard ('those rugged elms, that yew-tree's shade'), the pastures beyond Stoke Poges are surrounded by trees (❷ 3.5 miles). In late spring, they resemble a wood with clearings rather than agricultural land. Fulmer on the River Alderbourne is picture-pretty with neat old buildings and the ❸ Black Horse pub, which serves great food. The climb out of Fulmer takes you over the M40 and into the southern fringe of Gerrards Cross (❸ 6.1 miles).

Hedgerley Lane drops beside the high perimeter wall of Bulstrode Park before climbing to run parallel to, and then recross, the grumbling M40. It then swoops down to Hedgerley, another sweet village, where the ❹ White Horse serves robust pub food at lunchtime. The pub retains the feel of a village inn rather than a restaurant with a bar, serving beers from hand-pumps and cider direct from the cask; it also runs three beer festivals a year. At the bottom of the hill in Hedgerley, quiet Kiln Lane (❹ 9.4 miles – Hedgerley was once famous for brick-making) takes you to a short bridleway section. The surface is firm but rough; it never gets worse

Hedgerley.

The small area gets busy, but mainly around the car parks; elsewhere you can find remote spots in which to rest, feed and muse.

From the end of Burnham Beeches, back on the car-permitted roads (❼ 13.9 miles), the route heads through a typically Narniaesque portal provided by the Green Belt, on to the low-density Californian-style highways of Slough (❽ 15.5 miles). Pass the ❻ Dukes Head pub on Farnham Road and continue (❾ 17.3 miles). On Stoke Poges Lane, look out for the famous 1908 Horlicks factory. Some describe it as 'iconic'. Luckily, Sir John isn't here to hear. You're now back where you started, at Slough railway station (**END** 18.3 miles)

❶ **Gaudio's Continental Delicatessen**
31-33 Stoke Road, Slough, Berks SL2 5AH (01753 578697). Open 8am-6pm Mon-Sat.
❷ **St Giles' & St Andrew's Stoke Poges Church**
Church Lane, Stoke Poges, Berks SL2 4NZ (01753 642261, www.stokepogeschurch.org). Open phone for details.
❸ **Black Horse**
Windmill Road, Fulmer, Bucks SL3 6HD (01753 663183, www.blackhorsefulmer.co.uk). Open 11am-11pm daily.
❹ **White Horse**
Village Lane, Hedgerley, Slough, Berks SL2 3UY (01753 643225). Open 11am-2.30pm, 5-11pm Mon-Fri; 11am-11pm Sat; noon-10.30pm Sun.
❺ **Burnham Beeches**
Lord Mayors Drive, Farnham, Bucks (01753 647358, www.cityoflondon.gov.uk). Open Summer 10am-5pm daily. Winter 10am-4pm daily.
❻ **Dukes Head**
Farnham Road, Farnham Royal, Slough, Berks SL2 3AJ (01753 643138). Open noon-11pm daily.

than what you experience at the start, and you can ride it on any bike.

Once back on familiar tarmac and granite chips beyond the A355 (❺ 11.2 miles), it's a short run down to the entrance (❻ 12.5 miles) to ❺ Burnham Beeches. Twenty years ago, this square-mile site was divided by a network of motor roads; Olympic gold medallist Bradley Wiggins would cycle here from Maida Vale, as a teenager, for training. The various Drives were jammed at busy times. Later, they were closed to motor traffic, and now are slowly reverting to nature: they provide easy access for bikes, baby carriages and wheelchairs.

Burnham Beeches is wood pasture managed over the centuries for grazing, firewood and timber. Some of the pollarded trees are 450 years old. Thomas Gray described them as 'very reverend vegetables'. The woods are also managed for nature conservation.

The Cycling Calendar

Mass rides are great fun, and there are some great examples in and around London to suit all types of cyclists. Here's our selection of the best.

March-October
Evans Cycles Ride It!

www.evanscycles.com/ride-it.
A series of Sunday sportive rides (Saturdays are for the mountain bikers), held for most of the year at assorted locations across the UK. A variety of route distances are offered at each event, so all abilities are catered for.

Tweed Run.

April
Tweed Run

www.tweedrun.com.
In an age of carbon fibre, Lycra and aerodynamics, the Tweed Run eschews it all in favour of vintage bikes, tweed suits, flat caps and handlebar moustaches for a ten-mile ride in central London.

May
Davina's DIVA100

www.action.org.uk/davinas_diva100.
There'll be no *Big Brother*, but hopefully there will be plenty of supporters cheering you and television presenter Davina McCall riding in aid of Action Medical Research at Davina's DIVA100. It's a women-only bike ride starting and finishing in Cowdray Park, Sussex, with a choice between a 50km and a 100km route.

June
World Naked Bike Ride

www.worldnakedbikeride.org.
Help expose the problem of pollution caused by motor vehicles: expose yourself on one of the numerous World Naked Bike Rides taking place across the globe, from Latvia to Australia. The first ride took place in 2004, and London has hosted an event every year since then. Do you dare to bare?

World Naked Bike Ride.

Cycletta.

New Forest Rattler
www.newforestrattler.co.uk.
A proper cyclosportive event, with a choice of
a 47-mile or a 78-mile route around the beautiful
New Forest in Hampshire, starting and finishing
in Ringwood. It's kept relatively intimate with a
limit of 500 riders.

New Forest Rattler.

June, September
Cycletta
www.cycletta.co.uk.
Two brand-new, women-only, 40km bike rides: the
Cycletta North in Tatton Park, Cheshire, in June,
and the Cycletta South, taking place at Whipsnade
Zoo, Bedfordshire, in September. Supported by
Cycling Olympic gold medallist Victoria Pendleton,
the rides are on completely traffic-free roads.

July
Dunwich Dynamo
www.southwarkcyclists.org.uk/content/
dunwich-dynamo.
This 120-mile overnight ride is not for the faint-
hearted, or for those who don't like bats or the
dark. Starting in Hackney, east London, in the
evening, it arrives at the Suffolk coastal town of
Dunwich early the following morning – just in time
for a revitalising midsummer swim.

September
Mayor of London's Sky Ride
www.goskyride.com.
Originally known as the Hovis London Freewheel
in its first year in 2007, this central London bike
ride for the whole family – operated on closed
roads, and taking in such sights as Buckingham
Palace, Big Ben and St Paul's Cathedral along
its 15km route – attracted a whopping 85,000
riders in 2010. Expect it to continue growing in
the years ahead.

COUNTRY PLEASURES

King of the Hills

There is a peculiar, perhaps slightly masochistic, pleasure to the lung-busting, thigh-burning climb. It's what separates the riders from the dilettantes, the hardcore from the rest. And then, at the summit, there comes that perfect moment of achievement, followed by the sweat-drying, swooping descent. There's nothing near London to match the Alps, but the Chilterns provide the chance to crown yourself King of the Hills, if not King of the Mountains. This tour of the northern Chilterns is a catalogue of climbs and descents. Many are steep. The last section loops across mainline train tracks, so, if you're flagging, you can cut the ride short at Tring. But if you do, you'll miss the highlights of Ivinghoe Beacon and Ashridge Forest on the last leg to Berkhamsted.

START Priory Avenue, reached by a sudden short climb out of High Wycombe train station, gives a chance to survey this linear town, set in a steep wooded valley on the main road from London to Oxford. Plentiful beech woods and good communications – this was once the drovers' road from Wales – made it a centre of furniture making. ❶ Wycombe Museum, on your right, focuses on chair making and there's a private rival, the ❷ Chair Making Museum, down in the town; both are more interesting than they might sound. Slogging down the Oxford Road to West Wycombe, the elegant Palladian church of St Laurence appears on the hilltop directly ahead. Somewhere beneath are the ❸ Hell-Fire Caves. This chain of caverns, dug horizontally into the chalk, were the sometime headquarters of a notorious, and much mythologised, 18th-century aristocratic social club, whose meetings were allegedly orgiastic parties. The caves are now open as a visitor attraction.

The High Street of West Wycombe is lined with old buildings. It's easy to imagine it as a dusty cattle-and-coach road, although these days it's more often a car-and-van road. At the end of the village, turn north into the hills. If you want to reward yourself for getting this far, the garden centre by the turn has a nice ❹ café.

Slough Lane (❶ 4.1 miles), two turns off the Oxford road, is a rolling, scenic opening to the ride. Small Dean Lane, on the other side of the road to Aylesbury, starts innocently but ends with a brutal climb through Speen (❷ 8.4 miles) to Great Hampden, family home of John Hampden, whose refusal to pay 'ship money'

Start High Wycombe rail, HP13 6NN
Finish Berkhamsted rail, HP4 2JU
Time 6 hours
Distance 38 miles
Traffic & safety Some riding on busy roads, lots of narrow lanes
Terrain Frequent hills, many steep, with the riding mostly on narrow lanes, some with loose gravel
Transport *Start* High Wycombe rail. *End* Berkhamsted rail, or Tring rail if you want to cut the ride short
Good for Climbers

Cholesbury Camp.

to Charles I was one trigger for the Civil War. The tax had been paid, in cash or in ships, by coastal towns in wartime. Charles's mistake was to expand it to cover the whole country in peacetime. These hidden, wooded, dry valleys – locals call them 'chines' – certainly feel a long way from the ocean.

The route follows the edge of the Chequers estate, the prime minister's country residence (CCTV and notices about the Official Secrets Act will warn you when you're in the vicinity), before the next tough climb (❸ 12.8 miles) towards Dunsmore, which takes you past Coombe Hill and adjacent Low Scrubs. Coombe Hill has wonderful views over the Vale of Aylesbury, and Low Scrubs is a great site for bluebells in late April and early May, when many Chiltern woods are carpeted with an almost unbelievable purple haze.

Old roads and new roads

The Chilterns have long been a key to the geography and transport of the region. The Icknield Way, a prehistoric track turned modern-day walking route, runs south-west to north-east along their spine. Trunk roads and railway lines run outward from London to Oxford and Birmingham. A proposed new high-speed train line has released furious opposition. But despite all this ancient, current and threatened connectivity, much of the Chilterns remain remarkably isolated considering their proximity to London. Historically, they were known as a hiding place for outlaws and brigands, and supposedly contained pagan forest-dwellers right into the 17th century.

After the comically steep climb in and descent out of Dunsmure – at least, it's funny once you've completed it – and a sneaky crossing of the Wendover bypass (❹ 15.8 miles), it's another shady grind up to St Leonards and Cholesbury. Here, there is brick evidence of the continuity of history in the Anglican

COUNTRY PLEASURES

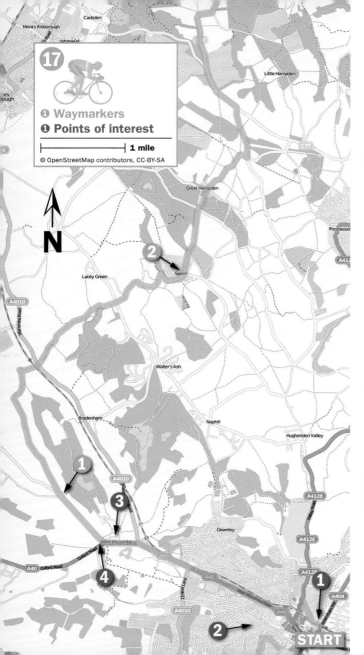

church that stands in an Iron Age fort, Cholsebury Camp. It's a good place to stop for a break: try the ❺ Full Moon pub, which has two restaurants.

Cholesbury is the last village in Buckinghamshire before the run down into Hertfordshire (❺ 22.2 miles). Both shires' names derive from deer (the hart of Hertfordshire and the bucks of Bucks). And, indeed, you're quite likely to see deer on this ride, especially early in the morning or towards evening: either the short-legged muntjac, originally a Chinese species that escaped from parks in around 1900 and can now be found in most woods across the area, or the larger, indigenous fallow deer. In fact, there are probably more deer in the Chilterns now than there have been for thousands of years.

Turning into Station Road (❻ 26 miles), just before you come to Tring train station, you'll see a new bridge crossing the Grand Union Canal. It's far below the roadway, in a cutting that gets deeper as it heads towards the Chiltern escarpment. The parallel railway track, the West Coast Mainline, has a similar earthwork. These cuttings are impressive, especially considering they were dug by men with picks and shovels, barrows and donkeys. A detour along the canal towpath leads to the impressive Tring Flight, a staircase of locks.

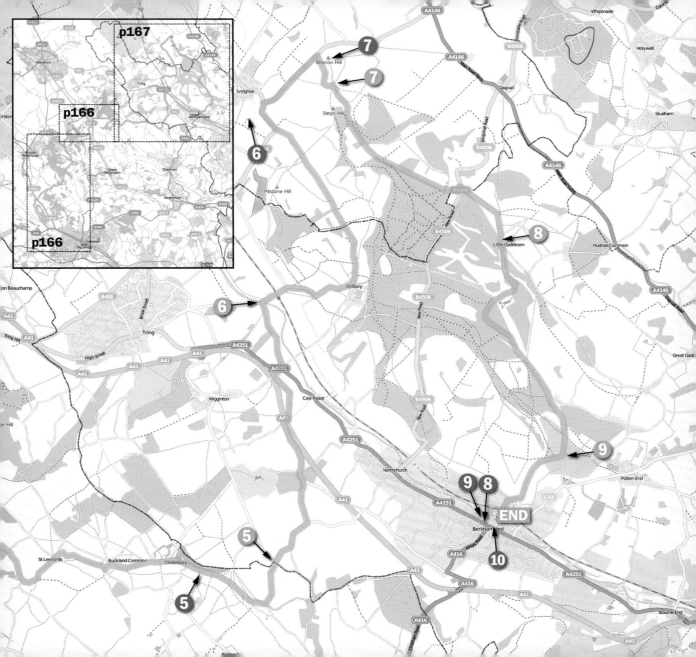

Route Directions

START Left out of High Wycombe railway station on one-way system

T-junction, traffic lights: right into Crendon Street

Left into Priory Avenue (through modal filter)

Crossroads: straight on still Priory Avenue

T-junction: left into Benjamin Road

Immediate T-junction: left into Temple End

T-junction: left (physically straight on) into Frogmoor

T-junction: right into Oxford Street

Roundabout: 3rd exit into Oxford Road – West Wycombe Road (A40)

Roundabout: 1st exit High Street (A40)

Right into Chorley Road (signpost Bledlow Ridge)

❶ **4.1 miles Right** into Slough Lane

Crossroads: straight on into Small Dean Lane

Crossroads: straight on into Slad Lane – Flowers Bottom Lane

In Speen

❷ **8.4 miles Left** into Hampden Road (signpost Gt Hampden)

Crossroads: straight on

T-junction: right (signpost Gt Hampden)

Crossroads: left (signpost S Mandeville)

T-junction: left (signpost Butlers Cross)

❸ **12.8 miles Right** (signpost Dunsmore)

In Dunsmore, **left** (physically straight on) on right-hand bend (signpost Chilterns Cycleway)

Roundabout: 2nd exit crossing A413

Then immediate right (signpost Farm Access Only)

❹ **15.8 miles Through gate**

T-junction: right (physically straight on) into Hale Road

Right into Hale Lane (signpost The Hale)

Bear left (signpost St Leonards)

T-junction: right (signpost Cholesbury)

Left into Stoney Lane (second left after Full Moon pub)

Left (signpost Heath End)

❺ **22.2 miles Crossroads: straight on** (signpost Northchurch)

Left (signpost Tring)

T-junction: left (signpost Aldbury)

T-junction: right into Bottom House Lane (under A41)

T-junction: right into Hemp Lane (signpost Aldbury)

Crossroads: straight on (signpost Aldbury)

Left into Beggars Lane (signpost Beggars Lane Businesses)

❻ **26 miles T-junction: right** into Station Road

Pass Tring rail station

In Aldbury, at **crossroads: left** into Stocks Road

T-junction: right (signpost Dustable)

Right into B489 (signpost Ashridge)

Right (signpost Ashridge)

❼ **31.2 miles Pass** Beacon Path on left

T-junction: left (signpost Dunstable)

Right (signpost Ashridge College)

❽ **34.2 miles** After Bridgewater Arms pub, **right** on to gated road (signpost Ashridge College)

❾ **37.5 miles Right** into New Road (signpost Berkhamstead)

Right into Brownlow Road (by Berkhamsted town sign)

Mini roundabout: 1st exit still Brownlow Road

END 38.3 miles Right into Berkhamstead railway station

The parallel valley to the east would have provided an easier line for the canal and railway through the ridge of the Chilterns. But that route was denied by the burghers of Hemel Hempstead, who were afraid the new infrastructure – or, more likely, the gangs of hard-drinking Catholic labourers coming to dig them – would lower the tone of their little town. Resistance proved futile: a century later, an even bigger project, a low-density new town, engulfed old Hemel.

Aldbury is pretty, nestling under the tree-lined heights of Ashridge. Over the hill, ❻ Pitstone Windmill, the oldest working example in the country, is a defiant reminder of an older form of power production.

The Beacon beckons

The slog up the Dunstable Road has more traffic than is ideal, but it's straight, and the lane is wide, so there's not much conflict. Ahead is the green whaleback of ❼ Ivinghoe Beacon, an isolated spur of the Chiltern escarpment nosing into the Vale of Aylesbury. The turn-off is where the road meets the horizon, and beyond you can see the ride's last major climb, continuing across the Beacon's south slopes. On cresting the Beacon ridge (❼ 31.2 miles), the great chalk-cut lion that marks Whipsnade Zoo in Bedfordshire is revealed. If you have time, a stroll along the Beacon is rewarded with views across the Midlands stretching towards Birmingham, Banbury and the Welsh Borders. Ashridge Forest (❽ 34.2 miles) is deep and quiet, and home to fallow deer.

Berkhamsted is another Chiltern road-and-valley town. Graham Greene grew up here and it provides a fictional home for BBC Radio 4's comic curmudgeon Ed Reardon. The run down from Ashridge (❾ 37.5 miles) is the most dramatic approach. You sail past a Norman castle, which remains impressive even though the building is in ruins and most of what

Wendover.

En Route

In winter, you can see the Bridgewater Monument from Stocks Road. This 108-foot-high column, with superb panoramic views from the top, is open at weekends from April to October. It was erected in 1832 to celebrate Francis Egerton, 3rd Duke of Bridgewater, who took the unprecedented risk of building the first canal – as opposed to improved river – in Britain. The Bridgewater Canal, which opened in 1761, ran direct from coal mines on his estates in Worsley, Lancashire into central Manchester. Many people thought he was mad to put himself deep in debt for such an improbable scheme, but the gamble paid off. The ability to move tons of coal cheaply to a ready market made huge profits, and launched both the canal age and the industrial system of centralised production.

remains are banks and ditches. The canal, railway and main street of Berkhamsted are squeezed into a narrow gap (**END** 38.3 miles) There are plenty of places to eat on the High Street, including a ❽ baker's, an ❾ ice-cream parlour and a ❿ brasserie. If you fancy rolling back towards London along the towpath of the Grand Union Canal, it's all downhill.

❶ Wycombe Museum
Priory Avenue, High Wycombe, Bucks HP13 6PX (01494 421895, www.wycombe.gov.uk/ museum). Open 10am-5pm Mon-Sat; 2-5pm Sun. Admission free.

❷ Chair Making Museum
Kitchener Works, Kitchener Road, High Wycombe, Bucks HP11 2SJ (01494 537957,

www.stewartlinford.com). Open 9am-5pm Mon-Sat; 11am-4pm Sun. Admission charge.

❸ Hell-Fire Caves
Church Lane, West Wycombe, Bucks HP14 3AH (01494 533739, www.hellfirecaves.co.uk). Open Apr-Oct 11am-5.30pm daily. Nov-Mar 11am-dusk Sat, Sun. Admission charge.

❹ Plant & Harvest Café
Chorley Road, West Wycombe, Bucks HP14 3AP. (01494 438635, www.plantandharvest.co.uk). Open 8.30am-5pm Mon-Fri; 9am-5.30pm Sat; 10am-4.30pm Sun.

❺ Full Moon
Hawridge Common, Cholesbury, Bucks HP5 2UH (01494 758959, www.thefullmoonpub.com). Open noon-11pm Mon-Sat; noon-10.30pm Sun. Food served noon-2pm, 6-9.30pm; noon-9pm Sat; noon-8pm Sun.

❻ Pitstone Windmill
Ivinghoe, Bucks LU7 9ER (01442 851227, www.nationaltrust.org.uk). Open June-Aug 2.30-6pm Sun, bank hols. Admission charge.

❼ Ivinghoe Beacon
Ashridge Estate, nr Ivinghoe, Bucks (www.nationaltrust.org.uk).

❽ Simmons Bakers
234 High Street, Berkhamsted, Herts HP4 1AG (01442 864970). Open 7.30am-5pm Mon-Sat; 9.30am-3pm Sun.

❾ Scoops Ice-Cream Parlour
208 High Street, Berkhamsted, Herts HP4 1AG (01442 877170). Open 7.30am-6pm daily.

❿ Brasserie Gérard
196 High Street, Berkhamsted, Herts HP4 3BA (0800 096 7989, www.brasseriegerard.co.uk). Open/food served 9am-11pm Mon-Sat; 9am-10.30pm Sun.

COUNTRY PLEASURES

The Rapha Phenomenon

'We are based in London, and were founded in London, but I don't really see us as a London brand or even a UK brand. If we're from anywhere, I'd say it's the south of France or Italy – cycling's heartland,' says Rapha co-founder and chief executive Simon Mottram.

Launched in 2004, the distinctive, luxury cycle clothing brand is a cycling success story. In 2006, it joined with iconic London bike shop Condor Cycles to create the Rapha Condor Sharp racing team, one of the UK's top pro squads.

'Before we started Rapha, I'd be in the Condor shop each month with my wallet open,' admits Mottram. 'Although the bike bits were great, I'd go away frustrated at the clothing. It became this gradual obsession. So when Condor started to stock our products, and gave us great support, linking with them for the team felt right – despite the shared London link, that wasn't the reason for us to get together. Now the shop seems to have turned into this testbed for other new brands.'

The capital has transformed too, into the heartland of cycling's evolution and revolution, says Mottram. 'When we started, the cycling market in London wasn't that great. In fact, it was possibly the worst place to be,' he says. 'But then everything changed, thanks to a combination of lifestyle trends, people becoming more anti-car, increased public transport problems, the Congestion Charge, the success of British cyclists at the Beijing 2008 Olympic and Paralympic Games. Today, London seems to be at the epicentre of the cycling world. It really is the place to be right now if you're a cyclist.'

Condor Cycles
www.condorcycles.com.
Rapha
www.rapha.cc.
Rapha Condor Sharp Pro Cycling Team
www.raphacondor.cc.

COUNTRY PLEASURES

⑱ 🚴 On the Straight and Narrow

If you want to ride out of London with the minimum of navigational stress, while avoiding roads with heavy traffic, old high streets often provide a good option. The fact that they were once used for carts pulled by draught animals and as routes for livestock means you can rely on them to avoid unnecessary hills and detours; even when you're sent off track by the current fashion for one-way streets, it's usually pretty easy to sniff your way back on to the old road. Barnet was once a hard day's travel from London and still feels like a destination. St Albans is one of the most important historic towns in the country and acts as a gateway to the villages and lanes of Hertfordshire.

START If you're peckish, Newington Green has a fine patisserie in ❶ Belle Epoque, and the ❷ Acoustic Café has outdoor tables and good parking. But if your priority is flight to the countryside, skip Stoke Newington and strike up Green Lanes, which starts from Newington Green's north-west corner. The street is old enough that its name may not be ironic. The great brick building beyond Clissold Park now houses the Castle Climbing Centre, but it was formerly the Metropolitan Water Board's pumping station. It marks the current terminus of the New River, the marvel of 17th-century hydrological engineering that brought clean Hertfordshire water to the centre of London. Green Lanes crosses the New River as the latter leaves Finsbury Park.

From Manor House to Wood Green, Green Lanes is a bustling shopping street sometimes known as 'Little Cyprus'. Conflict between the island's Greek-speaking Orthodox Christians and Turkish-speaking Muslims has driven waves of Cypriots to London. The problems of exile seem to have diluted the communities' grievances and now they live cheek-by-jowl without too many problems. Greengrocers' displays cover the pavements, and bakeries and cafés exude eastern Mediterranean warmth and hospitality. The road is long, narrow and busy, so ride carefully.

Beyond Turnpike Lane, Wood Green is more anonymous; the area around the Wood Green Shopping City is dominated by ubiquitous retail brands. The steeple of St Michael's Church marks the point to leave Green Lanes (❶ 3.6 miles). The church was designed by prolific Victorian architect Sir Gilbert Scott, and contains plenty of original stained glass. The green corridor that extends either side of Bowes Green Road, between Park Avenue and Braemar Avenue, marks the line

Start Newington Green, N16 9PT
Finish St Albans, Hertfordshire AL3 5DP
Time 3 hours
Distance 20 miles
Connects with ❾
Traffic & safety Busy high streets, country lanes and country 'B' roads
Terrain Hilly, but not steep
Transport *Start* Canonbury rail. *End* St Albans rail
Good for Fans of Roman roads and remains

of a tunnel. The original New River wound tortuously along the 100-foot contour. In the 19th century, as civil engineering matured and grand public works became routine, this course was straightened. This section of tunnel eliminated a long loop east as far as Edmonton. The New River continues north, parallel to its mother stream, the Lea, while our route begins the long climb to Barnet.

If bicycles represent the pinnacle of Victorian personal transportation, the Underground is its public counterpart. The route from Manor House follows the Piccadilly Line's 1930s extension into, and creation of, Metroland. Bounds Green station is a fine example of its modernist style. Crossing the North Circular Road signifies the start of outer London. Opposite Beaconsfield Road is an estate of luxury apartments – Princess Park Manor – set in 30 acres of grounds. The original Victorian bricks are so clean, you might mistake the domed bell tower and Italianate colonnades for a new-build. The developer's prospectus makes much of the buildings' history: conceived in 1845, designed by the winner of an architectural competition, and with a foundation stone laid by Prince Albert. Unfortunately, there is insufficient space in the brochures to mention its original name: Colney Hatch Lunatic Asylum. New railways allowed institutions like this to be located in green fields, and the asylum had its own station. The complex at Friern Hospital (as it was also known) remained in use until 1993. According to their interview in *OK Magazine*, Ashley and Cheryl Cole first met when they both lived in Princess Park Manor.

Next stop York
The Great North Road (❷ 7.4 miles) is a medieval post road running up from Islington through Highgate, Finchley, Totteridge and up to Chipping Barnet and

En Route

Head due north from London Bridge and you are following the old Roman road (aka the A10) for Lincoln and York. The first major village you pass is Stoke Newington, a place where people relocated if they didn't want (or couldn't afford) to live in the City, but wanted to stay close to the levers of power. Stoke Newington has a history of dissent.

The original Dissenters were radical Protestants, who believed that the Church of England was too hierarchical. Their influence peaked in the 17th century after the Civil War. Following the restoration of the monarchy in 1660, they were barred from universities and high office, and intermittently persecuted. Many Dissenters sailed for America to escape oppression; others went to Stokey.

Newington Green was enclosed in 1742, but some of the houses facing it are older. Nos.52-55 on the western side date from 1658 and form the oldest brick terrace in London. Isaac Watts, Dissenter and hymnologist, lived in the area. His greatest hits include 'O God, our help in ages past' and 'When I survey the wondrous cross'. Daniel Defoe was educated at a Dissenters' academy on the Green, and in later life pioneered the Puritan tradition of denouncing sin while describing it with relish. His novel *Moll Flanders* is a morality tale of prostitution, theft, bigamy and incest. The Unitarian Chapel on the north side of the Green was built in 1708. In 2008, its noticeboard announced that no more marriage services would be conducted there until the law on civil partnership was amended to allow same-sex couples equal access to religious weddings. The free-thinking tradition continues.

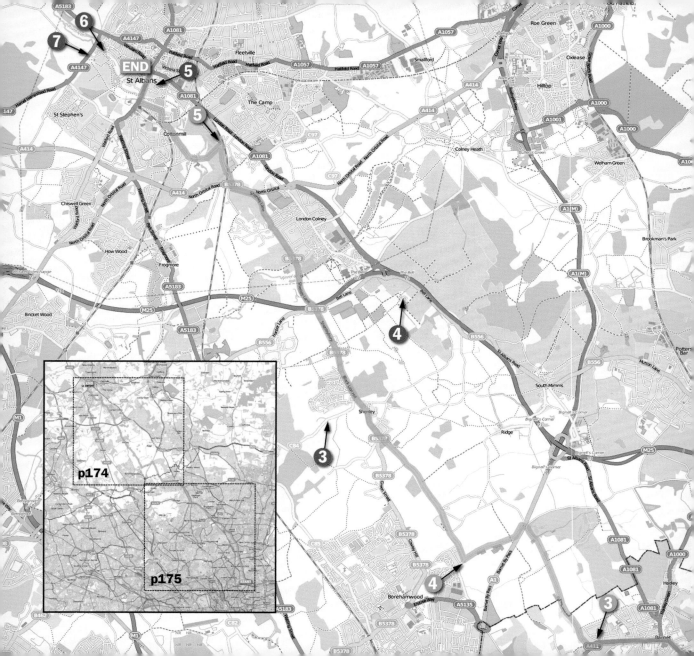

Route Directions

START Newington Green
Left into Green Lanes (A105)
Continue on Green Lanes – High Road to Wood Green, going past Wood Green tube station on right
❶ **3.6 miles Traffic lights: left** into Bounds Green Road – Station Road
Traffic lights, T-junction: left into Friern Barnet Road
Right into Beaconsfield Road
T-junction: left into Oakleigh Road North (A109)
❷ **7.4 miles Traffic lights, T-junction: right** into High Road – Great North Road – Pricklers Hill – Barnet Hill (A1000)
Traffic lights: left into Wood Street (A411)
❸ **10.2 miles Right** into Galley Lane
Cross A1 on footbridge
T-junction: right immediate left into Rowley Lane (heading south for the moment – nearside traffic on A1 will be heading in opposite direction)
❹ **12.7 miles T-junction: right** into Well End Road – Silver Hill – London Road – Black Lion Hill – Shenleybury
Cross over M25
Continue on Shenley Lane
Cross over A414
Continue on Napsbury Lane
❺ **18.6 miles T-junction: left** into Milehouse Lane – Cotton Mill Lane
Left into Prospect Road
T-junction: right Holywell Hill (A5183)
Traffic lights: left into High Street
END 20 miles Right into Market Place

High Barnet. High Barnet is indeed high: the highest point between London and York. On a map, Britain leans leftwards – Edinburgh is west of Bristol – but the quickest way to get up north from London is to keep to the east. Once you're out of Hertfordshire, the ride is flat all the way to north Yorkshire.

Before the road improvements of the 18th century, Barnet was a full day's journey from London, hence the rash of old inns. Just beyond the old town centre is a significant fork in the road; right for York, left for Lancaster. During the Wars of the Roses, in 1471, Edward IV won a decisive battle here, securing the throne of England for the House of York. The Manchester Road (A6) goes to St Albans, but we can take a quieter route, turning left before the church on to Wood Street. Fork right by the Arkley pub (❺ 10.2 miles) into Galley Lane and prepare to cross an important border.

Green and pleasant land

When you leave London on a radial route, a sudden shift from suburbia to green fields is often apparent. This is not an accident, it's the Green Belt – a band of parkland, farm land and recreational space in which any construction is strictly controlled. The Green Belt was part of the first London-wide plan, developed in the 1930s, to provide easy access to countryside for city dwellers, and to prevent a metropolitan sprawl over south-east England. Moving into the Green Belt can be particularly dramatic on summer nights, when sudden darkness (no city lighting) is accompanied by a dramatic drop in temperature as you lose the effect of buildings and pavements radiating heat stored during the day.

The footbridge over the new A1, a motorway supplement to the Great North Road, is designed for equine traffic, so watch out for slippery deposits.

Belle Epoque.

Well End Road (❹ 12.7 miles) rolls nicely and, before you reach Shenley, becomes the London Road – usually a good sign you're on a useful radial route. Shenley was once dominated by another gigantic mental institution; it was already half empty in 1979, when it provided locations for the youth prison flick *Scum*, and once it closed in 1998 it was redeveloped as a housing estate and self-financing park. The attractive park has a ❸ tea room where you can buy apple juice pressed from the orchards on site.

From Shenley, a screaming descent takes you down to the valley of the River Colne, which joins the Thames at Staines. Geologists speculate that when Britain was joined to mainland Europe, the Thames was part of the Rhine, and flowed in the opposite direction; later it may have flowed north around the highlands you've just traversed, following the present day lines of the Colne and the Lea. The theory also runs that the Thames only flashed through London when this loop was blocked by an ice-sheet. It's an undeniable fact that the Lea passes through Hatfield only six miles north-east of here, with no big hills in between. Cycling doesn't just give you an intimate feel for the shape of the land, it allows you time to ponder on such mysteries. The Colne Valley also holds the M25 and the training ground of Arsenal FC, so watch out for expensive cars driven by young men.

Turn right on Bell Lane just before the M25, if you want to visit the ❹ De Havilland Aircraft Heritage Centre, a quirky collection of old planes. Most were made by local company De Havilland, including the Mosquito, first developed in 1939. The Mosquito, one of the most effective planes of Word War II, had a wooden frame. It might be the last effective war weapon made from trees.

Entry into St Albans is via Sopwell (❺ 18.6 miles), where New Barnes Mill stands on the River Ver, a

Clissold Park.

tributary of the Colne that gave St Albans its Roman name, Verulamium. The appearance of St Albans Cathedral (known locally at the Abbey), which still dominates the town, is an uplifting sight, irrespective of your religious leanings, and it indicates that you've almost arrived. A short climb into town brings you to the Market Place with its 15th-century clocktower (**END** 20 miles).

The headquarters of the Campaign for Real Ale (CAMRA) is also in St Albans, so if you fancy a celebratory drink you're spoilt for choice. A handy option is the ❺ Goat Inn in Sopwell Lane. ❻ Kingsbury Watermill houses a museum containing the mill workings, and a Waffle House restaurant.

A highlight of Roman Verulamium's extensive remains is the ❼ Roman amphitheatre, a little further upstream. It's small – more 'Palace Theatre Watford' than 'Theatre Royal Drury Lane' – but there's enough standing to fire your imagination. On the way into town, the enigmatic stone walls on your right, at the junction of Cotton Mill Lane and Prospect Road, are part of Sopwell Priory, dating from the 12th century.

Their unheralded status, standing on a recreation ground, is a sign of St Albans' historic riches – anywhere else they'd warrant an entire visitor centre. You can laze in their shade for free.

❶ **Belle Epoque**
37 Newington Green, N16 9PR (7249 2222, www.belleepoque.co.uk). Open 8am-6pm Tue-Fri; 9am-6pm Sat; 9am-5pm Sun.
❷ **Acoustic Café**
60 Newington Green, N16 9PX (7288 1235). Open 8am-6pm daily.
❸ **Orchard Tea Room**
Shenley Park, Herts WD7 9DW (01923 852629, www.shenleypark.co.uk). Open 9am-4pm Mon-Fri; 8am-4pm Sat, Sun.
❹ **De Havilland Aircraft Heritage Centre**
Salisbury Hall, London Colney, St Albans, Herts AL2 1BU (01727 822051, www.dehavilland museum.co.uk). Open Mar-Oct 2-5.30pm Tue, Thur, Sat; 10.30am-5.30pm Sun. Admission charge.
❺ **Goat Inn**
37 Sopwell Lane, St Albans, Herts AL1 1RN (01727 833934, www.goatinn.co.uk). Open noon-11pm Mon, Tue, Thur, Sun; noon-11.30pm Wed; noon-midnight Fri, Sat. Food served noon-2pm, 6-9pm Mon-Fri; noon-9pm Sat; noon-4pm Sun.
❻ **Kingsbury Watermill & Waffle House**
St Michaels's Street, St Albans, Herts AL3 4SJ (01727 853502, www.kingsburywatermill.co.uk). Open Summer 10am-6pm daily. Winter 10am-5pm daily.
❼ **Verulamium Theatre**
Bluehouse Hill, St Albans, Herts AL3 6AE (01727 835035, www.romantheatre.co.uk). Open Summer 10am-5pm daily. Winter 10am-4pm daily. Admission charge.

St Albans Cathedral.

A celebration of great sporting moments

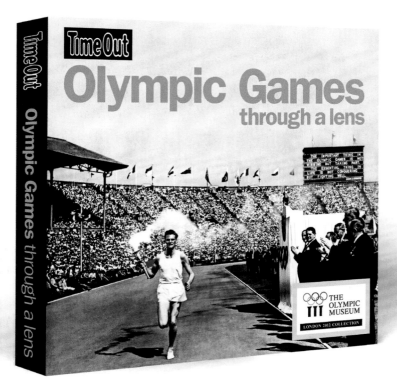

Fit for Purpose

You can't have one without the other: in the same way that your bike needs to be in good working order, you, the rider, are required to be up to the job too. We're not suggesting that you shave your legs right now (although you may feel that way inclined later), but improving your fitness with a view to tackling longer rides, or perhaps even competing, requires a little time and commitment.

Saddle up

So once you've ensured that your bike is perfectly adjusted, it's time for a little 'me time'. Your first longer ride, especially if you're not used to either the distance or the more stretched-out position of your bike, may lead to a few minor aches and pains, but these will disappear with time. Some gentle stretching before getting on the bike is a good idea. The lower back, in particular, is an area that could benefit from a little more stretching: the tried and tested touching of toes alternated with some rearward arching of the back will often do the trick.

You'll find that the more riding you do, the easier it becomes – and quite quickly. If you have a charity ride or bike holiday as an objective, go for a few weekend outings in the run-up. They don't have to be as long as the main event, but it helps to try and push the pace.

Stay strong

Not essential for the occasional weekend shortie, but for longer rides and tours it helps to condition the muscles that matter. Some core work such as Pilates helps support your back; squats and lunges work wonders for legs and bum.

Distance versus intensity

A gentle five-hour bike ride is very pleasant, but there needs to be some intensity about your riding and training if you want to get fitter, or are looking to mimic the speeds of races or sportive events. If you don't have much time to train (and most people are lucky to find even a couple of hours at the weekend), you'll need to make the best use of your time during the week.

That could mean getting up earlier to fit in a ride before work, or investing in a turbo trainer: an indoor trainer that attaches to your bike to effectively turn it into an exercise bike. You can either follow a spinning session on a DVD or create your own workout: perhaps an intense half-hour session incorporating intervals – a minute's hard effort followed by a minute's easy pedalling to recover – multiplied by ten, with a warm-up and warm-down either end. Of course, sitting on a bike indoors doesn't teach you any of cycling's essential skills, such as climbing, descending or riding close to others, so make sure you get out on the open road whenever possible.

Those intervals can be recreated on the road too: sprint against friends to a road sign, or give it everything to the top of the next hill. The less time you have, the more intense the session needs to be. Longer, slower rides are useful, but mix them up with shorter, more intense workouts if you really want to improve your fitness.

Riding to Roding

The best place to start a cycle tour is at your own front door; a rural railway terminus is a strong second. Chingford station – a 30-minute train ride from London's Liverpool Street – is situated where the high street of Station Road gives way to the rising scrub and hanging glades of Epping Forest. Even in this suburban setting, the end of the line carries a whiff of the frontier. The forest's woods, ponds and pastures allow city dwellers to indulge their bucolic fantasies. The area beyond Epping Forest remains in the forest's shadow and is still relatively quiet and rural. It is this gently rolling, green and underpopulated countryside that this ride explores.

START On 6 May 1882, Queen Victoria rode the train to Chingford station's rural isolation and announced, 'It gives me the greatest satisfaction to dedicate this beautiful forest to the use and enjoyment of my people for all time.' The open land south of Chingford station may have filled up with little palaces for commuters, but to the north it is almost all green.

Follow the forest edge on residential roads to cross Epping New Road (A104). Urbanites who prefer to run to their own timetable can get here by riding the A104 from Islington Green, where it's conveniently known as the Essex Road.

The next radial route is the High Road of Buckhurst Hill (❶ 1.5 miles) – formerly 'Buckets Hill'– where you can laze in the shade on the green, before swooping down Palmerston Road to cross the River Roding, which shares its flat-bottomed valley with the Central Line and the M11. The climb to the rustic village of Chigwell is on leafy Roding Lane beside Chigwell School, which has been on this site since 1692. Chigwell (❷ 4 miles) is a major setting in the novel *Barnaby Rudge*, and Charles Dickens described it in one of his letters as 'the greatest place in the world'. Dickens was a frequent visitor to Chigwell. The man was a relentless traveller, who relished the dawn of railway-enabled hypermobility.

Vicarage Lane leads up to Chigwell Row, past white-painted weatherboard cottages. This climb used to have a CTC (UK's National Cyclists' Organisation) sign 'This Hill is Dangerous' at the top, but the bends were eased long ago.

At the traffic lights by the Maypole pub (❸ 5.6 miles), a right turn would take you to the quaintly monikered Hog Hill cycle circuit, also known as the Redbridge

Start & finish Chingford rail, E4 6AL
Time 2.5 hours (much longer if you stop to explore)
Distance 29 miles
Connects with Road Racing (p214)
Traffic & safety Mostly minor country and suburban roads
Terrain Hilly. Essex is not flat
Transport *Start/end* Chingford rail
Good for People who like woods, fields and flying clouds

Cycling Centre. The London Borough of Redbridge – which takes its name from a crossing of the River Roding – was immortalised as the East End escapist's dream in Richard Bean's play *England People Very Nice*, which premiered at the National Theatre in 2009; a running gag sees first Irish, then Jewish, then Bengali East Enders, each affronted by the next wave of immigrants, relocate to Redbridge. The non-kosher cockney diaspora are served well by ❶ Shell's Shellfish, a friendly seafood stall in the car park of the Maypole pub. If you're planning a picnic, why not pack a lemon (vinegar is supplied for the traditionalists) and pick up a chewy pint of mineral-rich cockles or whelks?

The woods on the right are the stub of a wood pasture common, that was once as extensive as Epping Forest: ❷ Hainault Forest Country Park. The enclosure and deforestation of 90 per cent of Hainault Forest in 1851 – when 3,000 acres were cut down in six weeks to produce low-grade farmland – caused public outrage; with the spread of the railways and the demise of the stagecoach, the view of forests as unproductive and obstructive refuges for outlaws had started to give way to the romantic idea of the green wood as a resort and even a sanctuary from urban life. Beyond the trees are occasional long views south across Romford, Barking and Dagenham; to your left is the Roding Valley.

The ribbon development of Stapleford Abbotts is strung along the road from Ongar to Romford, and the next stretch of country road (❹ 9.7 miles) crosses the M25. Narrow Mill Lane then winds down to recross the Roding at Shonks Mill (❺ 13 miles). The mill ceased to operate in the 19th century and is long gone, but the mill race – an artificial side-stream to provide water power – remains, so there are two bridges to cross.

The Roding, which rises near Great Dunmow, gives its name to a string of Essex villages, and joins the Thames as Barking Creek. The flat, industrial Thames-side towns of south Essex contrast sharply with the pretty villages of the undulating interior. After a dog-leg crossing of the London to Ongar road, Berwick Lane climbs through woods toward Toot Hill. Where the lane bends sharp right, there is a bridleway straight ahead on an unmade 'country road' that offers rough riders the option of a bumpy shortcut to Tawney Common.

Watch the skies

The sloping triangular green at Toot Hill (❻ 16.7 miles) is equipped with a bench, where you might want to stop for a breather. Essex is not exactly flat, but hardly rises above 300 feet and, in the absence of high hills or deep valleys, skyscapes dominate. The proximity of the coast encourages towering cloud formations, and the fertile country, enriched by maritime trade, allowed at least some people time to stand and stare. 'Light and shade never stand still,' declared miller's son John Constable, grandfather of Impressionism. Constable's boyhood country – where the River Stour divides Essex from Suffolk – is 30 miles north-east of here, but his dynamic skies are often racing overhead.

Turning homeward, just beyond Toot Hill, is Tawney Common, where the ❸ Mole Trap Inn entices with roaring fires in winter, and a beer garden and terrace for the summer. Tawney Common is now enclosed and under cultivation, but the straight unfenced road around it retains a sense of open space.

The descent from the former common follows the line of a Roman road to London from Great Dunmow and High Roding. The next couple of miles cross the ancient parish of Theydon Garnon. The village was

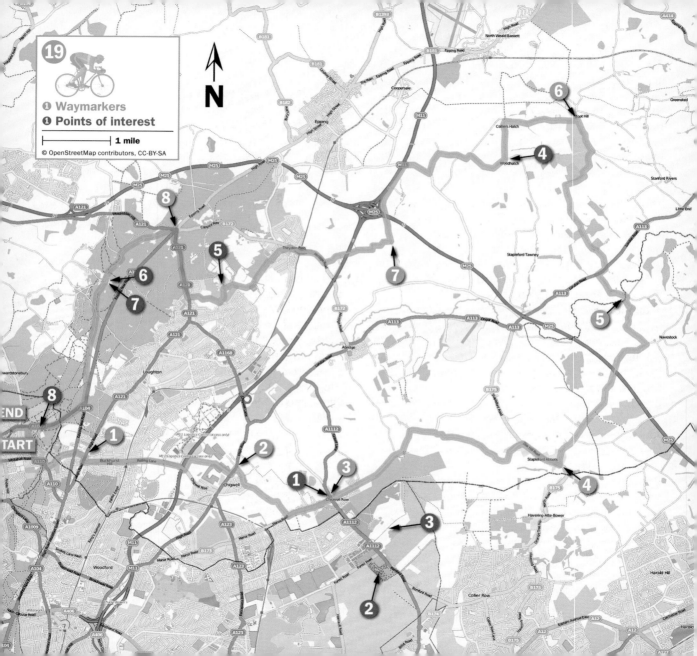

Route Directions

START at Chingford rail
Right into Station Road
Right into Beresford Road
Immediate left into Forest Avenue
Right into Forest Side
T-junction: left into Whitehall Road (A110)
Left into Brook Road
Traffic lights: straight over into Church Road
❶ 1.5 miles Right into High Road (A121)
Left into Palmerston Road – Roding Lane
Cross over M11
Left into Roding Lane
T-junction: left into High Road (A113)
❷ 4 miles Right into Vicarage Lane
T-junction: left into Lambourne Road (B173)
❸ 5.6 miles Traffic lights: straight on Lambourne Road – Manor Road – Bournebridge Lane
T-junction: right into Oak Hill Road (B175)
❹ 9.7 miles Left into Tysea Hill – Murthering Lane
Cross over M25
Left into Mill Lane
❺ 13 miles Left into Shonks Mill Lane
T-junction: right into London Road (A113)
Left into Berwick Lane (bridleway straight over on right-hand bend)
T-junction: left into School Road
❻ 16.7 miles T-junction: left by green into Epping Road (bridleway rejoins from left)
Left into Tawney Common
Continue to Mole Trap
Continue right on Tawney Common
Left into Banks Lane
T-junction: right into Mount Road

Left into Hobbs Cross Road (heading south parallel to M11)
Cross over M11
❼ 20.6 miles Right into Coopersale Lane
Cross over M11
T-junction: right into Abridge Road (B172)
Fork left into Loughton Lane – Debden Lane (opposite the Queen Victoria Pub)
Right into Clays Lane
Right into Golding's Hill (A121)
❽ 24.9 miles Roundabout: second exit into Woodridden Hill (A121)
Immediate left
T-junction: left
Fork left into Nursery Road
T-junction: left into Cross Roads
Slight right into Fairmead Road
Through gate
Right into Epping New Road (A104) heading south
Right into Ranger's Road – Station Road (A1069)
END 29.3miles Left into Chingford station

Epping Forest.

granted a market fair in 1305 and once dominated the area. It has been in decline since a 'new' road was constructed early in the 16th century, running from Loughton through Epping Forest. Traffic between London and Newmarket or Norwich diverted to this shorter route. The town of Epping grew along the new route and, by the time Epping was connected to London by rail in 1865, Theydon Garnon had definitely become a satellite. The main route re-emerged when the M11 was constructed, along with a motorway junction connecting it to the M25 orbital. A remnant of the village centre, All Saints Church – a right fork off Coopersale Lane (❼ 20.6 miles) – now overlooks the intricate concrete ramps. Through-travellers will see it, but few ever visit.

Old Bois

While Theydon Garnon has disappeared into relative obscurity, it's junior partner Theydon Bois (pronounced 'boys') has flourished. The combination of a forest hinterland and trains direct to the City make it an easy sell. Mains electricity didn't reach Theydon Garnon until 1950, and the residents of Theydon Bois – protective of its sense of isolation – continue to resist street lighting. We are back to the Essex 'Golden Triangle' of Buckhurst Hill, Loughton and Chigwell.

The lane between Theydon Bois and Loughton passes the entrance to ❹ Debden House, probably the best campsite inside the M25. One of its clearings is equipped with firepits, so you can enjoy a cheery bonfire before wandering off into Epping Forest's 6,000 acres. Bicycles are also available to hire. Hidden in the woods are two Iron Age earthworks, Loughton Camp and Amesbury Banks – the second of which is reputed to be the site of Boudicca's last stand against the Imperial Roman army.

Debden House.

A final steep hill takes you into the forest that skirts Loughton, and then to the Wake Arms roundabout (❽ 24.9 miles), and back on to Epping New Road. The petrol station serves snacks and drinks 24 hours a day. A mile of traffic-calmed back road emerges at the forest village of High Beach.

High Beach, surrounded by trees, has a metal shed where mountain bikers with mud-flecked faces drink tea and eat cake. Alternatively, the ❺ King's Oak Hotel offers pub meals, and has a garden. The ❻ Epping Forest Visitor Centre is also here. At the top of Fairmead Road stands another tea shack, where motorcyclists gather (in their hundreds on a sunny Sunday, with some riding down from the Midlands) to enjoy a cigarette and hot beverage with their chums.

Fairmead Road was closed to motor traffic 30 years ago, and is slowly reverting to dirt track. It can still be ridden (with care), even on the most delicate of bikes. When you reach its gated end, you can turn right into the woods to find the lake. Cycling is permitted on most of the forest paths, but be prepared to give way to horseriders or walkers. In this area in particular, close to the car park on Ranger's Road, you may encounter slow-moving pedestrians who deserve to be treated with respect.

If you want to keep your tyres clean, take Epping New Road, then Ranger's Road back to Chingford. Otherwise you can rejoin Ranger's Road beyond the lakes. ❼ Queen Elizabeth's Hunting Lodge beside Ranger's Road (originally known as the Great Standing) was built for Henry VIII in 1543. It was constructed as a grandstand or platform that allowed guests to view the hunt from a high vantage point, or to participate by shooting their crossbows from the upper floors – the 16th-century equivalent of a corporate hospitality box at White Hart Lane. The Tudor lodge is now a museum; the more recent roadhouse eaterie beside it is undoubtedly mock Tudor. Returning to Station Road (**END** 29.3 miles), take a final look back at the 'people's forest'.

Queen Elizabeth's Hunting Lodge.

❶ Shell's Seashells
Maypole pub car park, 171 Lambourne Road, Chigwell Row, Chigwell, Essex IG7 6DD (no phone). Open noon-7pm Thur; noon-9pm Fri, Sat; noon-8pm Sun.
❷ Hainault Forest Country Park
Romford Road, Chigwell, Essex IG7 4QN (8500 7353, www.hainaultforest.co.uk). Open Farm & Zoo Apr-Sept 9.30am-5pm daily. Oct-Mar 9.30am-3pm daily. Café Apr-Sept 10am-6pm daily. Oct-Mar 10am-3pm daily. Admission free.
❸ Mole Trap Inn
Tawney Common, Essex CM16 7PU (01992 522394, www.themoletrap.co.uk). Open 11.30am-2.30pm, 5.30-11pm daily. Lunch served 11.30am-2pm daily. Dinner served 6.30-9pm Tue-Sat.
❹ Debden House
Debden Green, Loughton, Essex IG10 2NZ (8508 3008, 8508 6770, www.debdenhouse.com). Open May-Sept.

❺ King's Oak Hotel
Pauls Nursery Road, High Beach, Essex IG10 4AE (8508 5000, www.kingsoakhotel.com). Open 11am-11pm daily. Food served 11am-9pm daily.
❻ Epping Forest Visitor Centre
Nursery Road, High Beach, Loughton, Essex IG10 4AF (8508 0028, www.cityoflondon.gov.uk). Open Apr-Sept 10am-5pm daily. Oct-Mar 10am-3pm daily. Admission free.
❼ Queen Elizabeth's Hunting Lodge
Rangers Road, Chingford, Essex E4 7QH (8529 6681, www.cityoflondon.gov.uk). Open Apr-Sept noon-5pm Wed-Sun. Oct-Mar 10am-3pm Fri-Sun. Admission free.

Eastward Hoo

From the unpretentious Georgian port of Gravesend to Rochester, where the Dover Road crosses the Medway, this route tours the Hoo Peninsula, the setting for much of Charles Dickens Great Expectations. *Lying between the Thames and the Medway, the Hoo Peninsula is not on the way to anywhere. Arrive when the sun is low and the wind is biting, and it still seems like the 'dark flat wilderness' that Dickens wrote about. This is a window into a post-industrial future, when nature reclaims what was once hers, and as such it has a bleak, melancholy beauty all of its own.*

START As you sweep down to the riverfront from Gravesend railway station, the old town, with its covered market, is to your right. From West Street you can take a foot ferry (bikes go free) to Tilbury, Essex. The ❶ Three Daws pub serves food and has a terrace overlooking the town's pier.

Gravesend has a beach backed by Promenade Park. A swing bridge (❶ 1.3 miles) takes you over the mouth of the marina to the start of the Thames & Medway Canal. The route, picking a way through the neglected industrial sheds of east Gravesend, is rough, overgrown and festooned with litter – hardly a great advert for the National Cycle Network. But this is, in fact, Route 1, connecting Dover to London, Edinburgh, John O'Groats and Orkney. Keep an eye out for industrial traffic on these estate roads, until you get on to the dirt path running beside the derelict canal and railway. The surface is rough but consistent. The Thames & Medway Canal, which took 25 years to complete, was intended to reduce a tricky, tidal 40 miles of river travel to a straight, steady seven miles. The idea was to make money from military traffic, but by the time the line opened, in 1824, the Napoleonic Wars were over. The canal was never a success.

Most English canals have a railway running parallel, as both need to follow a level path. Often the last time a canal made real money was when it was carrying materials in, and waste away, from the gangs of navvies digging the railway. The only notable earthwork on the canal – the Higham-Strood tunnel – is now dry and carries the train tracks from London to Rochester. The stone obelisk on the opposite bank marks the change in jurisdiction from the Port of London to the River Medway (❷ 4.3 miles).

Start Gravesend rail, Kent DA11 0HP
Finish Rochester rail, Kent ME1 1HQ
Time 4 hours
Distance 31 miles
Traffic & safety Mostly country lanes and cycle paths; traffic on short sections of rural 'A' roads
Terrain Rolling. Can be windy
Transport *Start* Gravesend rail. *End* Rochester rail
Good for Ornithologists, cloud-spotters, bibliophiles and dramaturgs

COUNTRY PLEASURES

Hoo's there

Lower Higham marks the beginning of Hoo. Salt Lane (a turn-off from the road to Cliffe) runs on an artificial ridge between great, square lagoons – the result of chalk extraction for cement making. Around the turn of the century, this area was identified as a possible site for a new London Airport, and, as often happens in these situations, the opposition campaign increased awareness of the 'waste' land's value. It's now run by the RSPB as the ❷ Cliffe Pools Nature Reserve. Some of the paths in the reserve are cycle-able, but you can't make a circuit without walking. If you want to park and explore the pools, there are bicycle racks in the car park. Signs for the Saxon Shore Way will lead you past this tortured landscape to Cliffe village.

Between Cliffe and Cooling there are pear orchards sheltered from the wind by screen trees. Cooling Castle (❸ 11.1 miles), built to defend against French raiders, shows where the shoreline was in the 14th century. St James's Church is assumed to be the inspiration for the opening scene of *Great Expectations*, where the orphan Pip is ambushed by Abel Magwitch, a terrifying escapee from the prison hulks that once lay in the tideway. The setting that taught Pip that 'the dark flat wilderness beyond the churchyard, intersected with dykes and mounds and

Gravesend.

Promenade Park.

Three Daws.

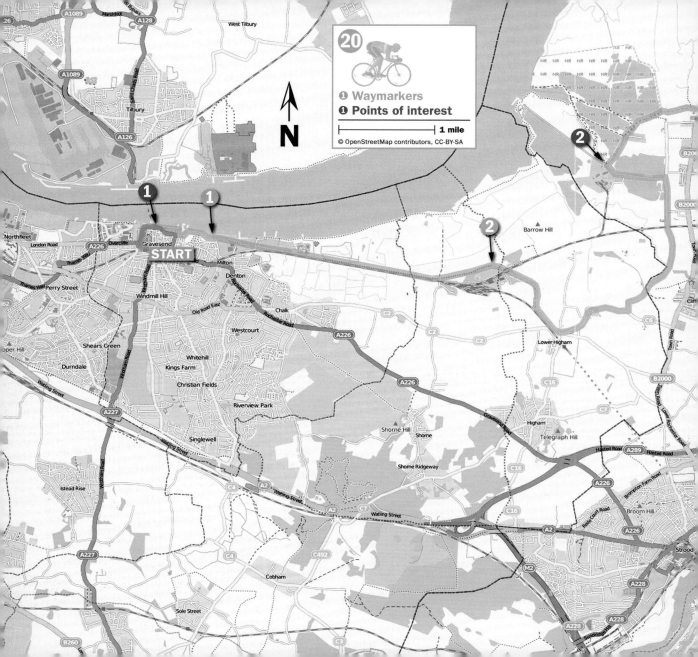

Route Directions

START From Gravesend rail station front entrance (north side by platform 2)

Left on Clive Road

Traffic lights: T-junction: right into Bath Street (A226)

Roundabout: second exit into West Street (A226)

Fork left into cycle track (after Three Daws pub)

Join Royal Pier Road

Bear left into the Terrace

Left into Commercial Place

Continue through Promenade Park along seafront

Exit the park to pass on the landward side of the Yacht Club

➊ **1.3 miles Cross** the swing bridge – Gordon Promenade East

Turn right at the end of the road behind galvanized fence

Bear left on to footpath

Continue along dirty urban footbath – Wharf Road

Right into Norfolk Road

Immediate left into Wharf Road (beside derelict canal)

➋ **4.3 miles Join** Canal Road

Right, immediate left at crossroads in Higham into Lower Rochester Road

Fork left shortly into Gore Green Road

Left into Buckland Road

Left into Salt Lane (signpost RSPB)

Bear right past RSPB car park

Fork left on to dirt road

Through gate (may be problematic for a big bike)

Bear left then sharp right (signpost Saxon Shore Road) into Pickle's Way

Medway Bridge.

Right into Pond Hill (in Cliffe)

Left into Reed Street – Common Lane

➌ **11.1 miles T-junction: left** into Cooling Road – Main Road – Cooling Road

Continue through High Halstow – The Street – Britannia Road

T-junction: left into Ratcliffe Highway (A228)

Left into Fenn Street – Ratcliffe Highway

Continue through St Mary Hoo

Right into Hoopers Lane (signpost 'Unsuitable for HGVs')

Left into Cuckolds Green Road

T-junction: right into Ratcliffe Highway

T-junction: left into Avery Way (Allhallows)

➍ **19.2 miles Continue past** the British Pilot pub

Cross pasture on rough track and climb sea wall

➎ **20.1 miles Retrace** past British Pilot pub

Continue on Avery Way

Left into Stoke Road – All Hallows Road

Bear left into Cuckolds Green Road

Right into High Street (by the Nags Head)

➏ **22.2 miles T-junction: right** into Grain Road (A228)

Left into the Street (signpost Upper Stoke)
– Stoke Road

T-junction: right still Stoke Road

Roundabout: first exit (signpost Hoo St
Werburgh) into Stoke Road

Mini roundabout: straight on (by Five Bells)

Continue through Hoo St Werburgh – Main Road

Roundabout: first exit Main Road

❼ **27.6 miles Merge** with A228 (use cycle track
if you prefer)

Left on down hill (just before flyover bridge)

T-junction: left into Upchat Road

Crossroads: straight on into Tower Hill
(take care at 'Stop' sign)

T-junction: left (physically straight on)
through Upnor

Join cycle path beside military base

Cross dual carriageway at light-controlled crossing

❽ **29.9 miles T-junction: right** on cycle path

Left into Upnor Road

Straight on (where road bends right) on to cycle path

Down steep hill

T-junction: right into Commissioner's Road

Immediate left into Wingrove Drive

Straight on into cycle path

Bear left into Canal Road

Traffic lights: T-junction: left into High Street

Cross Medway Bridge (use cycle track if you prefer)

Use crossing at east end of bridge to get into
High Street

Traffic lights: straight on into High Street
Dismount if necessary

❾ **31 miles END Left** Rochester rail station

gates, with scattered cattle feeding on it, was the
marshes; and that the low leaden line beyond, was
the river; and that the distant savage lair from which
the wind was rushing, was the sea...' still exists.
The major new addition, the towers of Coryton and
Canvey Island oil refineries, flaring at dusk, don't
make the scene any more homely. In the village, the
❻ Horseshoe & Castle pub serves real ale and food.

The big sky

High Halstow is the highest point on Hoo; beyond it,
you're able to survey the Thames from above. From
here you can cut the loop and take a shortcut to
Rochester following 'Cycle Route 18' signs, so check
the wind. Racing out with the wind behind you, only
to turn and have it hit you in the face like a hammer
is an easy mistake to make, and there's not much
shelter on Hoo. The sky gets bigger and, beyond St
Mary Hoo, you can occasionally see the Thames on
the left, the Medway on the right and – depending on
atmospheric conditions – the North Sea far ahead.

The first tall chimney in view is Kingsnorth power
station (due to close in 2016), which burns mostly
coal. A plan to replace it with a new coal-burning
facility attracted wide criticism, and in October 2007
six Greenpeace activists climbed the chimney and
painted the word 'Gordon' on the tower. They
intended to add 'Bin It', but were interrupted. A year
later, after a trial that included testimony on the
effects of climate change from an Inuit leader, a jury
found the Kingsnorth Six not guilty, accepting their
defence that they had lawful excuse for the criminal
damage. The other tower, to the left, is Grain power
station, which marks the limit of the peninsula.

Hoo All Hallows is an ancient hamlet, and its young
neighbour Allhallows-on-Sea had hoped to become a
holiday destination for Londoners when a branch line

opened in 1932. However, even in fine weather it has a bleak aspect, and World War II interrupted the project to build a new resort town. The train station, which stood opposite the British Pilot pub (❹ 19.2 miles), closed in 1961 and is now long gone. Continue over pasture to the sea wall to see Southend-on-Sea across the estuary. The beach is sandy in places. If you fancy a swim, check the tide tables, and time your arrival – at low water, it's a long, muddy walk to the sea.

Homeward bound

After a short retrace, past the British Pilot pub again (❺ 20.1 miles) to Hoo All Hallows, the homeward trip favours the Medway side, offering some shelter from the prevailing wind. Beyond the twin hamlets of Stoke, Lower (❻ 22.2 miles) and Upper, we run for a short

distance on a newly 'improved' road, the access for the Kingsnorth power station site. Follow signs for Hoo St Werburgh, go through the village and on to join the A228 (❼ 27.6 miles) at Chattenden. Here you have the choice to use the road or a parallel path. If you choose the path, take care, as you'll be riding against traffic coming in and out of side roads and entrances. Running downhill, past Chattenden, turn left before the over bridge to join Upchat Road; this will give the first view of Rochester's castle and cathedral across the winding Medway.

In Upnor, a short detour down the cobbled High Street takes you to ❹ Upnor Castle, an Elizabethan gun fort built to defend Chatham's dockyard and anchorages. Next door is the ❺ Tudor Rose pub, which is nearly as old and serves fresh food. At the end of Upchat Road, continue on the access road to

Cliffe Pools Nature Reserve.

the military base where the bike path (Kent Cycle Route 18) continues, to the right of the entrance, outside the perimeter fence. The path is marked with a 'Cyclists Dismount' sign. (A round sign gives a legal instruction: for example, a black bike logo on a white ground with a red border means 'No Cycling'. Blue rectangular signs, such the one here, give advice and are best treated as a disclaimer from the body responsible; so read 'If you choose to cycle on this sub-standard path, we won't be responsible for the consequences'.) In practice, the path is narrow, so take care and be courteous if you meet other traffic, but don't get off and walk unless you feel the need.

The dual carriageway at the end of the path is the access road for the Medway Tunnel, which was built by dropping prefabricated sections of rectangular tube into a trench dredged in the bottom of the river, creating the first immersed tube tunnel in England. It's closed to cycle traffic. A short ride north on the other side of the access road brings us to Parsonage Lane, a steep climb and then a narrow path with an ugly chain link fence on the left. The fence is necessary because close inspection through its overgrowth shows a deep chalk quarry. The path ends with a very steep descent. We're back on Route 1. Canal Street is reached by a path through new housing, built on the filled-in terminus basin of the ill-fated Medway Canal. On the eastern end of the Rochester bridge, a light-controlled crossing allows tricky access (walking is recommended) to the old High Street.

Rochester's ❻ castle and ❼ cathedral are a step away. Amuse yourself by counting the number of establishments that have (however bizarrely) squeezed Dickens references into their names (the writer had a house at Gadshill, just up the London Road). The greengrocer, Pip's, is a personal favourite, along with the ❽ Taste of Two Cities curry house.

Rochester High Street is one-way for motor traffic – the direction of flow changes in the middle – but two-way for cycle traffic, making a civilised finish to the ride. The train station END (31 miles) is to the left.

❶ **Three Daws**
7 Town Pier, Gravesend, Kent DA11 0BJ (01474 566869, www.threedaws.co.uk). Open 11am-1am Mon-Sat; noon-1am Sun.
❷ **Cliffe Pools Nature Reserve**
Salt Lane, Cliffe, Kent ME3 7SU (01634 222480, www.rspb.org.uk). Open 24hrs daily. Admission free.
❸ **Horseshoe & Castle**
Main Road, Cooling, Rochester, Kent ME3 8DJ (01634 221691, www.horseshoeandcastle.co.uk). Open 11.30am-3pm, 5.45-11pm Tue; 11.30am-11pm Wed-Sat; noon-10.30pm Sun.
❹ **Upnor Castle**
High Street, Upnor, Kent ME2 4XG (01634 718742, www.english-heritage.org.uk). Open Apr-Oct 10am-6pm daily. Admission charge.
❺ **Tudor Rose**
29 High Street, Upnor, Kent ME2 4XG (01634 715305, www.shepherdneame.co.uk). Open 11am-11pm Mon-Sat; noon-10.30pm Sun.
❻ **Rochester Castle**
Rochester, Kent ME1 1SW (01634 335882, www.english-heritage.org.uk). Open 10am-4pm daily. Admission charge.
❼ **Rochester Cathedral**
High Street, Rochester, Kent ME1 1SX (01634 843366, www.rochestercathedral.org). Open 7.30am-6pm Mon-Fri, Sun; 7.30am-5pm Sat. Admission free.
❽ **Taste Of Two Cities**
106 High Street, Rochester, Kent ME1 1JT (01634 841327). Lunch served noon-2.30pm Mon-Thur, Sat, Sun. Dinner served 6-11.30pm daily.

Pack a Pocket or Two

Panniers are great if you're on a long tour, but there's no doubt that the freedom of the open road is most delightfully experienced without a bag weighing you – or your bike – down. That's why classic bike jerseys typically come with three pockets on the back (where their contents won't interfere with your riding mechanics). You can easily and comfortably fit all you'll need for a day ride into these pockets, supplemented if necessary by a tiny under-saddle bag (look out for Fizik's clip-in saddle and bag systems).

❶ Spare tube and tyre levers

Better than faffing with a repair kit en route (patch the hole when you get home and you've got your next spare). You could use a self-adhesive patch instead, but these are only temporary – and don't help if the valve is damaged.

❷ Mini pump

Get a good pump that provides a decent pressure without causing too much swearing. Makes and models change quickly and price doesn't always indicate performance, so check out recent reviews on purchase sites such as wiggle.com; and note that size doesn't necessarily matter.

❸ Mobile phone

Protect your phone with a case, such as Prendas's cute phone sock, or invest in a handlebar mount. This is particularly useful if you're using online maps or one of several very useful bicycle apps, such as the Cyclemeter GPS Bike Computer, which does pretty much everything other than ride the bike for you, including some useful mapping, speedo and training features.

❹ A couple of bananas

There's a lot of rot talked about on-board nutrition, but for medium-length rides, a banana is not only a perfect, naturally packaged energy-giver, but something of a cult item. Flapjack is another cheap alternative to expensive sports bars. And some riders swear by jelly babies for a quick boost.

❺ Multi-tool

You pays your money and takes your choice, but make sure that you have all the sizes of Allen key your bike and its fittings require.

❻ Jacket

A windproof, showerproof or rainproof jacket, depending on the season and weather forecast, is a must. Breathability is more important than full weatherproofing, except in persistent rain (and only masochists go out in that), so the odds are it will be lightweight, and thus easily compactable into a pocket-sized roll. In warm weather, a gilet is a good alternative to protect you from early-morning chill.

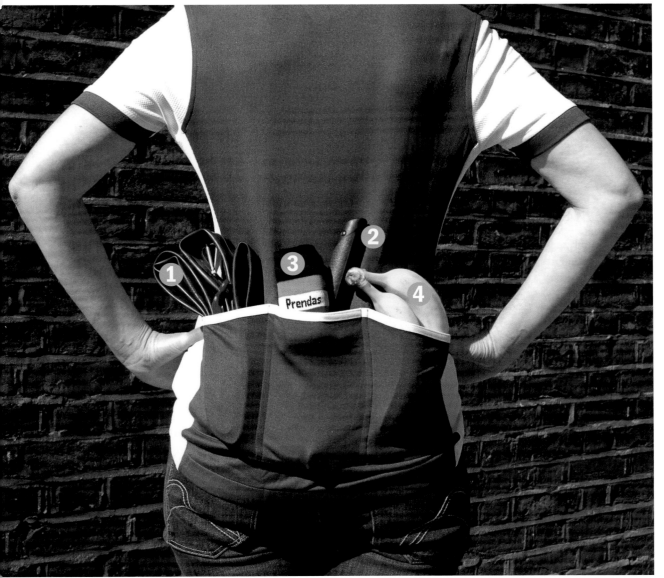

Wheels over the Weald

This is a straight run from Purley to the coast at Brighton. It mixes easy-to-follow 'B' roads with quieter lanes and includes a 'secret' cut through the North Downs. If you're not used to point-to-point cycle travel, don't waste energy thinking about the whole ride, just solve each problem in turn, relax and enjoy the trip. You may be surprised at just how quickly you're looking down at the sea.

COUNTRY PLEASURES

A key to enjoyable travel by bike is choosing a route to suit your mood. Roads that get you there quickest, are well signposted and follow the easiest line, are often the busiest. Quieter roads are likely to have more hills and bends, and demand more careful navigation. Some people are happy on 'good' roads and don't mind cars hurtling past, others only want to keep away from traffic and fumes. Mixing the two means you can appreciate the best of each; follow an easy road until you're fed up of noise, divert on to a quieter line until you're fed up of searching for the route. Southern England is full of highways of all classes, so it's usually simple to switch between the two.

The **START** – at Purley – is easily accessible by road from London. Just follow the A23 through Brixton and Streatham. It gets a bit dull bypassing Croydon, but the ride is never too onerous, especially if you get an early start on a summer's morning. If you want to save yourself for the nicest parts, hop on a train to Purley. The East Grinstead Road threads through Kenley, the last bit of the London Borough of Croydon, and into Whyteleafe, which is in Surrey. The pre-Green Belt linear development never quite decides whether it's town or country, and the carriageway is narrow for an 'A' road. There are shops, cafés and pubs all along the road; ❶ Salisbury's fish and chip shop in Whyteleafe is good, if it's open when you're passing. As Whyteleafe gives way to an industrial estate, the road widens to a dual carriageway, with a whole lane reserved for bicycles – a relief.

Cutting through the North Downs can be a problem. The easy routes are mostly monopolised by big, uninviting roads crammed with cars. Other lines are arduous. But the Woldingham gap has a good tarmac road, which is classed as a bridleway, and serves as the drive to a private school. It provides an ideal breakthrough point. The turn off the Woldingham Road is easy to find, being right under a railway viaduct (❶ 4 miles). The lane is easy, only the brutal speed bumps give a clue

Start Purley rail, CR8 2UD
Finish Brighton seafront, BN2 1TD
Time 5 hours
Distance 43 miles
Traffic & safety 'B' roads (which may be busy at times), quiet lanes and a surfaced bridleway section
Terrain Rolling roads, with an optional steep, shady climb of the Greensand Ridge near the start, and a steep climb of the South Downs near the end
Transport *Start* Purley rail. *End* Brighton rail
Good for Seaside lovers

South Downs, near Ditchling Beacon.

that it's not a public road. In case you're worried about trespassing, rest assured that, as a bridleway and a national or regional cycle route, it is a public right of way. However, the land off the bridleway is private, so don't go wandering.

The secret heart of England

The road empties out into the Weald above Godstone (❷ 7.1 miles). If you're anxious to get to the beach, you can turn left on the A25 and follow signs for the A22 across two big roundabouts. If you want something quieter and more scenic, keep running down by Godstone Church to Gibbs Brook, a tributary of the Eden that feeds the Medway in Kent, and climb the Greensand Ridge through chestnut woods on Tilburstow Hill Common. The Weald is a mysterious place, home to a strange strand of Englishness that is as much nature mysticism as it is patriotism. Writers as eminent as AA Milne, Rudyard Kipling and EM Forster have fallen under and hymned its spell. Its connections with Albion run deep, for the Romans never settled here, but just blasted roads through. It was the pig-keeping Saxons who colonised the forest slopes. The oak tree is the weed of the Weald. Trees were felled for ship building and to make charcoal for furnaces. Rivers were dammed for hidden hammer ponds, still a Wealden commonplace, which drove water-powered trip-hammers to forge steel for blades and cannon before the Industrial Revolution. This is the historic heart of British world domination.

The A22 is acceptable for the run to Newchapel, but the parallel lanes (❸ 11.7 miles) are nearly as quick and more convivial. They rejoin the B2028 beyond Newchapel (❹ 15.3 miles). Turners Hill is a sensible stopping point: it's around halfway and the top of a long gradual climb through Crawley Down, which makes getting going again relatively easy.

The ❷ Crown pub on the green at the top of the hill
(❺ 20 miles) is more interesting than it looks.
Running down from Turners Hill, the ❸ White Hart
– more a restaurant than a pub – is another option.

❹ Wakehurst Place is the country arm of the
Royal Botanic Gardens at Kew. Horticultural
enthusiasts may want to stop here, but the general
downhill inclination of the road, and the sense that
you're getting somewhere, encourages movement.
Watch carefully for the left turn off Lindfield High
Street (❻ 27.1 miles). If you reach the pond, you've
missed it. Stay on line and you can follow B2112
signs for Ditchling village through Haywards Heath,
but the alternative, Slugwash Lane, is a classic,
rolling through woods and fields while the distant
wall of the South Downs becomes more apparent
far ahead. Back on the B2112, the route south is
obvious (❼ 31.1 miles).

The South Downs become clearer as you cross
Ditchling Common. The looming ridge may be
daunting, but remember the sea is waiting on the
other side. The left turn at the south end of Ditchling
(❽ 35.2 miles) is more of a straight-on, but the
signpost to ❺ Ditchling Beacon is unambiguous.
The road up to the Beacon is steep and twisting;
the gradient on the climb keeps changing, which
breaks your rhythm, but means you can usually see
a shallower section ahead. It's shady at first, but
near the top the hedge on your left breaks, giving a
tremendous view back across the Weald, all the way
to the North Downs. The North and South Downs are
two stumps of a great chalk ridge that once rose to
3,000 feet. It wore away, leaving the wet clay Weald.

There's a National Trust car park at the top of
Ditchling Beacon – 814 feet – a good point to stop
for a breather and admire the view (though it's on the
right, so cross the road with care). A fast road across

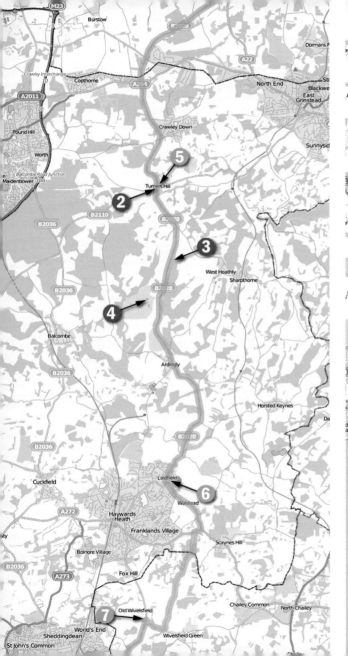
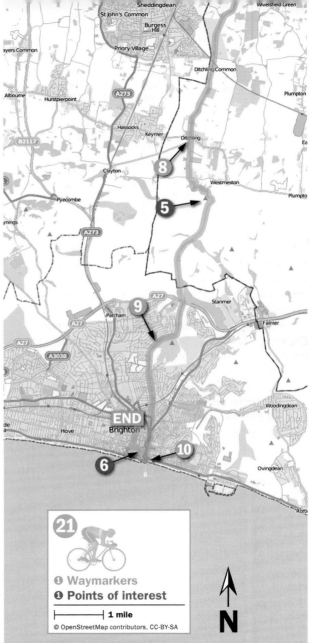

Route Directions

START Purley Station
Left into Whytecliffe Road South
Left into Godstone Road (signpost East Grinstead) (A22)
Roundabout: 2nd exit (signpost East Grinstead) still Godstone Road (A22)
Roundabout: 2nd exit (signpost Woldingham) into Woldingham Road
❶ 4 miles Fork right (under railway viaduct, signpost Woldingham School). This road is classed as a bridleway
After tennis courts on right…
Straight on between red brick piers (signpost Cycle Route 21)
T-junction: left (just past barrier)
❷ 7.1 miles T-junction: right (back on the public highway) into Flower Lane
Cross over M25
Cross over A22
Left, immediate right across A25 into Church Lane (signpost Godstone Church)
Right into Eastbourne Road (B2236)
Shortly left into Enterdent Road
T-junction: left (signpost South Godstone) into Tilburstow Hill Road
T-junction: right into A22
❸ 11.7 miles Right into Byers Lane (signpost Pet Cemetery)
Left into Brickhouse Lane (signpost Newchapel)
T-junction: right (signpost Horne) into Bones Lane
1st left into East Park Lane (no signpost)
❹ 15.3 miles T-junction: right (no signpost) into West Park Road (B2028)

Right into Effingham Road (B2037)
Immediate left, continue on West Park Road – Turners Hill Road (B2028)
Roundabout: 2nd exit continue on Turners Hill Road (B2028)
❺ 20 miles In Turners Hill
Mini roundabout: 2nd exit (physically straight on) into Selsfield Road – Lindfield Road – Ardingly Road – Buxshalls Hill – High Street (B2028)
❻ 27.1 miles In Lindfield
Left by post office into Lewes Road (no signpost) – Scamps Hill – Scaynes Hill Road – Bedales Hill (B2111)
T-junction: right (signpost Haywards Heath) into Lewes Road (A272)
Shortly left into Slugwash Lane (signpost 7.5T max)
T-junction: right (no signpost) into Green Road
❼ 31.1 miles In Wivelsfield
Roundabout: 1st exit (signpost Ditchling) (B2112)
Roundabout: 2nd exit (signpost Ditchling) into Common Lane (B2112)
❽ 35.2 miles In Ditchling…
Left into Beacon Road (signpost Ditchling Beacon)
Left, immediate right over flyover into Ditchling Road (signpost Golf Course)
❾ 40.2 miles Continue on Ditchling Road, which becomes A23 in Brighton
In Brighton at St Peter's Church…
Traffic lights: bear left continue on A23 to
END 42.8 miles Brighton seafront
To reach the railway station from Brighton Pier
   Old Steine; traffic lights: left into North Street; right into Queens Road; continue to station

Brighton.

the downlands makes the most of the descent, with a very gradual downhill. A tricky left and right over the A27 Brighton bypass brings you into the resort's suburbs. With pleasing completeness, the last climb of the ride, over the golf course (➒ 40.2 miles), reveals the English Channel. From here it's downhill all the way to the beach (**END** 42.8 miles). If you want to swim, there's a naturist beach east of the town centre, which means you'll have no wet clothes to carry home. There's hospitality of all categories in Brighton. Try ➏ English's Seafood Restaurant & Oyster Bar in East Street, west of the pier.

➊ Salisbury's Fish & Chips
2 Station Road, Whyteleafe, Surrey CR3 0EP (01883 622510). Open 11.30am-2pm, 4.30-10pm Mon-Fri; 11.30am-2pm, 4.30-9pm Sat.
➋ Crown
East Street, Turners Hill, West Sussex, RH10 4PT
(01342 715281, www.thecrownturnershill.co.uk). Open varies, phone for details.
➌ White Hart
Ardingly Road, West Hoathly, West Sussex RH19 4RA (01342 715217, www.thewhitehartinn.info). Open 11am-11pm Mon-Thur, Sat; 11am-midnight Fri; noon-6pm Sun. Food served noon-3pm, 6-9pm Mon-Sat; noon-4pm Sun.
➍ Wakehurst Place
Ardingly, West Sussex RH17 6TN (01444 894066, www.nationaltrust.org.uk, www.kew.org). Open Mar-Oct 10am-6pm daily. Nov-Feb 10am-4.30pm daily. Admission charge.
➎ Ditchling Beacon
(01323 870001, www.brighton-hove.gov.uk).
➏ English's Seafood Restaurant & Oyster Bar
29-31 East Street, Brighton, East Sussex BN1 1HL (01273 328645, www.englishs.co.uk). Open noon-10pm daily.

㉒ Humbling the Hill

COUNTRY PLEASURES

You've come this far. You've ridden through central London, you've reached the sea, and even followed in the tracks of Olympians. You've done things you never thought you could on two wheels. So now you want a real challenge. And here it is. This circuit is the toughest ride on this list. It uses dirt lanes and paths up and down the steep North Downs and Greensand Ridge. If you really want to test yourself, tackle it all on a bike. On the other hand, there's no shame in treating it as a bicycle-assisted country walk – the scenery will reward you. If you choose to do the ride, you'll need a mountain or cyclo-cross bike. If your aim is mechanically aided walking, a touring bike or hybrid is fine.

The River Mole rises near Gatwick and runs down to join the River Thames at East Molesley, opposite Hampton Court. The water has cut a steep-sided valley through the chalk hills of the North Downs, between Dorking and Leatherhead, known as Mole Gap. The combination of high hills and woods hanging off the flanks of the gap made it an early tourist destination. Horatio Nelson and Emma Hamilton stayed at the Burford Bridge Hotel, which stands on the Mole, at the foot of Box Hill. Jane Austen's Emma addressed Frank Churchill thus: 'We are going to Box Hill tomorrow: you will join us. It is not Swisserland, but it will be something for a young man so much in want of a change.'

From **START** Box Hill & Westhumble train station, it's short ride to ❶ Ryka's Café, opposite the hotel. The café is particularly popular with motorcyclists, although the scenery is better than the food. Burford Bridge is connected to Westhumble village via a cycle track and subway. Fanny Burney – the 18th-century pioneer of literary fiction – built a cottage in Westhumble with the proceeds from her hit novel of 1796, *Camilla*, and made a home there with General Alexandre D'Arblay, a penniless Frenchman who fled post-revolutionary turmoil.

If all this romance were not enough, the first turn of the ride is marked by the flint ruin of a 13th-century chapel. Off the tarmac road, the bridleway is steep and obstructed by roots. The path levels out on top of the North Downs, and passes ❷ St Barnabas Church, Ranmore, designed by Gilbert Scott, the architect of St Pancras station. As you'd expect with that pedigree, it's an exquisite example of Victorian neo-Gothic architecture.

Start & finish Box Hill & Westhumble rail, Dorking, Surrey RH5 6BT
Time 3.5 hours
Distance 21 miles
Connects with ⑭ ⑮
Traffic & safety Mostly on dirt roads classified as bridleways, with some potentially dangerous descents. Tarmac sections are on quiet country lanes, except for 100 metres on an 'A' road
Terrain Steep hills, woods and fields
Transport Box Hill & Westhumble rail
Good for Adventurers

Ranmore Common Road.

steep, with tree roots and erosion gullies making vertical steps. Stop at the top first. Take a view of the scenery and decide whether you want to commit to the descent. It's much easier to stop now than when you're halfway down. If you want to risk it, keep your weight pushed back, control your speed with your back brake and don't go too slowly. Walking also works (and it's better to walk than to go home in a helicopter with a neck brace). Sneaking under the railway and across the Dorking–Guildford Road brings a change of soil. The chalk is over. This is the start of the parallel, higher Greensand Ridge. As the path climbs above the ornamental mill ponds off Rookery Drive (❷ 5.7 miles), you can choose to fork right up a narrow, sunken lane that's now classified as a footpath, which absolves you of any obligation to ride, or continue on a bridleway. They both join Wolvens Lane, an unmade green lane that runs to Coldharbour.

Green lanes

It would be inexact to call this an 'off-road' ride. These are old country roads. When the rural economy was much more labour-intensive, there were agricultural labourers living in every hamlet. They walked. To work, to market, to church, maybe even to the village pub, and they went directly, so there was a dense network of lanes connecting anywhere to everywhere. After these people were replaced by machines, some country roads and lanes were adopted by the highway authorities, and sealed with tar and stones to make easy passage for cycles and automobiles. The rest usually became footpaths or bridleways. The density of these networks depends on the history of an area. For example, in Kent, where the land was enclosed early and most of it is held in small holdings, bridleways are rare, and almost all the old country roads became metalled lanes. But here in Surrey,

Over the edge

There's a discreet signpost off Ranmore Common Road for ❸ Tanners Hatch Hostel, which is half a mile up an unlit track in the woods; a great combination – for Londoners, at least – of accessibility and remoteness. From the Ranmore Common car park (❶ 3.3 miles), a track runs innocently into the woods, then plunges over the lip of the North Downs. It's

COUNTRY PLEASURES

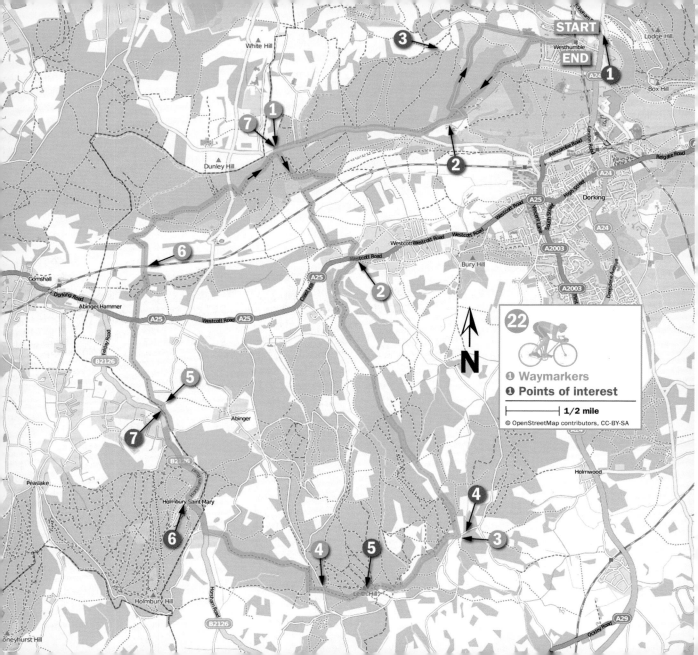

START

END

Westhumble

White Hill

Lodge Hill

Box Hill

Dunley Hill

Ashcombe Road

London Road

Reigate Road

Dorking

A24

South Street

High Street

A24

A2003

A2003

Westcott Road

Westcott Road

Westcott Road

Westcott Road

A25

A25

A25

Dorking Road

Abinger Hammer

Gomshall

Coast Hill

Bury Hill

Deepdene Avenue

Kelsey Road

B2126

Abinger

N

22

❶ Waymarkers

❶ Points of interest

1/2 mile

© OpenStreetMap contributors, CC-BY-SA

Peaslake

B2126

Holmbury Saint Mary

Holmbury Hill

B2126

Horsham Road

Leith Hill

Holmwood

oneyhurst Hill

Ockley Road

A29

where there were more big estates, many lanes have stayed green. Wolvens Lane, whose quickly changing variety of riding conditions make an interesting run to Coldharbour (**❸** 8.9 miles), is a prime example.

The **❹** Plough Inn at Coldharbour offers lunch, has a steakhouse restaurant open in the evenings and brews three characterful ales on site. Above the village is the highest cricket field in southern England, with short boundaries for rapid scoring. Beyond is Leith Hill. At 965 feet, it is the highest point on the Greensand Ridge. It's topped with **❺** Leith Hill Tower, an 18th-century folly that was designed as a viewpoint and – supposedly – to bring the hill up to 1,000 feet. Its soft brick is carved with a fine selection of antique graffiti. From the top, it's said you can see 13 counties. Even without climbing the tower, you get a long view south across the Weald to the South Downs, 25 miles away, hard up against the English Channel.

Take care descending as there are likely to be people around, even on quiet days. The next section of path begins at the lay-by car park (**❹** 10.5 miles) below the tower. It's mostly single-track along the top of the Greensand Ridge's southern face, and rolls along delightfully. The road section through Holmbury St Mary – the **❻** Royal Oak pub is on your left – is all downhill. The **❼** Volunteer pub (**❺** 13.4 miles) at Sutton Abinger offers a free bike wash facility and car parking, so – if you're car-dependent – it would make an alternative start and finish point. After the Volunteer, the path breaks into open country for almost the first time. You go across pasture, down by watercress beds, to recross the Guildford Road.

The only remaining obstacle, the wall of the North Downs scarp, lowers ahead as you recross the railway (**❻** 14.9 miles). A last section of woodland paths returns you to the Ranmore

Tanners Hatch Hostel.

St Barnabas Church, Ranmore.

Route Directions

START Leave Box Hill & Westhumble rail station and turn left on to Westhumble Street
Left into Chapel Lane
Left by the ruined chapel
When the drive bears left…
Fork right on to single-track bridleway
Keep right by the triangular green
Cross tarmac lane on the bridleway
T-junction: right on to road towards the flint church with a steeple
T-junction: right into Ranmore Common Road
Beyond second car park (National Trust, Ranmore Common)…
❶ 3.3 miles Left past steel barrier on to pressed-rubble bridleway
Take care on steep descent
T-junction: right through wooden gate
Left through gate
Under railway bridge
Right and left between farm buildings
Left on to tarmac road
T-junction: right into Balchins Lane
T-junction: left on to Coast Hill (A25)
❷ 5.7 miles Right into Rookery Drive
After crossing below the dam…
Left on to bridleway
Continue past ponds
At the triangular stand of trees…
Fork right up hill on footpath and…
Dismount or continue riding on bridleway
T-junction: left on sunken lane (Wolvens Lane) to…
❸ 8.9 miles At Coldharbour

Right (signpost Tower and Cricket Pitch)
Keep left by cricket pitch
Left up hill (past sign to Leith Hill Tower)
Continue past tower
At road…
❹ 10.5 miles Right and left on to bridleway through lay-by car park (signpost Greensand Way)
Right by the gate and yew tree
Left on to the hard farm road
Fork left to avoid 'Private' signs
Continue on rolling single-track
T-junction: left on Pasture Wood Road
T-junction: right on Horsham Road (B2126) through Holmbury St Mary
Just past the turn to the youth hostel…
Right (sign Maximum width 6.5)

T-junction: left into Water Lane
T-junction: right by the Volunteer pub
After 20 yards…
❺ 13.4 miles Left into bridleway
Fork right on to single-track bridleway by black metal gates
T-junction: left on to bridleway
Left and right through the farmyard
Cross dam above watercress beds
Cross A25 with care on to bridleway
Beyond the second wooden gate…
Keep left at triangular green
Left at first corner of the green on to single-track going down into woods
T-junction: right on to farm road
❻ 14.9 miles Over railway bridge
Fork left up hill
T-junction: right by brick ruins
When path levels out…
Right at bridleway crossroads with wooden post
Keep left to reach White Down car park
Cross road and continue on single track marked 'self-guided trail'
Join bigger track merging from right
❼ 17.1 miles Continue to reach Ranmore Common car park
Right on to Ranmore Common Road
Left towards Ranmore Church (signpost Westhumble)
Continue down hill
T-junction: right on to Chapel Lane
END 21 miles Return to Box Hill & Westhumble rail station

Common car park (❼ 17.1 miles). From here, you can retrace to Westhumble and the train station (**END** 21 miles), but the tarmac lane running past Ranmore Church provides a more relaxing finish than the rough country road you came up.

❶ Ryka's Cafe
Old London Road, Dorking, Surrey RH5 6BY (01306 884454, www.boxhill.co.uk). Open 8am-7.30pm daily.
❷ St Barnabas Church, Ranmore
Ranmore Common Road, Dorking, Surrey RH5 6SP (01306 884360). Open phone for details.
❸ Tanners Hatch Hostel
Ranmore Road, Dorking, Surrey RH5 6BE (0845 371 9542, www.yha.org.uk).
❹ Plough Inn
Coldharbour, Surrey RH5 6HD (01306 711793, www.ploughinn.com). Open 10am-11.30pm Mon-Thur; 10am-12.30am Fri, Sat; noon-10pm Sun. Lunch served noon-3pm Mon-Thur; noon-3.30pm Fri-Sun. Dinner served 7-10pm Tue-Sat.
❺ Leith Hill Tower
Leith Hill, nr Coldharbour, Surrey (01306 712711, www.nationaltrust.org.uk). Open times vary, check website for details. Admission charge.
❻ Royal Oak
Holmbury St Mary, Surrey RH5 6PF (01306 730120). Open noon-11pm Mon-Sat; noon-10.30pm Sun. Food served noon-2.30pm, 6-9pm Mon-Sat; noon-6pm Sun.
❼ Volunteer
Water Lane, Sutton Abinger, Surrey RH5 6PR (01306 730985, www.the-volunteer.co.uk). Open 11.30am-11pm Mon-Sat; noon-10.30pm Sun. Food served noon-2.30pm, 6.30-9.30pm Mon-Fri; noon-9.30pm Sat; noon-4pm Sun.

COUNTRY PLEASURES

Allez, Allez!

For beginner cyclesportsters

Here's where to start if you want to take it to the next level. Venues for, and tips on, the four Olympic Cycling disciplines, plus a look at London's exciting new Velodrome, in the Olympic Park.

Road Racing

If you want to get more involved in road racing, the best place to start is the Redbridge Cycling Centre (affectionately known as Hog Hill) on the eastern outskirts of London. Opened in 2008, it is effectively the replacement for the Eastway circuit, which was redeveloped as the Olympic Park's VeloPark (which will become a public facility after 2012). While Eastway held fond memories for many of London's older cyclists, the Redbridge circuit is an excellent replacement, ensuring that a new generation of riders can cut their racing teeth in a safe environment.

That was where Eastway's beauty lay, and where Hog Hill has taken over: purpose-built for cycling, it's a long, well-surfaced road circuit, with no traffic. There are routes of various lengths to suit different users, but the main, two-kilometre loop is used for the road races – it is this you will need to learn to love if you fancy yourself as a future Tour de France contender.

But Redbridge is not aimed at racing cyclists only, as a glance at the week's schedule reveals: activities range from lessons to teach people of all ages how to ride a bike, to school excursions, to elite racing. There's also an off-road track for mountain biking and BMXing. When the road circuit isn't booked for such events – and as cycling becomes more popular, it often is – you can train on it for a small fee. This will also give you an idea of what lies ahead before your first race.

The course itself features a few rises and falls to keep you on your toes, but with long, sweeping corners, and sufficient width, it's quite safe. There's a sting in the tail, though, that those familiar with the circuit will warn you about: the finish line comes after a last 100 metres up a pretty stiff incline, which saps the energy from your legs with each lap, and makes for a very tough sprint finish at the end of the race.

For those looking to try road racing for the first time, Redbridge is ideal. Apart from being traffic-free, the fact that it's a circuit means you are never too far from help should you suffer a mechanical problem, crash or just struggle to keep up. The latter is likely in your first couple of road races, as you get used to the speed and rhythm of racing.

New riders automatically start as fourth-category – or 'fourth-cat', as you'll soon be calling yourself – but winning points will bump you up into higher categories should you find your racing legs straightaway.

In the absence of a Go Race event, look for a fourth-cat-only event: this will be marginally easier than the more common races for third- and fourth-cat riders. Note that even the lower-level racing will be fast, and you will need to be in good shape just to finish a race with the bunch. There's no cycling equivalent of a pub football Sunday league. Just thank your lucky stars that you're not racing against the elite riders in the 'E/1/2/3' race, which will normally follow your '3/4' event. Drag your tired legs to the café to re-fuel on cake and coffee, and then watch the big boys and girls demonstrate how it should be done.

The Redbridge Cycling Centre has excellent facilities, with changing rooms and showers in the pristine new clubhouse next to the finish line, along with the all-important café. The start/finish area is the perfect spot for spectators, should your friends and family wish to see you in action, and cheer you on to the win... or commiserate, as the case may be for some time. But persevere. Few experiences in cycling are as satisfying as the day you complete your first road race and are still in the thick of the action at the end.

British Cycling
www.britishcycling.org.uk.
Redbridge Cycling Centre
Forest Road, Hainault, Ilford, IG6 3HP (8500 9359, www.redbridgecyclingcentre.co.uk). Open 9am-8pm Mon-Thur; 9am-5pm Sat, Sun. Admission Casual use £3.80; see website for full price list and bike hire.
Redbridge Cycling Club
www.redbridgecc.org.uk.

Entry-level racing

British Cycling has a couple of initiatives for beginner cyclists: the Go Ride scheme for under-16s covers BMXing, cross-country mountain biking and other disciplines in addition to road racing. Adult entry-level cyclists should investigate the Go Race initiative. A number of such races are organised by the Redbridge Cycling Club, as part of the RCC Road Race Series at Hog Hill, during the summer. Just turn up, pay your entry fee, and ride. Otherwise, races require you to have a British Cycling racing licence.

ALLEZ, ALLEZ!

Mountain Biking

If there was one thing that took cycling out of the ghetto and into the limelight, it was the mountain bike. Now it seems like everyone has one, but a good proportion of those fat-tyred, suspension-forked beasts never get any dirt on their wheels. That's a shame, for few things can beat the sheer joy of finding yourself out on a mountain bike in the middle of nowhere on a warm summer's evening. The North Downs are within easy reach of the capital, so it's not difficult to find trails to explore.

However, if you don't want your first experience of mountain biking to involve juddering down an ever-steepening hill with no idea when it's going to stop, there are more structured places to get a feel for the discipline. Among them is PORC (Penshurst Off Road Cycling), located near Penshurst, Kent. Set in 40 acres of woodland, it provides a fun, safe environment for all riders – no matter what their off-road preferences – with the safety of the car park and civilisation never too far away.

Londoners can reach PORC quickly and easily, by car (leave the M25 at junction 5 towards Tonbridge) or rail (it's a 20-minute bike ride from Penshurst station). Camping is even offered on site, so you need never be far from the trails if you feel like treating yourself to a mountain bike mini-break.

Purists may not think this is proper mountain biking, but even they will be impressed by PORC's mix of natural and man-made trails – sheer delight for downhiller/freeride types. The trails for 4X (downhill elimination races fought out between four competitors at once) are held in reverence by riders, and have been used for a round of the British 4X Series. The 4X course has recently been improved too: extended and widened to promote more overtaking manoeuvres, while the dirt jumps have been re-dug.

PORC also hosts Women on Wheels weekends, designed to give women a taste of off-road riding, or to help them improve their skills.

Mountain bike clubs

Although the idea of a London mountain biking club may seem a contradiction in terms, PORC isn't the only organisation near the capital that caters for mountain bikers. In west London, the members of the West Drayton Mountain Bike Club are a busy bunch, enjoying regular rides in the locality, as well as trips to races and events up and down the country. They all come together for a regular pub night at the Crown pub in Cowley – purely to plan rides and races, you understand.

On the edge of north-east London, Epping Forest Mountain Bike Club has the forest of the same name on its doorstep. It sells itself as a gathering of riders, rather than a formal club, and is firmly aimed at over-35s wanting to enjoy some off-road riding. Youngsters should look elsewhere.

If you want to head much further afield, there are plenty of dedicated off-road biking centres across Britain. Mountainbiking Wales (www.mbwales.com) has six purpose-built sites in Wales, of which Coed-y-Brenin in Snowdonia is the oldest and most popular, with riders travelling from all over the country to spend a couple of days exploring the all-weather

PORC.

trails. Glentress Forest (www.glentressforest.com) in the Tweed Valley in the Scottish Borders is also an off-road mecca, and Highland Mountain Biking (www.mtb-highland.com) has information on purpose-built trails further north still.

Epping Forest Mountain Bike Club
www.epping-forest-mbc.co.uk.

PORC (Penshurt Off Road Cycling)
Grove Road, Penshurst, Kent TN11 8DU (01892 870136, www.porc.uk.com). Open 9am-dusk daily. Admission charge.
West Drayton Mountain Bike Club
www.westdraytonmbc.co.uk.
Women on Wheels
www.women-on-wheels.co.uk.

Tips from the Pros

Three of the top UK-based pro cyclists offer advice to help you get the most out of your riding. Swede **Magnus Bäckstedt**, of the new Team UK Youth (www.teamukyouth.co.uk), is a Tour de France stage winner and 2004 Paris-Roubaix champion. Briton **Kristian House**, who races for Rapha Condor Sharp (www.raphacondor.cc), was the British Road Race Champion in 2009. **Dan Lloyd** is also British and rides for top American pro team Garmin-Cervélo (www.slipstreamsports.com).

Magnus Bäckstedt

Improve your riding

Dan: 'For anyone looking to improve their cycling, I'd say that you need to be as consistent as you can. Try to do a couple of rides a week, rather than just one six-hour marathon on a Sunday – even if that means time on the turbo trainer on, say, a Tuesday and a Thursday evening. If you've not got much time, perhaps only an hour, then you need to hammer it for that hour instead of just pootling.'

Magnus: 'If you're not from a family where a parent or older brother or sister already rides a bike, then the way to progress in the sport is to join a club. That's not to say that you can't ride on your own if you prefer, as there are many good books and magazines to learn from.'

Kristian: 'My key tip is to suggest getting fitted properly on your bike. You see people in some very awkward positions, which, long-term, might turn them off cycling completely. Joining a club is a great way to easily get advice from people on such things. There are hundreds of clubs, all happy to welcome new members, and everyone involved in the sport tends to be willing to help people out.'

Start racing

Dan: 'Sportives are a really good way of getting a feel for road racing, or make a pretty good alternative if you don't fancy full-on competition. Unlike in road racing, if you're not having a good day in a sportive, then there'll always be other groups of riders going at your speed, so you don't need to worry about getting left behind.'

Kristian: 'Sportives are the perfect way to start out on the road to competition: a great way to take the next step. They're not strictly competitive, but some people take them quite seriously. Then there are things like 'evening 10s': regular ten-mile time trials that most clubs hold on a weekday evening. They're great for testing yourself – week in, week out – against other people, but also against your own best time over the distance, so you can easily see your progression.'

Best places to train

Magnus: 'One of my favourite places to ride in London is Richmond Park. Whenever I'm staying in London, that's where I head for a couple of hours of training. With its seven-mile circuit, it's a great place to ride.'

Dan: 'I used to live in the Hampton area of south-west London, just beyond Richmond Park, where the London 2012 Time Trial route will be. The roads around Esher and Cobham are fantastic for cyclists, and you often see big groups training there.'

Kristian: 'My favourite training routes are where I'm originally from: towards Canterbury in Kent via the North Downs. Those are still my training

Dan Lloyd

routes when I'm home visiting my family. There are some really beautiful roads that you can ride to or from London, or get to by train with your bike.'

Gadgets, gear and gizmos

Dan: 'I know they're one of my team sponsors, but a Garmin bike computer is very useful. The ones with GPS mapping are really helpful for pro racing, as you can see what's coming up next in terms of where the wind's coming from. For a sportive or a training ride, you can see when a climb is going to end, and what's coming up next – so it can be a really useful tool for training too.'

Kristian: 'For me, the vital pieces of kit for people starting out are gloves, glasses and a helmet. As you go further afield, having the right clothing becomes essential. Getting caught out in the wrong weather in the wrong clothes can completely put someone off getting on their bike again.'

Kristian House

Track Cycling

London is in the enviable position of now having not one, but two, purpose-built velodromes. The newest, the state-of-the-art Velodrome in the Olympic Park in Stratford, east London, is ready and waiting for the London 2012 Olympic and Paralympic Games, and British fans are holding their collective breath in the hope of Team GB winning more gold medals to add to its haul from the Beijing 2008 Games.

The other velodrome has also seen Olympic use, at the London 1948 Games. Originally constructed in 1891, the historic outdoor track at Herne Hill Velodrome, in south-east London, is currently where tomorrow's London-based track stars are learning their trade. Herne Hill occupies a special place in riders' hearts, and will continue to do so once the two tracks co-exist. For a while, though, it looked as if it might close, due to its deteriorating state. However, the Save the Velodrome campaign (www.savethevelodrome.com), mounted by local residents and riders, has been successful, and track cyclists are once again enjoying the 450-metre circuit, safe in the knowledge that British Cycling will pay for track resurfacing.

As the place where Reg Harris won silver in the Sprint at London 1948, and where current Olympic gold medallist and Tour de France star Bradley Wiggins first started bike racing, at the age of 12 – not to mention the thousands of others who have ridden, and continue to ride, here – the cycling community felt compelled to save this piece of cycling history, which can now serve to help mould the future of British track racing once again.

Herne Hill Velodrome.

However, Herne Hill still needs all the support it can get to ensure that money is available to develop it further, so that it complements the new London 2012 Velodrome as a place to develop young riders and as a permanent venue for riders on the 'other' side of London.

Getting racing

While the training and racing at Herne Hill is open to all, first-timers are requested to attend a Saturday morning induction session to familiarise themselves with the track and its etiquette. There are sessions for youngsters and other novices, where they can try the banked track on their own standard bikes. Bikes are also available for hire for individual sessions (or even for a whole season), but once the track bug has bitten, it won't be long before a keen rider starts calling upon the friendly advice and knowledge of the track coaches and regulars, and collecting the components to build his or her own personal bike. The simplicity of a single-speed track bike is one of the ingredients of the poetry of track racing.

Numerous coached training sessions are held throughout the week. Most are run by Vélo Club Londres, which is based at, and runs, the velodrome. VCL is always pleased to welcome new members, of any age. In summer, Wednesday nights are race nights, with races for senior riders and several youth categories – all hard-fought, but contested in a spirit of fair play. Those new to the sport may want to watch first, to get an idea of how it works and the rules for the different kinds of races.

The track is also home to the Herne Hill Youth Cycling Club, for riders aged six to 16. The club meets on Saturdays to ride on an off-road course next to the track, with many members graduating to other forms of riding and racing as they get older.

Senior riders get the chance to show what they can do off-road when cyclo-cross races are held during the winter.

Herne Hill Youth Cycling Club
www.hhycc.com.
Herne Hill Velodrome
Burbage Road, SE24 9HE (www.hernehill velodrome.com). Open check the website for sessions and events.
Vélo Club Londres (VCL)
www.vcl.org.uk.

BMX

Stockwell Skate Park.

Bicycle Motocross, to give BMX its full and proper name, has always enjoyed ups and downs in terms of popularity, but becoming a fully fledged Olympic sport at the Beijing 2008 Olympic and Paralympic Games has given it the kind of permanency proponents of the sport have wanted for so long.

Multiple world champion Shanaze Reade has ensured her name stays on the lips of anyone talking about British BMX Racing. She was expected to add Olympic gold to her victory list at Beijing 2008, but crashed in the final. The London 2012 Games give her another chance to shine, with the purpose-built BMX Track where she will be hoping to win that gold medal she craves so badly. Once the Games are over, the BMX Track, as part of the Olympic Park VeloPark, will be open for public use, helping to bring the sport to more youngsters.

for the Peckham BMX club, which was set up by local parents to provide their kids with a safe, local environment in which to have fun. The track has already borne fruit in the shape of Peckham local and future Olympic hopeful Tre Whyte, who is now based in Manchester with British Cycling as part of its Olympic Development Program (ODP).

The excellent 400-metre-long track in Brockwell Park is home to the Brixton BMX Club. Open to all ages, the club meets every Saturday and Sunday morning during summer.

Local races at clubs such as Brixton and Peckham only require you to have a BMX track-ready bike, plus the necessary safety equipment, which includes a full-face helmet and long-sleeve top. Race categories exist across all age groups, subdivided by wheel size: either the traditional 20-inch wheel or the 'cruiser' 24-inch wheel. Races are basically long sprints, lasting around 30 seconds (depending on the length of the track). The added difficulty, of course, is the multiple jumps and berms that need to be negotiated. Those who move on to enter regional or national events will need to have a British Cycling racing licence. More information on licences, and getting into BMX in general, including the location of your nearest club, can be found on the British Cycling website. A local club and its riders will be only too happy to offer help and advice.

BMX may now be an Olympic discipline, but it has lost none of its friendly, encouraging atmosphere, so it's the ideal cycling discipline in which to take your first steps towards competition.

British Cycling
www.britishcycling.org.uk.
Peckham BMX club
www.peckhambmx.co.uk.

Urban sport
In the meantime, BMXing in London has managed to retain its original urban flavour. Outdoor tracks such as Bird in Bush, in Peckham, and Stockwell Skate Park and Brockwell Park, both in Brixton, offer young cyclists the opportunity to improve their skills, meet like-minded riders and even give racing a go.

Bird in Bush, located on the road of the same name in south-east London, is the meeting place

London 2012: Track and Road Cycling

Velodrome.

Anyone lucky enough to obtain what will be one of the hottest tickets of the London 2012 Olympic and Paralympic Games – for the Olympic Track Cycling events, where British medals are a near certainty – will also be able to get up close and personal with the striking new indoor Track Cycling venue, the Velodrome. The venue will host both the Olympic Track Cycling (2-7 August; ten events: five for women, five for men) and the Paralympic Track Cycling (30 August-2 September; 18 events: ten for men, seven for women and one mixed).

Located in the Olympic Park in Stratford, east London, the 6,000-capacity Velodrome was the first London 2012 venue in the Olympic Park to be completed. It was officially opened by Lord Coe in February 2011, and christened by Beijing 2008 gold medal-winning cyclists Sir Chris Hoy and Victoria Pendleton.

Track design

The track was designed by Ron Webb, the pre-eminent track-building guru, who has created some of the world's fastest cycling tracks. The sheer beauty of the building is immediately apparent. The lovely, red cedar panelling on the exterior lends it a Scandinavian, ark-like appearance, while, inside, the track brings on a more aggressive, gladiatorial feel. The amount of light comes as a surprise. Where many velodromes are gloomy, the new London track basks in natural light from the large windows at either end of the building.

The design team asked Sir Chris Hoy for his input when designing the Velodrome, and his suggestions of having the seats stretch all the way around the track, and that the doors should be designed so as to maintain an even temperature inside the hall, have been incorporated. Hoy's most important request, however, according to the track designers, was that an athletes' toilet should be included in the infield. One was duly added.

Both riders and spectators will get a taste of what is to come at the Games when the Velodrome hosts a round of the UCI Track World Cup in February 2012. Tickets are likely to be snapped up for the event, which has in recent years been held at the Manchester Velodrome. Everyone is keen to see how the new track does.

The road ahead

Fans who don't have tickets for the Track Cycling can cheer themselves up with the knowledge that the Road Cycling events are free to watch – along with a handful of other London 2012 events, including the Marathon, Race Walk and a section of the Triathlon.

The Time Trial, taking place on 1 August on a course based around Hampton Court Palace in south-west London, will provide opportunities for British cyclists too. Emma Pooley, 2010 Time Trial World Champion, will be a contender in the women's event, while Alex Dowsett, the young time-trialling star, will have notched up a couple of seasons as a pro, and will be a medal hope in the men's event.

The Road Race, starting and finishing on the Mall in central London, will be a much more open affair, though Team GB has strength here too. On 28 July, all eyes will be on Mark Cavendish, hoping that the sprinter can bring home gold. Lizzie Armitstead, silver medallist in the Road Race at the 2010 Commonwealth Games, will be the one to watch in the women's race, held the next day.

Central London Essentials

For urban explorers

They're not necessarily pretty, but they're the routes you need to know if you tackle central London on a regular basis. From clever cut throughs to the most useful bike lanes, this is your commuting cheat sheet.

Central London Essentials

Believe it or not, central London can be a great place to ride. Traffic is usually slow-moving, cycle infrastructure is improving and you usually have a choice of routes, through streets that are never dull. The main problem is knowing where you're going. Master our key arterial routes and you'll soon throw your Oyster card away.

The quickest routes between major destinations are usually main roads. To the cyclist, these provide the advantages of easy navigation, clear priority at junctions and generally alert road users. To ride comfortably on these thoroughfares, you need to be a confident and decisive rider. It helps if you know where you're going, because getting in the appropriate lane early reduces conflict with other traffic.

On smaller streets, there are more hazards; people are less careful, and which road user goes first and which one waits is often less obvious. On the other hand, you usually have more time to assess situations and communicate with others than on roads with faster traffic. In short, smaller roads have more potential for danger and conflict with other road users, but the hazards you face on big roads are potentially more deadly.

If you're comfortable on a bike and know how to share space with others, you can be safe on any road. If your riding skills, understanding of the rules of traffic or confidence are deficient, you won't be safe anywhere.

Route selection is less to do with safety, than your mood and the purpose of your journey. The ten routes mapped on pages 230-234 show useful links across central London that, where possible, avoid the most complex junctions. They're not the only routes, and

we certainly don't claim that they are the best for every rider and every occasion – but they do work. Note the short one-way section in the Argyle Square area close to King's Cross.

The routes are the same in each direction, apart from three exceptions.

Routes ❷/❷
Route 2 (Waterloo to King's Cross) runs north through Covent Garden on Drury Lane. The ride in reverse (Route 2a) goes south via Lincoln's Inn Fields. The latter has two sections where you have to walk: Great Turnstile, south of High Holborn, and Grange Court, which connects Lincoln's Inn to Aldwych near the London School of Economics.

Routes ❹/❹
The routes between Hyde Park and King's Cross, through Marylebone, Fitzrovia and Bloomsbury, also needs separate eastbound and westbound routes. However, you don't need to walk any sections.

Routes ❺/❺
The routes between Hyde Park and Liverpool Street take different lines through Soho and Mayfair. Most of the narrow streets of Soho are one-way, and pedestrian traffic dominates the area. Route 5 (riding east) involves a very short stretch on Wardour Street against the one-way traffic, where walking is the only legal way to get through. The link east from Soho Square to St Giles is currently blocked for building work on Crossrail. When it reopens, it may provide a more direct line without going south on Greek Street. On Route 5a (heading west), you may need to walk near Carnaby Street.

The Routes

❶ Waterloo – Hyde Park
Belvedere Road; Westminster Bridge; Bridge Street; Parliament Square; Great George Street; Birdcage Walk; Constitution Hill; Hyde Park Corner; Hyde Park
Works in reverse

❷ Waterloo – King's Cross
Waterloo Bridge; Aldwych; Drury Lane; Museum Street; Great Russell Street; Montague Street; Russell Square; Bernard Street; Brunswick Square; Hunter Street; Judd Street; Cromer Street; Whidborne Street; Argyle Street

⓴ King's Cross – Waterloo
Belgrove Street; Argyle Square; Argyle Street; Whidborne Street; Cromer Street; Judd Street; Hunter Street; Brunswick Square; Lansdowne Terrace; Lamb's Conduit Street; Red Lion Street; High Holborn; Great Turnstile; Lincoln's Inn Fields; Serle Street; Carey Street; Grange Court; Houghton Street; Aldwych; Strand; Waterloo Bridge

❸ Liverpool Street – Waterloo
Old Broad Street; Threadneedle Street; Victoria Street; Queen Street; Southwark Bridge; Bridge Road; Southwark Street; Stamford Street; Broadwall; Upper Ground; Sutton Walk
Works in reverse

❹ Hyde Park – King's Cross
Stanhope Place; Seymour Street; Wigmore Street; Cavendish Square; Cavendish Place; Mortimer Street; Goodge Street; Tottenham Court Road; Chenies Street; Ridgmount Street; Store Street; Keppel Street; Malet Street; Montague Place; Russell Square; Bernard Street; Brunswick Square; Hunter Street; Judd Street; Cromer Street; Whidborne Street; Argyle Street

⓬ King's Cross – Hyde Park
Belgrove Street; Argyle Square; Argyle Street; Whidborne Street; Cromer Street; Judd Street; Leigh Street; Marchmont Street; Tavistock Place; Tavistock Square; Gordon Square; Byng Place; Torrington Place; Tottenham Court Road; Howland Street; New Cavendish Street; Marylebone High Street; George Street; Portsea Place; Connaught Square; Stanhope Place

❺ Hyde Park – Liverpool Street
Upper Brook Street; Grosvenor Square; Brook Street; Hanover Street; Regent Street; Great Marlborough Street; Noel Street; Berwick Street; Wardour Street; Sheraton Street; Carlisle Street; Soho Square; Greek Street; Shaftesbury Avenue; New Oxford Street; Bloomsbury Way; Theobald's Road; Red Lion Street; High Holborn; Holborn Viaduct; Newgate Street; King Edward Street; Aldersgate Street; Cheapside; Poultry; Threadneedle Street; Old Broad Street

⓭ Liverpool Street – Hyde Park
Old Broad Street; Threadneedle Street; Poultry; Cheapside; Newgate Street; Holborn Viaduct; High Holborn; Shaftesbury Avenue; Wardour Street; Broadwick Street; Marshall Street; Ganton Street; Carnaby Street; Great Marlborough Street; Maddox Street; Grosvenor Street; Grosvenor Square; Upper Grosvenor Street; Park Lane

❻ King's Cross – Liverpool Street
Belgrove Street; Argyle Square; Argyle Street; Whidborne Street; Cromer Street; Judd Street; Hunter Street; Brunswick Square; Lansdowne Terrace; Lamb's Conduit Street; Red Lion Street; High Holborn; Holborn Viaduct; Newgate Street; King Edward Street; Aldersgate Street; Cheapside; Poultry; Threadneedle Street; Old Broad Street
Works in reverse

**❼ Spur to London Bridge
(connects with Route 3)**
Liverpool Street; Bishopsgate; Gracechurch Street; King William Street; London Bridge

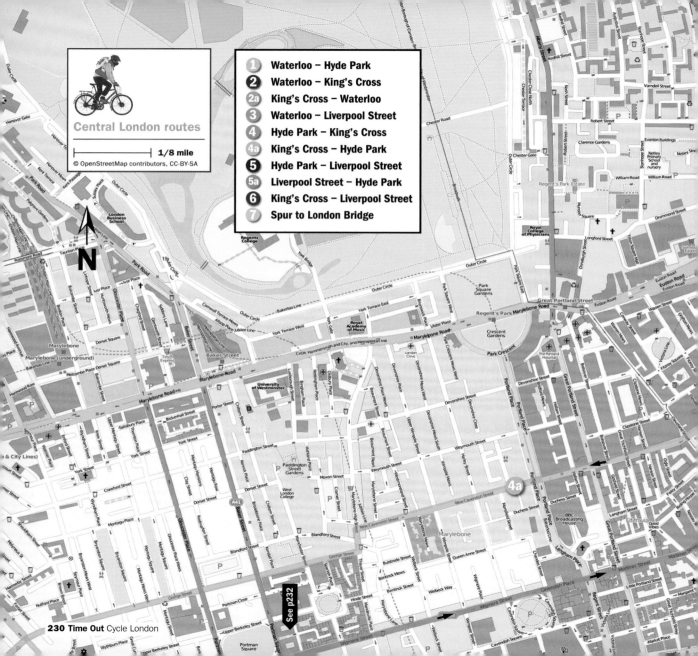

Central London routes

|—————————————| 1/8 mile

© OpenStreetMap contributors, CC-BY-SA

N

1 Waterloo – Hyde Park
2 Waterloo – King's Cross
2a King's Cross – Waterloo
3 Waterloo – Liverpool Street
4 Hyde Park – King's Cross
4a King's Cross – Hyde Park
5 Hyde Park – Liverpool Street
5a Liverpool Street – Hyde Park
6 King's Cross – Liverpool Street
7 Spur to London Bridge

See p232

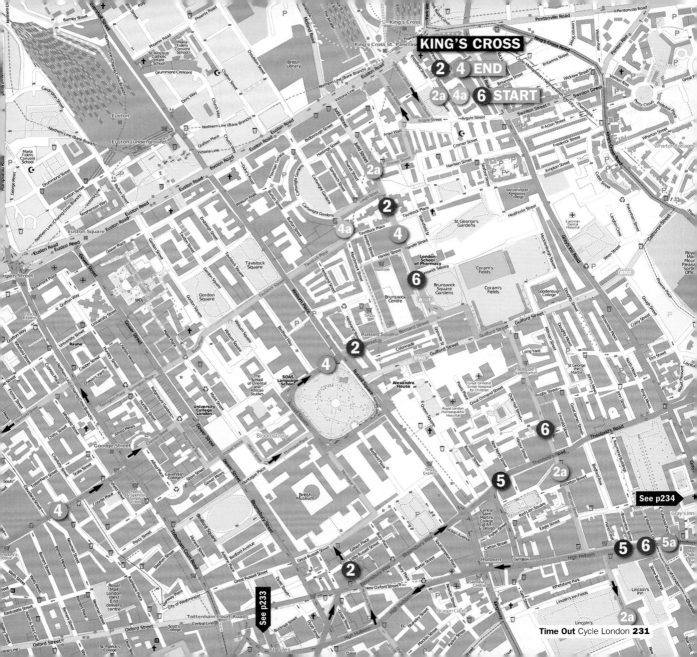

KING'S CROSS

2 4 END

2a 4a 6 START

See p234

See p233

See p232

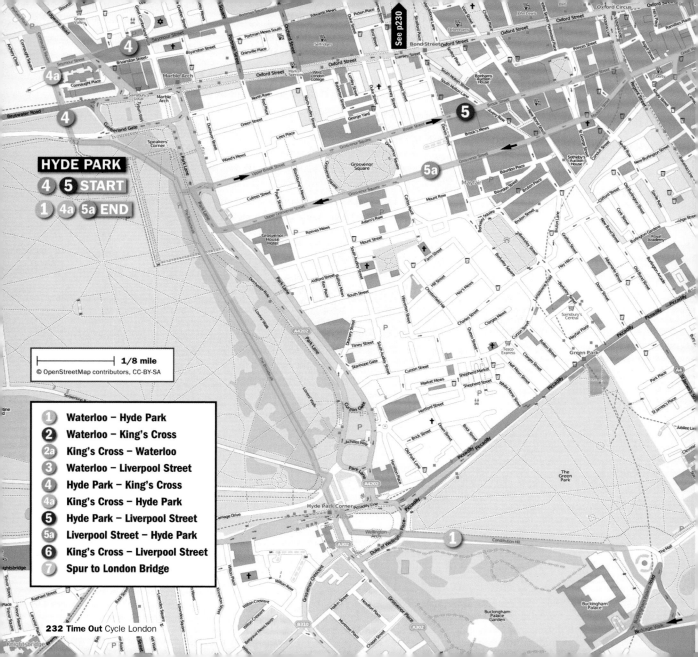

See p230

HYDE PARK

4 5 START

1 4a 5a END

1/8 mile

© OpenStreetMap contributors, CC-BY-SA

1 Waterloo – Hyde Park
2 Waterloo – King's Cross
2a King's Cross – Waterloo
3 Waterloo – Liverpool Street
4 Hyde Park – King's Cross
4a King's Cross – Hyde Park
5 Hyde Park – Liverpool Street
5a Liverpool Street – Hyde Park
6 King's Cross – Liverpool Street
7 Spur to London Bridge

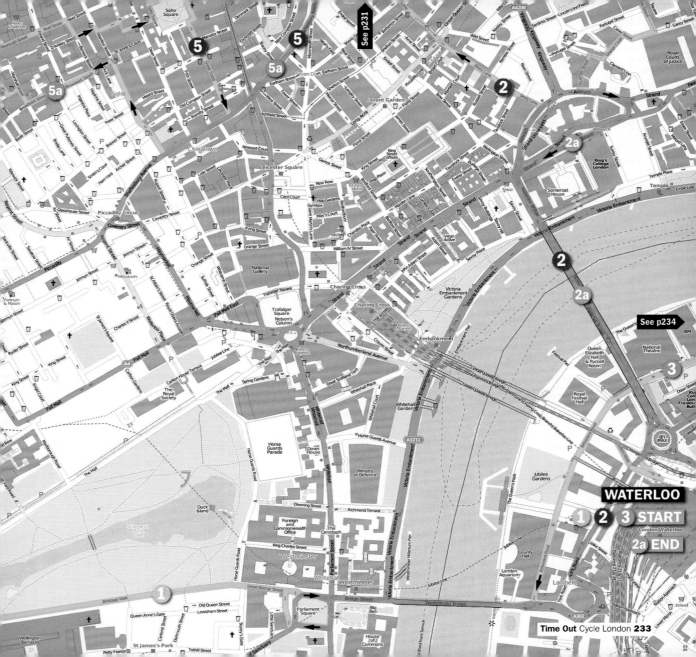

See p231

See p234

WATERLOO

1 2 3 **START**

London Waterloo

2a **END**

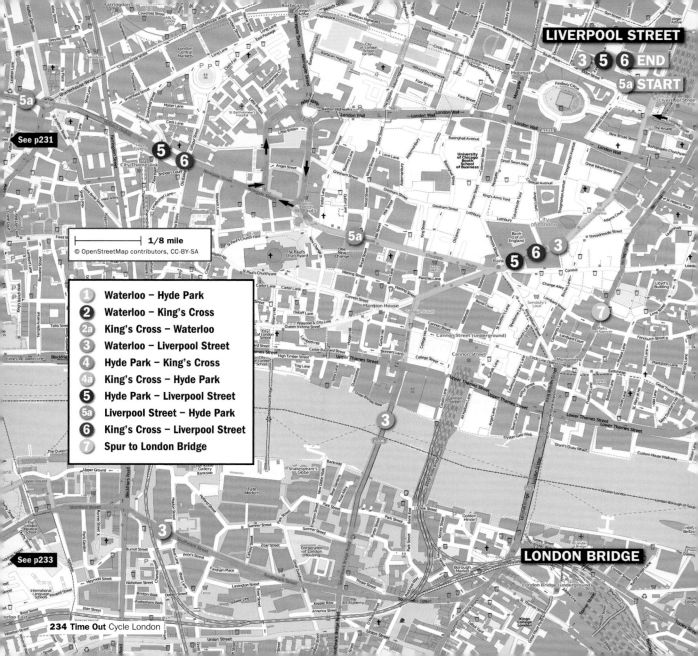

3 5 6 **END**
5a **START**

See p231

1/8 mile
© OpenStreetMap contributors, CC-BY-SA

5a

1 Waterloo – Hyde Park
2 Waterloo – King's Cross
2a King's Cross – Waterloo
3 Waterloo – Liverpool Street
4 Hyde Park – King's Cross
4a King's Cross – Hyde Park
5 Hyde Park – Liverpool Street
5a Liverpool Street – Hyde Park
6 King's Cross – Liverpool Street
7 Spur to London Bridge

See p233

LONDON BRIDGE

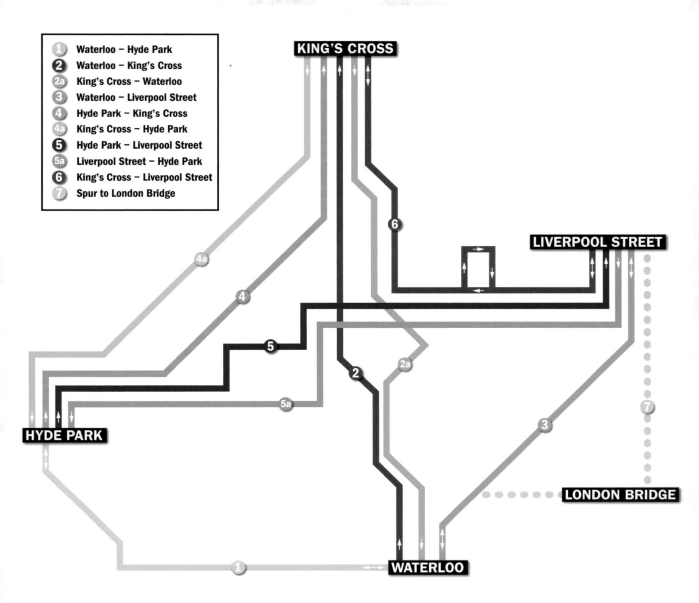

1 Waterloo – Hyde Park
2 Waterloo – King's Cross
2a King's Cross – Waterloo
3 Waterloo – Liverpool Street
4 Hyde Park – King's Cross
4a King's Cross – Hyde Park
5 Hyde Park – Liverpool Street
5a Liverpool Street – Hyde Park
6 King's Cross – Liverpool Street
7 Spur to London Bridge

KING'S CROSS

LIVERPOOL STREET

HYDE PARK

LONDON BRIDGE

WATERLOO

What Bike?

If you've decided to take the plunge and cycle part of (or even all) the way to work, welcome to the fold: you're a bike commuter now.

The daily slog into the workplace is not the place for your carbon fibre-framed pride and joy. You need a workhorse. Simplicity and efficiency are essential: through sheer frequency of use, this bike is going to take one hell of a beating.

Single-speed and fixed-wheel bikes

Learn a lesson from bike couriers, as well as (to the couriers' disgust), fashion-conscious Shoreditch types, by choosing a 'fixie'. Fixed-wheel bikes have just one gear, and no freewheel; your pedalling action is transmitted directly to the back wheel with no need for the usual derailleur gearing system. If you pedal faster, the bike speeds up; if you slow down or stop, so does the bike – meaning adepts can do without a back brake. Once you've mastered the riding technique, the control you have will amaze and delight, and you'll soon be singing the fixie's praises, you dedicated follower of fashion, you. But it's the lack of gears, and therefore moving parts, that is the real draw. Less to go wrong means less to maintain.

A fixed-wheel bicycle may not be to everyone's tastes – there is an art to riding it that needs perfecting for it to be safe – so perhaps a single-speed bike would be a better choice. This is basically a fixie with a freewheel. You need to ensure you have a separate back brake if you plump for this latter option, though – and both versions need a working front brake too.

Best brands: the Specialized Langster (£500) is well worth a look, and has a 'flip-flop' back wheel, so that you can choose between single-speed or fixed. Trek's 4th District (drop bars) and 5th District (flat bars) also give you the 'flip-flop' option and cost a similar price.

Expect to pay: a decent, ready-made fixed or single-speed bike will set you back around £300-£400. Prices vary greatly, depending mainly on the choice of frame material or wheel specification.

Folding bikes

Folding bikes are a viable option if you commute in part by train, tube or bus, as they're allowed on all forms of public transport at all times of the day. Non-folding bikes are permitted on trains and some tubes, but at restricted hours. Make sure the model you buy is light enough to carry up (and down) any steps you might encounter. Around the 15kg mark should be just about comfortable.

Best brands: British brand Brompton and US manufacturer Dahon are excellent, and have been making folding bikes for decades. Brompton still makes all its bikes in its west London factory near Kew Bridge. Newcomer Kansi, another British brand, is also worth investigating.

Expect to pay: the relationship between price and weight is inversely proportional: the more you pay, the less the bike weighs. Dahon's Mu Uno and Kansi's 1twenty are both light, no-nonsense, single-speed folders, priced around £500-£530. Brompton's classic model, the three-speed M3L, costs around £800.

Kit Bag

For the urban commuter cyclist, there are plenty of accessories that are designed to make life on the road safer and that little bit more pleasant.

Lighting-up time
Lights are essential at the best of times, but if you're going to be a regular bike commuter, then invest in at least a couple of sets of decent lights for those dark early morning starts and miserable midwinter evening slogs home. Names to look out for are Knog, Blackburn and Cateye; it's a false economy to buy a blinking mini-set in the pound shop, although a few of those dotted around your bike and on your person in addition to your main rig will only help. The more lights you have, both for visibility and back-up, the better, in case of flat batteries or pothole-ejected lights. Your main front light should be a full-beam, not an LED.

Bag it up
A commute normally means carrying a bag, and while a standard backpack fits the bill, courier culture has influenced many riders to plump for a messenger bag – a large, single-strapped bag slung crosswise across the back. For couriers, these give quick and easy access to the parcels within; for the rest of us, they distribute the load better than a backpack, especially if you're riding drop bars. Oh, and they look good. Timbuktu's are reliable and ubiquitous; women like the smaller Rickshaw version, from www.minx-girl.com.

Alternatively, get a pannier (or two), attached to a rear or front rack. Long considered the domain of old-fashioned touring cyclists, today's panniers offer a stylish and practical way to transport your stuff (whether a laptop, a change of clothes, bike tools or a 200-page document), letting your bike shoulder the load instead of you.

Modern pannier bags are hard-wearing and water-resistant, with snap-on clips to make it easy to take them on or off. Look for makers Agu and Blackburn, or Dutch company Basil, which does a vast range of colourful and stylish models that are particularly popular with women. English favourite Brooks, established in 1866 and revered for its leather saddles, also produces beautifully crafted saddle and bar bags, and modern takes on rucksacks and courier bags – all in leather.

Lose that skunk stripe
Using a bike as your main form of transport in London has its downsides – the main one being the weather. So how can you ensure that you get to your destination as fresh as your non-cycling work colleagues? A changing room and a shower work wonders, but in wet weather a set of mudguards will help keep the worst of the road muck off your suit (and your bike's moving parts).

Today's usually plastic mudguards have evolved from the mountain bike scene, and now border on being a cool accessory. The big name here is British brand Crud, which makes a range of different shapes and sizes for different types of bikes, and rather than ruin the look of your bike, these mudguards actually go some way towards enhancing it. Cool and dry – what's not to like?

The Word from the Streets

Seb Cherchi-Bersch

Seb Cherchi-Bersch founded bicycle courier company BycaBoy (www.bycaboy.com) in 2007, and he still gets out daily to pound the streets of London. Seb used to work in senior management at a small business, but resigned in an effort to live the dream: to get paid to ride his bike.

'Becoming a bike courier fulfilled that dream,' he says, 'and it's been everything I'd expected and hoped for, and more. But things have changed a lot in the five years since I started as a bike courier. It's been an amalgamation of things. With budgets generally being cut across the

board in businesses, things like the use of courier companies tend to be one of the first things to go. A big part of it too has been the fact that, increasingly, people can transfer large files safely and securely across the internet. That's made a huge difference.'

Courier café culture

'When I started, there used to be much more of a bike courier community; it was a real lifestyle choice,' Cherchi-Bersch says. 'There was all the illegal racing and the courier drinking holes; people would ride 90 miles during the working day, and then think nothing of riding down to Brighton after work, having a drink, and then riding home again.'

These days, you're as likely to find London's bike couriers hanging out together on the web – at places like www.movingtargetzine.com – as you are at the capital's cafés and pubs.

Those hangouts still exist, though, and notable among them is Fullcity in Clerkenwell. Ostensibly a bike shop, it quickly became a favourite for bike couriers after opening in 2009, serving also as a coffee shop and meeting place as couriers wait between jobs. The workshop is always ready to help couriers and non-couriers alike with repairs, spares and advice galore.

Other, more traditional bike shops include the world-famous Condor Cycles (www.condorcycles.com), which Cherchi-Bersch praises for having helped him out of a mechanical jam on more than one occasion. Brick Lane Bikes (www.bricklane bikes.co.uk) is an essential go-to shop for all your courier, single-speed and fixed-gear needs – technically, it's on Bethnal Green Road rather than Brick Lane itself, although only just.

A dangerous job

For all the freedom, bike-tech geekiness and black-cab-knowledge-rivalling fun that comes with working as a bike courier, it's worth keeping the dangerous aspect of the job at the front of your mind at all times. 'It is a dangerous profession,'

says Cherchi-Bersch. 'But if you look at the number of people working in the industry, and then consider how many serious accidents there are, it's, luckily, relatively low.

'You're out from 8am until 8pm, and from the moment I leave home to the moment I get back inside my front door, I think that people are out to get me. But it's a career choice, and out on the streets, just like in all walks of life, you have good and bad road users. The bus drivers and taxi drivers – the people who work on the road every day – are quite tolerant and careful, despite what some cyclists might think. I rarely have problems with them. It's the other, less regular drivers in central London who are the worst.

'The biggest danger of all, though, is pedestrians. They're just kamikaze. They're oblivious to road users. I've seen them create the most unbelievable accidents due to cars swerving and then hitting other cars… I've seen situations that simply look like war scenes.

'But when it comes to riding, a lot of it is down to common sense. I do ride aggressively – I'm very assertive in my manoeuvres. But I will signal my intentions every single time, using the good old-fashioned Highway Code signals. I think bike couriers have a pretty good track record: there are relatively few injuries or deaths. But you can't be too careful when cycling in a big city like London.'

Fullcity
72 Leather Lane, EC1N 7TR (7831 7081). Open 8am-7pm Mon-Fri.

Nuts and Bolts

The essential information toolkit for London cyclists: recommended bike shops, mechanics, events and contacts, and advice on security, bike buying, cycle routes, transport and more

Nuts & Bolts

BIKE-BUYING

Where to buy

Generally, bikes are slightly cheaper online than in shops, but there are many advantages in going to a good retailer. One, you'll be founding a relationship that should last for years, through upgrades and services and on the local bike scene. Two, you'll benefit from the staff's expertise. Three, perhaps most crucially, you'll get to try the bike for size and maybe give it a test-ride. And four, you should get a free service to re-tune the bike once the cables have settled in. Manufacturers release bicycle collections annually; unless you really care about sporting the latest model, take advantage of summer sales to buy end-of-lines cheaply.

Sizing & fit

Bike geometry is complicated and frame size standards vary. There are all sorts of equations out there purporting to deliver the ideal fit. However, our best advice is to visit one of our recommended bike shops or another trusted retailer, where the staff should have plenty of sizing experience and use their knowledge to help select the size that's right for you (what might seem comfortable while you're perched atop the saddle on the shop floor for five minutes may be agony after an hour on the road). Your bike dealer will also be able to help you set the saddle to the right height – at a position that is no lower than the handlebar and allows you to retain just a little flex at the bottom of the pedal stroke.

Consider the reach – or 'stretch' – of your bike: how easily can you reach the handlebar, and is your neck comfortable as you look forward? Your weight should be roughly evenly distributed between your hands on the bars and your backside on the saddle. Moving the saddle forwards or backwards and changing the length of the handlebar stem (women, whose legs are longer relative to their torsos, often need a shorter one) should lead to you finding the optimum position.

For cycle fitting services, see p252.

Gears

Single-speed and fixed-wheel bikes certainly look cool. However, if the type of riding you want to do or the area in which you live involves a lot of hills, then you should probably go geared. Derailleur gears are standard, and work beautifully when properly adjusted. But it's also worth considering hub gears if you're an everyday commuter: enclosed within the rear hub, they're lighter in both weight and action than before, and they're extremely reliable, maintenance-light and long-lasting.

You'll hear the word 'groupset' bandied about. The word refers to different gearing and brake systems; especially when, as is common, they're specced to each bike as a complete package. Some manufacturers issue the same model at a variety of different price points: these are largely determined by the groupsets (as well as by other key variables, such as the quality of the wheels). Anything by Shimano should be reliable (our only gripe being the impenetrability of its instructions), but Campagnolo and SRAM also have their fans.

Materials

When buying a new bike – or, for that matter, a used one – a key decision will revolve around the material used for the frame. The decision isn't as simple as it first appears, as all the different materials have their plus points and negatives.

Steel has been making a comeback of late, thanks to a great price-to-durability ratio and a general trend towards retro materials; on the downside, steel frames are the heaviest of the bunch, although this is mitigated if high-quality tubing is used. Aluminium is lighter, more common and less classically attractive since the tubing needs to be thicker, while carbon-fibre frames are built for speed but not necessarily for durability or carrying loads. Finally, there's titanium: light, strong, efficient, comfortable… and very expensive.

Buying second-hand

Second-hand bikes are widely available through websites such as eBay and a few shops, such as Lock 7 (*see p246*). Check the seller's history to avoid as far as possible purchasing a stolen bike.

Just like kicking the tyres on a new car, people will often look at a bicycle's tyres as a measure of its roadworthiness. But the truth, more often than not, is that people will be selling their bike because they don't use it any more: the wheels may be punctured, the cables frayed or broken, and the gears and brakes out of adjustment. All are quickly, easily and fairly cheaply resolved – and it's easy enough to buy a new pair of tyres.

Instead, check for play in the bottom bracket and headset – although these are both relatively easily remedied, too, if a bit more costly – and pay particular attention to the frame, checking closely for any cracks, dents or sections that are about to rust away.

As they are more expensive to replace than to other parts, concentrate on the wheels, and gear and brake systems, looking for obvious damage and signs of terminal wear such as worn-down cog teeth.

BICYCLE SHOPS

We can personally recommend this selection of bike shops, but we don't claim it to be exhaustive. Ask around for local recommendations if your area isn't covered. Where noted, shops have a workshop.

Cycle cafés sometimes sell bikes and accessories, and most of them have a workshop. *See p248.*

Bicycle Magic

6 Greatorex Street, E1 5NF (7375 2993, www.bicyclemagic.com). Open 9am-6pm Mon-Wed, Fri; 9am-6.30pm Thur; 10am-5pm Sat.
A good general store close to Aldgate East tube. Bikes include the great-value Planet X range. Workshop.

Bikefix

48 Lamb's Conduit Street, WC1N 3LJ (7405 1218, www.bikefix.co.uk). Open 8.30am-7pm Mon-Fri; 10am-5pm Sat.
This friendly and long-established shop puts an emphasis on bikes that are built more for comfort than speed, and also has an excellent workshop.

Bobbin Bicycles

397 St John Street, EC1V 4LD (7837 3370, www.bobbinbicycles.co.uk). Open 11am-7pm Tue-Fri; 11am-6pm Sat; noon-5pm Sun.
Gloriously, self-consciously old-school bikes and accessories, which include floral panniers and helmets in the shape of bowler hats. No workshop.

Bon Vélo

27 Half Moon Lane, SE24 9JU (7733 9453, www.bonvelo.co.uk). Open 8am-6pm Mon, Tue; 9am-6pm Wed-Fri; 10am-6pm Sat.
A new bike shop in Herne Hill, offering a carefully chosen selection of bikes and accessories alongside a full workshop.

Brick Lane Bikes

118 Bethnal Green Road, E2 6DG (7033 9053, http://bricklanebikes. co.uk). Open 9am-7pm Mon-Fri; 11am-6pm Sat; 11am-5pm Sun.
Fixed-wheel central, Brick Lane Bikes offers everything a hipster rider could possibly desire. Including, if you ask nicely, brakes. Workshop.

Brixton Cycles

145 Stockwell Road, SW9 9TN (7733 6055, www.brixtoncycles.co.uk). Open 9am-6pm Mon-Wed, Fri, Sat; 10am-7pm Thur.
Nearing 30 years in business, this terrific co-op offers everything from commuter-staple cycles to comparatively rare Surly machines and all manner of accessories. Workshop.

Cloud 9 Cycles

The Arches, 17 Castlehaven Road, NW1 8RA (8090 9560, www.cloud9cycles.com). Open 11am-7pm daily.
New and used bikes, including custom builds, plus a workshop.

Condor Cycles

49-53 Gray's Inn Road, WC1X 8PP (7269 6820, www.condorcycles.com). Open 9am-6pm Mon, Tue, Thur, Fri; 9am-7.30pm Wed; 10am-5pm Sat.
Now into its seventh decade, Condor remains among the leaders of the London pack, offering its own highly desirable bikes alongside a stellar range of clothing and accessories. Great service too. Workshop.

Cycle Surgery

Strype Street, E1 7LQ (7375 3088, www.cyclesurgery.com). Open 8am-7pm Mon-Fri; 9am-6pm Sat; 11am-5pm Sun.
The increasingly ubiquitous Cycle Surgery chain offers a solid but not altogether exciting range of bikes, clothes and accessories. There are workshops at all branches, but services offered vary.
Other locations: throughout the city.

Cyclopedia

262 Kensington High Street, W8 6ND (7603 7626, www.cyclopediauk. com). Open 8am-7pm Mon-Fri; 9am-6pm Sat; 11am-5pm Sun.
Bikes of all types, and helpful service. Workshop.
Other location: 256 Fulham Road, SW10 9EL (7351 5776, www. cyclopediauk.com). Open 8am-7pm Mon-Fri; 9am-6pm Sat; 11am-5pm Sun.

Cyclopolis

54 Balham High Road, SW12 9AQ (8673 7153, www.cyclopolis.co.uk). Open 8am-8pm Mon-Fri; 9am-6pm Sat; 10am-5pm Sun.
A fine little local bike shop down in Balham, with a workshop.

Decathlon

Canada Water Retail Park, Surrey Quays Road, SE16 2XU (7394 2000, www.decathlon.co.uk). Open 9am-9pm Mon-Fri; 9am-7pm Sat; 10.30am-5pm Sun.
The French sports multiple offers a good range of reasonably priced bikes, accessories and kit of decent quality.

Edwardes

221-225 Camberwell Road, SE5 0HG (020 3330 4121, www.edwardes camberwelllondon.co.uk). Open 8am-6pm Mon-Sat.
Edwardes looks a little like a pile-it-high merchant from the outside, but the range of bikes and the service make it worth the trip. Workshop.

Evans Cycles

62 Mortimer Street, W1W 7RR (7637 1940, www.evanscycles.com). Open 8am-9pm Mon-Fri; 9am-6pm Sat; 10am-6pm Sun.
This ubiquitous all-rounder has come on a lot in recent years, not least in its much-improved service. Some stores have workshops.
Other locations: throughout the city.

50cycles Electric Bikes

82 Hill Rise, Richmond, Surrey, TW10 6UB (0333 900 5050, www. 50cycles.com). Open 9.30am-5pm Mon-Fri; 10am-5.30pm Sat.
Standard and folding electric bicycles and accessories.

Fitzrovia Bicycles

136-138 New Cavendish Street, W1W 6YD (7631 5060, www.fitzrovia bicycles.com). Open 8am-7pm Mon-Fri; 11am-6pm Sat.
The former Cavendish Cycles remains a good all-rounder, whether you're in the market for a new bike or just a back light. Workshop.

Foffa Bikes

Unit 11, Pinchin Street, E1 1SA (7481 2516, http://foffabikes.co.uk). Open 11am-7pm Tue-Fri; 11am-6pm Sat, Sun.
A newish East End enterprise, Foffa

specialises in fixed-wheel and single-speed machines, including its own-brand bikes. Workshop.

Kiwi Cycles
152 Victoria Park Road, E9 7JN (8525 5944, www.kiwicycles.com). Open 9am-7pm Tue-Fri; 10am-4pm Sat, Sun.
Single-speed, fixed-gear and racing bike shop located hard by Victoria Park, specialising in full builds, restorations and repairs. Workshop.

London Fields Cycles
281 Mare Street, E8 1PJ (8525 0077, www.londonfieldscycles.co.uk). Open 8am-6pm Mon-Fri; 10am-6pm Sat; 11am-5pm Sun.
This neighbourhood fixture offers a comprehensive selection of mainstream bikes and accessories, plus a popular (read: book ahead) workshop.

London Recumbents
Ranger's Yard, Dulwich Park, SE21 7BQ (8299 6636, www.londonrecumbents.com). Open 10am-5pm daily.
The clue's in the name. Workshop.

Mosquito Bikes
123 Essex Road, N1 2SN (7226 8765, www.mosquito-bikes.co.uk). Open 9am-6pm Mon-Wed, Fri; 9am-7pm Thur; 10am-6pm Sat.
A longtime Islington favourite, Mosquito offers accessories, clothes and a drop-dead gorgeous range of bikes (it's a stockist for cult US firm Independent Fabrications, for instance). Workshop.

On Your Bike
52-54 Tooley Street, SE1 2SZ (7378 6669, www.onyourbike.com). Open 7.30am-7.30pm Mon-Fri; 10am-6pm Sat; 11am-5pm Sun.
This large store by London Bridge station offers a solid, all-round selection of bikes and gear, plus a reliable and reliably popular workshop.

Push Cycles
35C Newington Green, N16 9PR (7249 1351, www.pushcycles.com). Open 8am-6pm Mon-Fri; 9am-5.30pm Sat.
One of our favourite new bike stores, Push delivers a small but nicely chosen range of bikes (including Mercians), along with accessories and a downstairs workshop.

Retrospective Cycles
1C Park Ridings, N8 0LB (8888 5424, www.retrospectivecycles.com). Open 9am-6pm Mon-Fri; 9am-1pm Sat.
Imported vintage European road bikes together with unrefurbished pieces for restoration projects.

Route Canale Cycles
Regent's Canal towpath, between Whitmore Bridge & Kingsland Road Bridge, N1 5SB (http://routecanalebicycles.wordpress.com). Open 9am-6pm Tue-Fri; 10am-5pm Sat, Sun.
Hard-to-find bike parts and accessories. Workshop.

Sargent & Co
74 Mountgrove Road, N5 2LT (7359 7642, www.sargentandco.com). Open 10.30am-6.30pm Wed-Sat.
Classic steel frames and bikes lovingly restored with or without gears behind an equally classic and lovingly restored shopfront. There's a bike valet service and workshop.

Spencer Ivy
15 Pennyfields, E14 8HP (020 3021 3388, www.spenceriyy.com). Open 10am-6pm Mon-Fri.
Beautiful, own-make, electrically assisted bikes with a vintage feel.

Southbank Cycles
194 Wandsworth Road, SW8 2JU (7622 3069, www.southbankcycles.com). Open 9am-6pm Mon-Sat.
Friendly can-do local bike shop with workshop.

Stratton Cycles
101 East Hill, SW18 2QB (8874 1381, www.strattoncycles.com). Open 9am-6pm Mon, Wed, Thur, Sat; 8am-7pm Tue, Fri.
Exemplary local do-it-all bike shop, with bend-over-backwards service. Workshop.

Two Wheels Good
143 Crouch Hill, N8 9QH (8340 4284, www.twowheelsgood.co.uk). Open 8.30am-6pm Mon-Fri; 9am-6pm Sat; 11am-5pm Sun.
A brace of friendly and knowledgeable shops/workshops.
Other location: 165 Newington Church Street, N16 0UL (7249 2220,

www.twowheelsgood.co.uk). Open 8.30am-6pm Mon-Fri; 9am-6pm Sat.

Velorution
14-18 Great Titchfield Street, W1W 8BD (7637 4004, www.velorution.biz). Open 8.30am-6.45pm Mon-Fri; 10.30am-6.30pm Sat.
Town bikes, work bikes, family bikes and folders, along with some lovely accessories. Workshop.

BICYCLE SHOPS (ONLINE)

Accessories only
www.cyclechic.co.uk
www.probikekit.com
www.zyro.co.uk

Bikes & general
www.bikegoo.co.uk
www.cyclestore.co.uk
www.cyclesuk.com
www.cycleworld.co.uk
www.edinburghbicycles.com
www.fisheroutdoor.co.uk
www.jejamescycles.co.uk
www.merlincycles.co.uk
www.ridelow.co.uk
www.rutlandcycling.com
www.tredz.co.uk
www.ukbikestore.co.uk
www.wheelbase.co.uk

www.wiggle.co.uk

Books, posters & artwork
www.cycling-books.com
www.dynamoworks.co.uk
www.excellentbooks.co.uk
www.frankpatterson.co.uk
www.philipdeacon.co.uk

Clothing
www.alwaysriding.co.uk
www.gearforgirls.co.uk
www.hellojoe.co.uk
www.minx-girl.co.uk
www.velodog.cc

Gifts & cards
http://shop.cafepress.co.uk/cycling
www.cyclegifts.co.uk
www.cyclinggifts.co.uk
www.retrobicycles.co.uk
www.wheelygoodcards.co.uk

Specialist bikes & unusual accessories
www.cyclingmadeeasy.co.uk
www.theoldbicycleshowroom.co.uk
www.tartybikes.co.uk
www.tokyofixedgear.com

CYCLE CAFES
The beauty of cycle cafés is that you can often get small repairs attended to while you avail yourself of coffee, flapjack, cycle chat and free Wi-Fi.

Container Café
View Tube, The Greenway, E15 2PJ (07834 275687, www.theviewtube.co.uk/visit/eat). Open 9am-5pm Mon-Fri; 10am-6pm Sat, Sun.
Scrummy food in the View Tube on the perimeter of the Olympic Park; it's on the Greenway, and cycle hire is available by arrangement from BikeWorks (8983 1221, www.bikeworks.org.uk), at least until spring 2012.

Cyclelab & Juice Bar
18A Pitfield Street, N1 6EY (020 3222 0016, www.cyclelab.co.uk). Open 7.30am-6pm Mon-Wed, Fri; 7.30am-8pm Thur; 10am-4pm Sat.
Funky super-healthy juice bar; funky bikes too plus a workshop.

Fullcity
72 Leather Lane, EC1N 7TR (7831 7081). Open 8am-7pm Mon-Fri.
Courier central, which speaks for their coffee, vibe and servicing skills. Also bike sales.

Lock 7
129 Pritchard's Road, E2 9AP (7739 3042, www.lock-7.com). Open 8am-6pm Wed-Sat; 10am-6pm Sun.
The food is simple but tasty and the coffee well made at this large café by the Regent's Canal, which offers used bikes and a popular workshop service.

Look Mum No Hands!
49 Old Street, EC1V 9HX (7253 1025, www.lookmumnohands.com). Open 7.30am-10pm Mon-Fri; 9am-10pm Sat; 10am-10pm Sun.
This friendly café, strong on cakes, salads and pies, has become a bit of a cycle community clubhouse, hosting events and screening live races. It's licensed (good beers), so a good evening hangout for all.

Micycle
47 Barnsbury Street, N1 1TP (7684 0671, www.micycle.org.uk). Open 10am-5pm Mon-Sat; noon-5pm Sun.
A few cycles (Bianchi and Kona, mostly), a small café and a workshop that, unusually but laudably,

NUTS AND BOLTS

allows members to use the shop's tools to carry out their own repairs for free.

Towpath
Regent's Canal towpath, between Whitmore Bridge & Kingsland Road Bridge, N1 5SB (no phone). Open 8am-dusk Tue-Sun. Closed Nov-March.
Kick back with a some fine Italian-influenced snacks and a coffee while you get your bike fixed at Route Canale (*see p245*) next door. Strung along the towpath, it's great for people- and bicycle-watching, especially with a glass of wine on a summer evening. Pictured on this book's cover.

CYCLING CLUBS
Addiscombe Cycling Club
www.addiscombe.org.
South London and Surrey rides for all abilities.
Central London Cyclists' Touring Club
www.centrallondonctc. org.uk.
All-day cycle rides for all abilities every Sunday.
Cycling Club Hackney
www.cyclingclubhackney. co.uk.

Weekly club rides and an active youth division.
Greenwich Cyclists
www.greenwichcyclists. org.uk.
Casual weekly cycle rides catering for all abilities.
London Dynamo
www.londondynamo.co.uk.
Weekly rides, time trials and sportives for the relatively confident.
London Phoenix
www.londonphoenix.co.uk.
Training rides, races and time trials.
Pollards Hill Cyclists
www.pollardshillcyclists. org.uk.
All-day, sociable leisure rides in and around town.
Velo Club Londres
www.vcl.org.uk.
VCL ride on the road and the track at Herne Hill.
Willesden Cycling Club
www.willesdencycling club.co.uk.
West London's largest cycling club.

CYCLE ROUTES
Mayor Boris Johnson introduced the Transport for London Cycle Superhighways in July 2010. These clearly defined, blue-painted bike lanes are designed to bring cyclists safely into central London from all points of the compass. The first two to open linked Barking and Tower Gateway, and Merton and the City; in July 2011, Bow to Aldgate and Wandsworth to Westminster will open, with the rest due to follow by 2015.

A network of local and national cycle routes moves riders around town. Look out for the blue signs and green road markings. The superhighways overtook this internal network in priority, and some work remains to be done before it is fully developed, but it generally succeeds in getting you safely around town.

London's cycle paths are shown on a set of 14 excellent free maps available from Transport for London's website, www.tfl.gov.uk, and Tube stations. They are used by TfL's online journey planner, which generates custom maps if you select the bicycle option.

CYCLE TO WORK SCHEME
The Cycle to Work scheme is part of the UK government's Green Transport Plan. It effectively allows you to purchase a bike tax-free, in monthly instalments (usually 12) deducted from your pay, on the understanding that you will be using your new bike to commute to work. You can't join as an individual; your company needs to sign up, through administrators such as Cyclescheme (www.cycle scheme.co.uk) and Bike 2 Work Scheme (www.bike 2workscheme.co.uk). You will need to choose a bike from the range offered by the scheme.

FESTIVALS & EVENTS
For rides, *see p162 and p250.*

London Bicycle Film Festival
www.bicyclefilmfestival. com/london. Date Oct.
A film festival dedicated to all things cycling. Started in New York in 2001, the

Bicycle Film Festival is now held in cities all over the world, showing a fantastic selection of bike-related films. The Barbican has been a regular host of the London event. Valet bike parking is laid on.

London Nocturne

www.londonnocturne.com. Date June.
Smithfield market becomes a race circuit once a year in this must-see event for London cycling fans. There are plenty of opportunities for amateurs to take part – folding-bike races, bike messenger races, longest skid competition – but simply spectating on a balmy London summer evening with a cold beer is one of the capital's bike-related musts. The main event later in the evening is the men's elite road race – all floodlit and exciting – but arrive late afternoon to get a prime spot along the barriers.

Tour of Britain

www.tourofbritain.com. Date Sept.
The world's top-name pros compete in Britain's biggest and best bike race. London hosts the final stage, so there's everything to play for. Spectating is free.

LONDON CYCLE HIRE SCHEME

The Transport for London Cycle Hire scheme, launched in 2010, has filled the streets with 6,000 distinctive turquoise bicycles, which are available at 400 docking stations around central London (roughly Zone 1 on a Tube map). There are plans for extension eastwards to the Olympic Park by 2012.

The bikes are available round the clock to anyone over 14 who can ride without assistance, and come with dynamo lights and small baskets. You can take out a subscription or pay as you go.

For more information, to register as a subscriber or to purchase pay-as-you-go, visit www.tfl.gov.uk or call 0845 026 3630.

Subscriptions

An annual subscription costs £45. This buys you access using an electronic key which will be posted to you. You can also get subscriptions for a day (£1) or a week (£5), which will lie dormant until used; useful if you usually ride your own bike but occasionally find yourself stranded.

Within your subscription period, a 30-minute ride is free: keep docking the bike and there's no limit to how many trips you can take. Otherwise, it's £1 for an hour, rising to £50 for the maximum hire period of 24 hours. Keep the bike for longer and you may face a £150 fine; if you don't return it, it's £300.

Pay-as-you-go

You can purchase casual access to the bikes online, by phone or at a docking station. A day's access costs £1 and a week's £5. Once you've paid, insert your card to receive a keycode for each journey and bike hired; punch this in to unlock the bikes. Usage costs are as for subscribers, above.

How it works

Find a docking station either by looking around – they're near-ubiquitous – using the map available on the website, or with an app, of which there are several, offering various nifty features including cost calculators. We recommend the one called London Cycle. Then release a bike with your key or your pay-as-you-go code (*see above*). If the rack's empty, the terminal will direct you to the nearest available bike.

To return, find an empty space at any docking station and park your bike, pushing the front wheel firmly into the docking point. Wait for the green light to come on, which indicates that the bike is secured. If the rack is full, the terminal will show you where to find the nearest station with free places. You'll be given an extra 15 minutes to get there.

If you get a puncture, or your bike needs some TLC, take it to the nearest dock and press the fault report button. The bike will then be locked until it's repaired, and you will be offered a replacement.

NUTS AND BOLTS

MAINTENANCE

Toolkit

Even if you rely on the pros to service and maintain your bike, you will need to keep a few basic tools at home. Allen keys and standard and Phillips screwdrivers are essential for making sundry adjustments such as saddle height. An adjustable spanner can help with these, and is also necessary for removing wheels if you don't have quick-release skewers; you'll need tyre levers for replacing an inner tube after a puncture. You should know how to fix punctures as a back-up even if you usually entrust them to a shop; also keep a spare tube and, if you're up for patching, a puncture repair kit. For a step-by-step guide to mending a puncture, *see p50*. A pump, of course, is standard kit, preferably a floorstanding track pump, far more powerful and easy to use than a hand pump.

A portable multi tool – the cyclist's equivalent of a Swiss army knife – may well be your next purchase, neatly combining a few of the more common-sized Allen keys, a Phillips and flat-head screwdriver, and a chain tool: the basics for getting you home after a minor mechanical drama.

If you want to develop your skills, you'll want to invest in tools specific to your bike's fittings and the job you want to do; your local bike shop can advise. Maintaining brakes, replacing worn cables and adjusting gears are easily within the reach of the averagely handy cyclist. To assess what jobs might be within your capabilities, *see p99*.

Servicing

Unless you are an able mechanic, you should have your bike serviced at least once a year, depending on how much you use it. A service routinely checks for any safety problems, fixes them, and identifies failing componentry. Prices start at around £30, not including any further work or parts required; upwards of £60 is normal for central London.

Cleaning & lubing

If you only learn how to do one maintenance task, make it cleaning and lubricating your bike's transmission, which is key to the smooth functioning and longevity of the mechanics at the heart of the miracle of human-powered transport.

A good bike-specific degreaser – like those from Muc-Off or Finish Line – will soon have your gears looking shiny again. Spray it on to the chain, cassette sprockets (on the hub of the back wheel) and front and rear derailleurs, then get to work with an old toothbrush or, like the pro team mechanics, a relatively stiff paintbrush. Purpose-designed tools are available to reach between the cassette sprockets to shift any clods of dirt that a degreaser can't reach.

The key to it all is the chain. The best way is probably to take it off, using a chain tool if necessary, and soak it in degreaser, but there are chain-cleaning tools that don't require the chain's removal. You fill them with cleaning fluid, clamp them over your chain, and then turn the pedals backwards so that the links move through the internal brushes. Either of these methods is more effective than stabbing at your chain with a toothbrush while it's on the bike.

Once your transmission is clean and shiny, you'll need to re-lube it. Use a bike-specific product rather than a generic household brand. Spray a single coating along the lower length of the chain while turning the pedals backwards (protect the floor), then wipe off any residue with a rag. Then target the jockey wheels and pivoting parts of the rear derailleur, plus the pivots on the front derailleur.

Cleaning and lubing the transmission is worth doing as often as you can bear it, but at the very least apply a new squirt of lube every couple of weeks to keep things ticking over until the next degreasing session. As for the brakes, keep the pivot points lubed, taking care not to let any get on to the brake pads or rims. Leave it to your mechanic to grease the cables and bearings.

Classes
BikeWorks and Cycle Systems (for both, *see p254*) both offer courses leading to professional qualifications.

Bike Yard East
1A Goldsmiths Row, Hackney City Farm, E2 8QA (07949 764631, www.bikeyardeast.com). Open 8.30am-6pm Tue-Fri; 11am-4.30pm Sat.
We can personally vouch for the hands-on courses and private classes offered at this little shed.

Cycle Maintenance Courses
07989 687506, www.learn cyclemaintenance.co.uk.
Bike mechanic and enthusiast Stephen Cumberland helps you to get to know your bike inside-out in his one-day maintenance courses, held in various east London venues, including cycling café Look Mum No Hands! (*see p246*).

He can also come to your home.

Ealing Bike Hub
07880 797437, www.ealingbikehub.co.uk.
Monthly maintenance lessons – beginners, advanced, and an intensive two-day course.

ONLINE & DIGITAL RESOURCES

Apps
With GPS-based mapping and location services, and built-in networkability, apps are a boon for the cyclist. There are more arriving all the time, but these are our current favourites. Some are for iPhone only but Android is catching up fast.
Bicycle Gear Calculator
The Bike Computer
The Complete National Cycle Network
Bike Doctor
Bike Hub
Bike Your Drive
Bikegps
Cyclehireapp.com
Cyclemeter
London Bike Shop
MotionX

Blogs
www.cyclinglondononline.

wordpress.com
www.ibikelondon. blogspot.com
www.londoncyclechic. blogspot.com
www.londoncyclist.co.uk
www.velochick.wordpress. com
www.velorution.biz

Campaigns
www.fillthathole.org.uk
www.stop-smidsy.org.uk

Communities & forums
www.bikeradar.com
http://forum.ctc.org.uk
www.lfgss.com
http://londonbikehub.com
www.totallysporty.com

News & reviews
www.bikehub.co.uk
www.bikeradar.com
www.londoncyclesport.com
www.roadcyclinguk.com
www.road.cc.
www.thecyclingexperts. co.uk
www.cyclingweekly.co.uk

Route planning
http://cyclejourney planner.tfl.gov.uk
www.cyclestreets.net
http://routes.bikehub. co.uk

Route sharing
www.bikely.com
www.mapmyride.com

ORGANISED RIDES
There are several types of organised ride, from charity and leisure events – a good way to tackle your first long-distance outing – to sportier, timed runs called audaxes and sportives. The difference between these two is primarily one of attitude. Sportives, which have been enjoying a boom, are populated largely by riders wanting to meet and beat their own personal challenges. Some are comparatively flat and extremely fast; others are more challenging with stiff climbs and hair-raising descents. By comparison, audax rides, some of which are billed as randonnées (the distinction is often elusive), are mellower and attract a more traditional rider. They can be tough, in terms not so much of speed but of distance: they can top 600km, although the most common length is 200km (and some offer much shorter options).

Organised rides typically sign their routes and may close roads to other traffic; they may arrange en route snacks, mechanical assistance and first aid, and a 'sag wagon' to pick up riders unable to finish the course. Sportier rides will time riders electronically and may publish the results.

For London and the South-east's standout individual rides, see p162.

Audax UK
www.aukweb.net.
Bike Events
www.bike-events.com. Expertly organised and supported rides to suit all levels, including families, many in the South-east.
British Heart Foundation
www.bhf.org.uk. The BHF organises over 40 rides a year, many of them in the South-east, including some classic 'London to...' rides (eg Brighton, Paris, Brussels). Like many charities, they encourage you to raise sponsorship money in addition to paying a reasonable ride fee.

CTC
www.ctc.org.uk. The Cyclists' Touring Club publishes a list of the many and varied rides its member groups organise, from family to sporty.
Cycling Weekly
www.cyclingweekly.co.uk. Listings and news of cyclosportive events.
Cyclosport
www.cyclosport.org. One-stop shop for sportives, with a results service.

RENTAL
The Transport for London Cycle Hire scheme (see p248) is ideal for short rentals if you don't mind a heavy bike: if you want a wider choice of mount or a longer hire period, or a guided tour, try the companies listed below.

Cloud 9 Cycles
The Arches, 17 Castlehaven Road, NW1 8RA (8090 9560, www.cloud9cycles.com). Open 11am-7pm daily.
London Bicycle Tour Company
The Wharf, 1A Gabriel's Wharf, 56 Upper Ground, SE1 9PP (7928 6838, www.londonbicycle.com). Open Apr-Oct 10am-6pm daily; Nov-Mar 10am-4pm daily.
On Your Bike
52-54 Tooley Street, SE1 2SZ (7378 6669, www.onyourbike.com). Open 7.30am-7.30pm Mon-Fri; 10am-6pm Sat; 11am-5pm Sun.
Velorution
18 Great Titchfield Street, W1W 8BD (7637 4004, www.velorution.biz). Open 8.30am-6.45pm Mon-Fri; 10.30am-6.30pm Sat.

Specialist
City Bike Service
2 Fairchild Place, EC2A 3EN (7247 4151, www.citybikeservice.co.uk) Open 8.30am-6pm Mon-Fri; 9am-5pm Sat. Hybrid, folding and racing bikes.
Foffa Bikes
Unit 11, Pinchin Street, E1 1SA (7481 2516, http://foffabikes.co.uk). Open 11am-7pm Tue-Fri; 11am-6pm Sat, Sun. Single-speeds and fixed gears.
London Recumbents
Ranger's Yard, Dulwich Park, SE21 7BQ (8299 6636, www.london recumbents.com). Open 10am-5pm daily. Recumbent bikes for hire.
Tally Ho! Cycle Tours
216 Carlisle Lane, SE1 7LH (07969 230828, www.tallyhocycletours. com/london/bicycle-hire). Reservations required: email london@tallyho cycletours.com. Tours on classic Pashley cycles.

SERVICES

Bike parking
London Bridge Cycle Park
Entrance: Tooley Street, at end of Weston Street tunnel (7378 6669, www.onyourbike.com). Open 7.30am-7.30pm Mon-Fri; 10am-6pm Sat; 11am-5pm Sun. This staffed indoor bicycle parking facility has space for 400 bicycles and is CCTV-monitored, with access controlled by card. It costs £1.50 per day, and you need to register. There are changing rooms on site; On Your Bike's shop and workshop

(*see p245*) are on the doorstep.

Coaching
British Cycling
www.britishcycling.org.uk/coaching.
The number of highly qualified cycling coaches in and around London is increasing all the time. Word of mouth is the best way to find the right one but to search a one-stop shop for local British Cycling-qualified coaches, visit the national federation's website.

Cycle rescue
ETA Cycle Rescue
0800 212 810, www.eta.co.uk/breakdown/cycle_rescue.
Breakdown cover for bicycles, available either as part of ETA's cycle insurance or on its own. If you break down, have an accident or have your bike stolen, Cycle Rescue will take you to the nearest repair shop or home.

Fitting/sizing
Bike Whisperer
www.thebikewhisperer.co.uk.

Take your bike to Scherrit and Corinne Knoesen's base in Ealing, and with a few tweaks and perhaps some new componentry they can transform your riding comfort and performance.

Cycle Fit
7430 0083, www.cyclefit.co.uk.
Cycle Fit uses its extensive experience and modern technology to analyse your posture and pedal stroke to make you more efficient and prevent injury.

Roller-racing
Rollapaluza
0843 289 7112, www.rollapaluza.com.
Rollapaluza organises events that put two cyclists head-to-head over a simulated 500m distance on a pair of custom rollers.

SECURITY
There's really only one surefire way to prevent your bike being stolen, and that's never to let it out of your sight. Bike theft is rife and rising in London, with pro gangs using increasingly sophisticated methods (as a new

police task force set up specifically to deal with the problem is finding out). If you commute and your workplace offers secure cycle storage, use it.

If you have to leave your bicycle in the street, the sad truth is you need to be prepared to lose it. Some people ride a cheap everyday bike and only take out their pride-and-joy roadster at the weekend ; some tape over decals to make expensive models look run of the mill. Good strategies, but not guaranteed to work. An appeal for solidarity: don't buy from street traders or the likes of Gumtree. Someone like you may be mourning their loss.

Locks are essential if you leave your bike on the street (or in your garden shed, or anywhere else not fully secured), but none are 100 per cent unbreakable. Cable locks, even thick ones, can be stretched and broken with relative ease, and combination locks went out with *Dixon of Dock Green*. Your best bet (though not infallible,

however stentorian its marketing) is a D-lock – named for its shape – which fits tight to the frame without offering much leverage for a crowbar or space for a cutting tool. This will at least deter casual criminals packing a bolt cutter. You tend to get what you pay for with a D-lock; good ones well upwards of £50. Look for one with a unique key.

Pass the lock through the frame and rear wheel and anchor it to an immovable object such as a bike rack, lamp post or railings (beware poles bearing roadsigns; bikes can often be lifted up and off them). If your wheels have quick-release levers, remove the front wheel and put it into the D-lock or replace the lever with a keyed version such as a Pitlock. Or you could carry a second, smaller D-lock or a cable lock – it's a question of where you put yourself on the continuum of risk and hassle. Remove your saddle if it's got a quick release, or change the fitting to a standard bolt.

Insurance

Cycle insurance is expensive, and the cost needs to be weighed against the benefit. Some household policies (such as Sainsbury's) include it as standard, but there may be an excess and a maximum claim; others offer it as an add-on. Make sure the bike is covered both in and out of the home. Both the Cyclists' Touring Club (*see p248*) and London Cycling Campaign (*see p254*) have affiliated specialist insurers; another to look at is www.cycleguard.co.uk.

Insurers may require details of your bike, so take a photo and keep a record of the frame number. If you post details to www. immobilise.com, the police can track you down if they find your stolen bike (it can happen). Police also run free security-marking and microchipping sessions.

TRAVELLING WITH YOUR BIKE

By air

Most airlines charge for transporting your bike; rule of thumb, the more budget the airline, the more this will cost. Charges are usually higher if the bike is not booked in advance.

At the time of writing, British Airways is allowing bikes to be carried free of charge, provided the total weight is within your baggage allowance. It also permits two cabin bags.

Airlines – and common sense – require your cycle to be packed in a bike box or bag. This can be as basic as the cardboard box in which bikes are supplied to shops, as long as you pad like mad with pipe lagging and bubble wrap. A variety of commercial bike travel bags and hard cases are also available.

You will need to partially deconstruct your bicycle. This takes time and care; don't leave it until the morning of your flight. Wheels need to be taken off, tyres deflated; depending on the size of your bag or box, you may also need to remove the pedals, saddle and handlebar. Remember to pack tools for re-assembly, and your Pitlock key.

By train

Different rail companies have different rules, so check with your operator.

On local services within the south-east, bikes are generally permitted on off-peak services (only folding bikes at peak times). Some operators have a designated cycle area, sometimes with fixing straps; convenient, but if it is already in use you may not be allowed to put bikes elsewhere on the train.

Bikes are carried free on long-distance services, usually in the guard's van. Advance booking is sometimes compulsory and always advised.

You can take your bike with you on Eurostar if you remove the saddle, pedals and handlebar, and fit it into box or bag no more than 120cm long. Otherwise, space allowing, you can pay £30 each way for carriage of the complete bike.

By tube

London Underground permits carriage of bicycles outside the peak hours of 7.30am to 9.30am and 4pm to 7pm Monday to Friday – on certain lines only, and not on escalators. The deeper lines and sections, including the whole of the Victoria line, are not accessible; lines nearer the surface, such as the Metropolitan, Circle and District lines, are. For specifics, consult the Transport for London's 'Bicycles on the Tube' map, downloadable from its website. Also consult TfL for details of carrying bikes on Overground services, on which restrictions apply.

Folded bikes can be carried throughout the tube network at any time.

By car

Most bikes will fit in most boots if you take both wheels off. Folding down the back seats often requires just the front wheel to be removed. Put down an old sheet to keep oil off the seats.

A better option is to invest in either a roof-mounted or rear-mounted bike rack (for the latter, ensure your numberplate is visible). Brands like Thule (www.thule.co.uk) and Saris (www.saris.com) are up to the task.

USEFUL ORGANISATIONS

Bike Club
www.bikeclub.org.uk. Bike Club is aimed at helping ten- to 20-year-olds enjoy different forms of cycling in a fun, safe environment, whether it's mountain biking, BMXing or learning essential bike maintenance.

Cycling Embassy of Great Britain
www.cycling-embassy. org.uk.
A new, forward-looking campaign to improve the UK's cycling infrastructure – and ultimately to make the idea of cycling more appealing to those who don't already ride. It was inspired by the Cycling Embassy of Denmark – where they have it pretty much spot-on.

Cyclists' Touring Club
www.ctc.org.uk.
The CTC has been promoting cyclists' rights since its formation back in 1878. As the creators of the first cycling proficiency test, cycle training initiatives remain high on the list of priorities, along with advice and help for cyclists – from right-of-way disputes to legal aid and insurance. Touring is, obviously, a speciality.

London Cycling Campaign (LCC)
www.lcc.org.uk.
LCC is the London cyclist's best friend, working to make the capital a safer, more pleasurable environment for cycling, combating bicycle theft, lobbying government to educate other road users and fronting forward-looking campaigns to help promote London as a world-class cycling city.

Sustrans
www.sustrans.org.uk.
Sustrans' National Cycle Network totals more than 12,000 miles of quiet, often traffic-free routes across the UK, while in London, the GOAL (Greenways for the Olympics and London) programme is inspired by the London 2012 Olympic and Paralympic Games to provide cycle and walking paths in the vicinity of the Olympic Park.

WORKSHOPS & MECHANICS

Workshops will all do basic services and repair; many will also be able to build wheels and some can put together whole bikes. A good mechanic who gets on with you and your bike is to be treasured; find out their name and ask for them next time.

Most bike shops also have workshops; for shop listings, *see p242.*

Bicycle Workshop
27 All Saints Road, W11 1HE (7229 4850, www. bicycleworkshop.co.uk). Open 10am-2pm, 3-6pm Tue-Fri; 9am-5pm Sat.

Bike Yard East
1A Goldsmiths Row, Hackney City Farm, E2 8QA (07949 764631, www.bikeyardeast.com). Open 8.30am-6pm Tue-Fri; 11am-4.30pm Sat.

Bikeworks
Unit 8, Gun Wharf, 241 Old Ford Road, E3 5QB (8983 1221, www.bikeworks.rg. uk). Open 8.30am-6.30pm Mon-Thur; 8.30am-5.30pm Fri; 10am-5pm Sat.

London Bicycle Repair Shop
2-3 Benson House, Hatfields, SE1 8DQ (7928 6898, www.londonbicycle. com). Open 8am-7pm Mon-Thur; 8am-6pm Fri.

Mobile mechanics
Bike Ade
(07767 214724, www. bikeade.co.uk). Covers Zones 1 & 2 in central London; Zones 3 & 4 by arrangement. Available 9am-5pm Mon-Fri.

Cycle Systems
www.cycle-systems.co.uk. Covers Greater London. Emergency call-outs available 10.30am-5.30pm Mon-Fri; bookings by appointment daily.

Cycledelik
0800 0910 500, www.cycledelik.com. Covers Greater London with a call-out charge for some areas, incl east & south-east London. Available 6am-11pm daily.

Mobile Cycle Service
0800 321 3303, www.mobilecycleservice. co.uk. Covers central London. Available 9am-8pm Mon-Fri; weekends by appointment.

Rides Overview

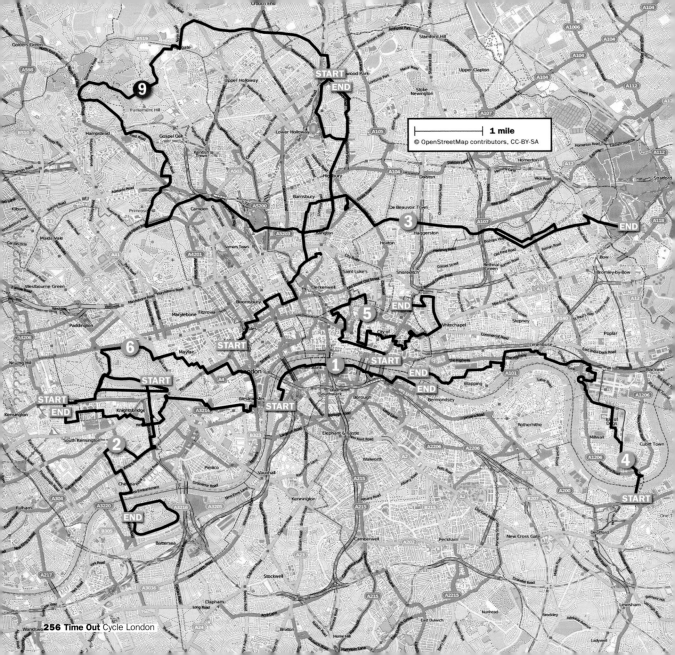